# GODARD'S CONTEMPT: ESSAYS FROM THE LONDON CONSORTIUM

# GODARD'S CONTEMPT: ESSAYS FROM THE LONDON CONSORTIUM

Edited by Colin MacCabe and Laura Mulvey

Blackwell Publishing was acquired by John Wiley & Sons in February 2007. Blackwell's publishing program has been merged with Wiley's global Scientific, Technical, and Medical business to form Wiley-Blackwell.

Registered Office
John Wiley & Sons Ltd, The Atrium, Southern Gate, Chichester, West Sussex, PO19 8SQ, United Kingdom

Editorial Offices
350 Main Street, Malden, MA 02148-5020, USA
9600 Garsington Road, Oxford, OX4 2DQ, UK
The Atrium, Southern Gate, Chichester, West Sussex, PO19 8SQ, UK

For details of our global editorial offices, for customer services, and for information about how to apply for permission to reuse the copyright material in this book please see our website at www.wiley.com/wiley-blackwell.



First published 2012 by Blackwell Publishing Ltd

Library of Congress Cataloging-in-Publication Data

Godard's Contempt: essays from the London Consortium / edited by Colin MacCabe and Laura Mulvey.
p. cm. – (Critical quarterly book series; 5)
Includes bibliographical references.
ISBN 978-1-4443-3931-4 (pbk.)
1. Mepris (Motion picture) 2. Godard, Jean Luc, 1930—Criticism and interpretation.
I. MacCabe, Colin. II. Mulvey, Laura. III. London Consortium.
PN1997.M43553G64 2011
791.4302'33092–dc23

2011043324

A catalogue record for this title is available from the British Library.

Set in 10 on 12 pt Palantino
by Macmillan India
printed in Singapore
by Fabulous Printers Pte Ltd

# Contents

# Preface

The essays collected here started life as 4,000 word papers for a London Consortium core course titled "Godard's *Contempt*: Text and Pretext" which we taught in the academic years 07/08, 08/09 and 09/10. We thought them worth gathering together in a book not simply for their intrinsic value but as an example of the kind of work that the Consortium is producing in its Master of Research course. This is the second occasion on which *Critical Quarterly* has showcased work from the Consortium but on the first occasion (CQ Volume 42, No. 2 (Summer 2000)) it was master's dissertations that were published to show the range and originality of the work being produced within the Consortium. But formally, the dissertation is the least original of the elements that go to make up the Consortium's M.Res.

When the London Consortium was founded in 1995* it determined that all students in a given year would have to take, as a cohort, a set of core courses which would constitute the most distinctive feature of the degree. All core courses are team taught in an effort to pluralise scholarly authority and, indeed, normally the teachers are from different disciplines. Both of us are affiliated with film studies but both of us would stress the determining effects of our undergraduate degrees in our intellectual formation and in the difference of our intellectual formation (for Laura history and for Colin philosophy and English). It should also be stressed that this course was not conceived as being a course in film studies. Like all the other core courses the aim was to use an object, a text, a concept as a way of enabling the students to develop their own thinking.

The core courses seek to demonstrate the way in which any complex cultural object whether it be from the elite cultural tradition or from contemporary popular culture, be it an author or a concept, requires a multiplicity of disciplinary approaches if the object is to be grasped in its complexity. The students in the course on Godard's *Contempt* would in their first year in the Consortium also take courses on St Paul, the Cultures of Collecting, Catastrophe and Flat Baroque: special effects and the rigging of the Whole Wide World. In each the students would write a 4,000 word essay started some three weeks into the course and finished some two weeks after the final class.

---

*The London Consortium was initially a joint venture between the Architectural Association, Birkbeck College, the British Film Institute and Tate. In 1998 the British Film Institute withdrew and was replaced by the Institute of Contemporary Arts. In 2008 The Science Museum joined.

If the desire to showcase the kind of work of which students in their first year of research at the London Consortium are capable was one element in the decision to collect these essays together, another lies in the film that we took as our text. Frank Kermode holds that one of the features of a classic is its "patience of interpretation". These essays demonstrate to what extent *Le Mépris* exercises such patience, the wealth of interpretation that it generates.

Finally it should be said that this book records the pleasure that we enjoyed in teaching together for the Consortium, not only the Godard course 2008–2011 but also an earlier course on *The Satanic Verses* 1995–2000.

August 2011

## Note

Godard's film of the Moravia novel *II Disprezzo* is referred to in these essays by both its English and French titles (*Contempt* and Le *Mépris*). We decided not to standardize the title but to let authors choose how to refer to the film.
Colin MacCabe and Laura Mulvey

# Introduction: Essays from the London Consortium

The London Consortium was, from the bureaucratic perspective, an initiative of the British Film Institute. When Wilf Stevenson became director in 1989, in succession to Tony Smith, he determined that the Institute should become a graduate institution with research built into its every activity. The first and most important result of this was the setting up of an M.A. in Film and Television, which took its first students in 1992. The M.A. was, in part, an attempt to address a generational crisis. Many of those who had created the Institute were retiring and their long expertise was in danger of being lost. That early generation had not, by and large, gone to university but they combined a passionate and intelligent love of film with an obsessional commitment to accuracy and a deep knowledge of the industry. The commercial nature of film production, distribution and exhibition means that to work in film is inevitably to mix aesthetic and economic considerations. The BFI's mission to encourage the love of film meant that this mixing was the daily bread of the institute.

The M.A. attempted to reproduce these mixed knowledges through four month placements in the various departments of the Institute: the archive, the library, distribution, exhibition (both repertory and festival), production. These placements had two conditions – first they had to be real tasks, which the host department considered a priority, but for which they did not currently have the resources and second the student had to formulate a theoretical question to which the placement practice would help to provide an answer. These placements were the key innovation and, from an educational point of view, marked an attempt to address one of the serious defects of the model of film study developed by *Screen* in the early and mid seventies. This model, which proved the template for much of film studies in the Anglophone world, from the United States to India, placed enormous emphasis on textual analysis. While retaining this emphasis on the text the M.A. inflected it both through history (with courses on film's conversion to synchronized sound in the late twenties and British Television in the Sixties) and, most importantly, through practice (the placements). Because of its importance for the future of the Institute, it was thought proper to allocate a small but significant permanent resource to the degree – some £70,000 to cover the salary of the director of the course and a full time administrator. Student scholarships were raised from the industry.

With the M.A. launched, a second and more ambitious collaborative initiative attempted to create research degrees that would place film in a genuine interdisciplinary setting. Much of the excitement of the initial *Screen* moment had been that film, as a medium that required both economic and aesthetic analysis, was a privileged site for the work around Marxism that had burgeoned in the sixties. If *Screen* and the Centre for Cultural Studies at Birmingham had disagreements about the role of evaluation, this disagreement came after an agreement that the analysis of cultural objects required the use of the disciplinary tools from both the humanities and the social sciences. The development of film studies as a discipline in the late seventies and eighties had paradoxically but inevitably led to a marginalisation of film in the academy. Allocated its own place it no longer was at the centre of intellectual debates in the humanities and social sciences. Further, the academicisation of film studies had led to the abandonment of the audiences that it had always addressed outside the academy. In the seventies this had been a generation of politicized cinephiles but if that political moment had passed, the British Film Institute still harboured the older ambitions of adult education and, through its cinemas and publications, it still addressed considerable audiences that were not limited to, or defined by, the academy.

The multi-disciplinary research degrees grew out of a series of partnerships that were formed in order to give this new initiative the range of competences and audiences necessary. Birkbeck College had collaborated with the BFI for decades. It shared the adult education ethos of the BFI, it had been the obvious academic partner for the M.A. degree and it could provide academic teaching across the entire range of the humanities and social sciences. The Architectural Association was seeking a larger pulpit both for the new thinking around architecture and for the Association's experimental educational practices. Finally the Tate Gallery was on the verge of the huge expansion that would see it open three new museums and wished to engage with the highest level of academic research. Most significantly, the Tate, like the BFI, wished to bring the results of this research to the large audiences that it addressed.

The first and perhaps most important decision was to dispense with any model which involved the teaching of theoretical texts independently of specific analyses. The texts which had been so influential in the seventies: Derrida, Foucault, Lacan, Barthes, Althusser had all been written as part of defined intellectual traditions and in a context where these traditions would feed into a political revolution understood as imminent. The failure of that political moment both in France and America had led by the late seventies to the development of "Theory" where, within the university, the unfortunate fact that all the major political battles had been lost could be ignored in the elaboration of politicized debates which either referred to Marxist battles long past or evolved towards the new identity politics. While committed to the highest level of theoretical rigour, the London Consortium (as the four partners named the new institution) was not interested in teaching "Theory". Indeed in a world where that "Theory" was largely academic orthodoxy, one of its educational tasks would be to persuade its students to unlearn some of the orthodoxies they had been previously taught. It was decided that each cohort of students would take a series of four core courses. These courses would take texts or objects that required students to draw on a range of disciplines and expertises. This training would equip them either to advance to a Ph.D or complete a master's dissertation. The first set of core courses were as follows:

1) Kant's *Critique of Judgment*. Kant's text was chosen both for the degree of interest it had recently generated and because it posed very clearly the arguments around aesthetic relativism to which the Consortium was committed. It also served as a straightforward exercise in reading a difficult philosophical text.
2) *Whiteness*. This course tracked whiteness at the beginning of the twentieth century across the fields of hygiene, race and art. Students were taught to follow an idea across a whole range of different objects and fields.
3) *Tate Modern*. The Consortium took its first students in 1995 as the Tate was in the midst of planning its huge new development. This planning was used to provide a concrete example of the ways in which audiences are conceived and formed.
4) *The Satanic Verses*. Reading *The Satanic Verses* immediately raised questions both about the early history of Islam and about Indian cinema. The novel thus became a springboard for introducing students to the problems of approaching new and unfamiliar knowledges. It also served as a straightforward exercise in reading a difficult text.

While film did not occur as a discrete topic, it was at the centre of all four courses: as Indian Cinema in *The Satanic Verses*, as Griffith's *Birth of a Nation* in Whiteness, in the relation between film and art in a contemporary museum in Tate Modern, and in relation to general questions of evaluation in *The Critique of Judgment*. The BFI's commitment to this new venture was to a postgraduate school which would place the contemporary image (film, art, architecture) at the centre of its investigations and which would consider ways in which these investigations could reach wider audiences. Nonetheless it was recognized that this experiment, unlike the M.A., was more tangential to the BFI's future and there was no permanent allocation of resource. There was a development budget of £25,000, which the Consortium repaid, and initial administrative support. Within three years the Consortium was entirely self supporting and it would indeed make contributions each year to its constituent members. Laura Mulvey, then Director of the BFI MA, and I taught *The Satanic Verses* from 1995–2000 and when we finished we agreed that we would repeat the experience with the difference that it would be a film which would be the difficult text that provided a springboard to unfamiliar knowledges. Our determination to choose a film was in part a reaction to the fact that the British Film Institute had chosen to withdraw from the London Consortium in 1998.

A radical change of policy at the BFI began with the election of New Labour in 1997. New Labour had long made clear that it had no interest in any argument for either education or culture which was not linked directly either to inward investment or to assorted series of socially inclusive targets. In both their definition of investment and in their bureaucratic understanding of deprivation, New Labour was the worst post-war British government for education and culture. New Labour's chosen errand boy to carry out their philistine policy in relation to film was Alan Parker. Parker was long known for his dislike of the BFI and his antagonism to any intellectual engagement with film. His appointment as the new Chair of the British Film Institute provoked horror and laugher in equal measure. The laughter grew noticeably less as he abolished all the production and education functions that had contributed so much to the Institute's worldwide reputation as a centre of thought about film and television. He did this with a disregard for evidence and argument that was to mark New Labour at every level of its policy-making. At one particularly charged meeting, he defended the abolition of the M.A. on the ground that, at £70,000 a student it was too expensive. He might had had a point if his figure was right because that would have had the M.A. costing in excess of £1m a year. When it was pointed out to him that the figure was £70,000 for the whole degree he immediately forsook argument to bully and bluster. Alastair Campbell would have been proud of his argumentative abilities.

Parker, however, was unable to touch the London Consortium and the BFI was replaced by the Institute of Contemporary Arts. While the Consortium continued, after the BFI's departure, to adhere to an intellectual progamme focused on the modern image in the three disciplines of art, film and architecture, the absence of the BFI meant that in practice much of the most interesting work in the Consortium's first decade focused on art and architecture.

It was, thus, in part to re-focus the Consortium on film that Laura and I offered a new core course on Godard's *Contempt* in 2007. Godard's film suited our purposes from three different angles of education. First, where *The Satanic Verses* had offered questions about the early history of Islam, *Le Mépris* opened up the whole question of Homer and his transmission in Western culture. Second, *The Satanic Verses* led directly into the history of Indian cinema, *Le Mépris* into the history of Hollywood. Finally, both texts would engage students in questions of evaluation so central to the Consortium. *Le Mépris* is an adaptation and an adaptation about an adaptation. This story of making a film of the Odyssey led directly into the world of Homeric scholarship. Although adaptation itself is a process as old as fiction with almost all narratives up until the Renaissance the telling of already told tales, film has produced a new and specific form of this retelling. In Shakespeare or Sophocles the fact that a text is an adaptation does not differentiate it for all (in Sophocles's case) or almost all (in Shakespeare's case) their plays are adaptations. Further the relation of the adaptation to the source text is not part of the immediate interest of the text; there is no notion of fidelity at work either in production or reception. Film, however, arrives when the fictional form of the novel (which proclaims in its name its commitment to originality) and the aesthetic ideology of Romanticism had combined to render adaptation irredeemably aesthetically inferior. If high modernism in texts such as *Ulysses* (the Odyssey) and *The Waste Land* (the Grail Legend) had reasserted the centrality of adaptation, these experiments had little echo in mainstream literary culture. Film, very early however, developed a form of adaptation where the relation to the source text was central either in terms of the aesthetic value of the original (a Shakespeare play, an Austen or Dickens novel) or its recent commercial success (the series of films from *The Girl with the Dragon Tattoo* novels) or both (*The Lord of the Rings*). It is worth distinguishing this kind of adaptation from the older pre-Romantic adaptation which cinema also uses when some literary property forms a pretext for a script whose relation to the source is tangential and contingent. In all Godard's other films where there is a literary source text (as for example *Sauve qui peut (la vie)* which is notionally related to Bukowski's short stories or *Pierrot le Fou* which claims some relation with Lionel White's novel *Obsession*) his adaptation is of this older kind.

*Le Mépris*, however, is different, and the difference is linked to its most important economic and cultural reality: that it was a film starring Brigitte Bardot. The use of stars is not in any way foreign to Godard. Jean Seberg was an international star when he cast her in *À bout de souffle* and Jean Paul Belmondo became one on the film's release. Throughout his career Godard has had recourse to stars thus, for example, when he returned to the cinema in 1979 he cast three of the hottest stars of contemporary French cinema: Jacques Dutronc, Isabelle Huppert and Nathalie Baye to relaunch his film career. *Le Mépris*, however, is the only film of Godard's in which both the economic structure of the film and the cultural project are entirely dependent on its star: the actress who was then the most famous French and European actress of the moment and who, while such judgments are difficult to quantify, enjoyed a fame not equaled by any successor.

Surprisingly Bardot was not part of the initial pitch. Godard wished to make a New Wave film with a Hollywood budget and proposed to his producer Beauregard the Moravia novel *Il Disprezzo* as the vehicle to realize this ambition with Frank Sinatra and Kim Novak as the stars who would embody the couple and thus raise the finance. If it is easy for someone who was a teenager at the early sixties to remember the incredible aura that Bardot enjoyed, it is difficult now to summon back a time when Moravia was considered not only a major European novelist but also a hot cinematic property. No less than three other Moravia novels were to become films in 1963 and Moravia's fee of 500,000 francs was two and half times Godard's. Whatever Moravia's reputation, there can be little doubt that the novel's interest for Godard, over and above its value as a film property, lay in the autobiographical resonances of a story of the collapse of a relationship from intense love to unbridled contempt. Anna Karina, Godard's wife when the film was shot, is adamant that the dialogues of the long central scene between the couple in the apartment are largely taken directly from her life with Godard. Both Bardot, with some resentment, and Piccoli, with none, have made clear that they knew they were playing the couple whose love had blossomed during the shooting of *Le Petit Soldat* and *Une Femme est Une Femme* but which, after a miscarriage and affairs, was now collapsing.

Beauregard knew that a budget of the size Godard wanted would require both his Italian producing partner Carlo Ponti and an American co-producer in the shape of Joe Levine. At budgets this size casting is all and Ponti countered the suggestion of Sinatra and Novak with an Italian pairing of Sophia Loren and Marcello Mastroanni. It was at this moment that Bardot's name was mentioned. It is impossible to overstate Bardot's iconic stature in 1963. Suffice to say that no European actress before or since has been the focus of such media attention. She made it clear that she was not going to commit to a film without a conventional script. Throughout his career Godard has mocked the producer's need for a script before shooting. Perhaps his best joke is that as the producers consider the script so important the first thing he will do when the film is finished is get a transcript made and sent round to them. In general Godard works from very general summaries that sketch out the themes and preoccupations of his films. It is these themes and locations together with the cast that provide the architecture of the film with usually the most minimal narrative articulation. Dialogues, from *À bout de souffle* on, are written just before shooting on a daily basis. So keen, however, was Godard to make his New wave film on a Hollywood budget, a keenness accentuated, one can surmise, by the possible casting of Bardot that for the first and only time in his career he produced a full length shooting script, a script that went through four different versions.

Bazin, in his classic article in praise of adaptation "Pour un cinema impur" was not interested in adaptations which merely used the source text as a prompt nor in slavish attempts at fidelity, rather he looked for those adaptations which used the medium of film to develop and extend as well as cut and reduce the literary text so that film adaptation and source book form an "ideal construct". Godard's adaptation of Moravia follows Bazin's dictum in being a real engagement with the Moravia text that is neither mere prompt nor slavishly followed original. However, Godard's adaptation is rare if not unique in cinema history in that the engaged adaptation is at the service not of producing an "ideal construct" but in some sense of ruining the assumptions of the source text to produce a film completely at odds with the book that inspired it. Will Viney in this volume describes the relation to the source text as elliptical and inconsistent.[1] What is certainly true is that while Moravia's basic story of love turning to contempt is preserved, everything else is systematically transformed and eradicated. Most importantly, Moravia's psychological investigation is abandoned almost entirely with only fragments of voice over from Paul as a kind of ironic echo of the book's dominant voice. The sub-plot of the shooting of the film of Ulysses is completely transformed. While the shortening of the narration from one year to two days can find simple justification in the film form, the internationalization of what had been an almost entirely Italian story makes American cinema, and its attempt to dominate European film, one of the major themes of the film. Most important, however is the struggle over classic and modern between producer and director. In Moravia's novel it is the producer who argues for a classic interpretation of Homer's epic and the director who wants a modern psychological interpretation. In Godard's version it is the director, magnificently embodied in Fritz Lang who argues for a classic interpretation and the crass producer, Prokosch who wants a modern psycho-sexual version.

This debate opens up onto nearly three millennia of the transmission and interpretation of what are the foundational texts of Western culture. The film was used as a pretext to consider the changing interpretations of Homer's text from the Greeks right to the present day. In class, special emphasis was placed on the twentieth century theories which revealed that these supreme totems of written culture were in fact predominantly oral in form.[2] The fertility of the return to the Greeks can be read in James Wilkes's essay which goes back to the Homeric deities to find a function – the possessing of superior knowledge by sight, eidenia – which can be used to describe those moments in the Godard's text when the camera cannot be identified with any character's point of view.[3]

An attention to the Homeric tradition broaches the whole question of transmission and interpretation from the beginning of Western culture. More specifically for the interpretation of Godard's film, attention to Godard's own practice of adaptation in a film about adaptation leads to a questioning of any reading which would simply identify with Lang's determination to film Homer's text as it is. Godard's own practice, and indeed the fragments of Lang's film that we see, reveal this to be impossibility. However attractive the appeal to an immutable classicism, it is as dead as the Hollywood that has rejected Lang. The film itself argues for a continuous dialectic and condemns Paul for his failure to understand this. As Raphaelle Burns writes "if Paul is tempted by classicism he cannot reflect *on* classicism and cannot thereby overcome the tragic and fatal separation of the modern and the classic which modernity seems to have imposed. Godard on the other hand, relentlessly explores the inexhaustible nature of the classic, its power to continue poetically into the modern".[4] Oliver Harris argues that Blanchot and his engagement with Hölderlin are a crucial element in this relation to the classical past "Blanchot's intricate probing of the creative process, along with his own use of fragmentation and his pointed engagement with the classical past all feed into *Le Mépris*'s reflections on cinema. Godard set out to make movies like books by Blanchot, and succeeded".[5]

In class *Contempt* served as our tutor text firstly as an introduction to the Western literary tradition and to the intermedial agon between text and image that is so central to Godard's practice. Second and perhaps more importantly, however, it served as an introduction to the history of the cinema. *Le Mépris* declares itself in its opening epigraph as a history of cinema and, in long retrospect, it can be seen as the first step towards what may be Godard's most enduring masterpiece his *Histoire(s) du cinema*. It is from this perspective that Laura Mulvey writes her concluding essay in this book. In choosing to look at the history of the cinema as a network of quotations Mulvey is not simply following Godard but what came to be the emphasis of all three classes and many of the essays collected here. Mulvey brilliantly weaves her tale of quotations together to show how densely allusive and argumentative this apparently simple text is. Godard's later *Histoire(s)* are premised as a history of failure, the history of film's failure to prevent or to represent the genocide of the Jews in Hitler's Germany. The horror of Nazism is present in *Le Mépris*, it is part of the history that Lang brings to the film but the historical failure the film focuses is much more precisely the present and is signaled in the opening epigraph attributed to Bazin: "Cinema substitutes for our gaze a world that corresponds to our desires". The voice over which introduces the film continues "*Contempt* is the history of this world" Much has been made of the fact that this quote is not in fact anywhere in Bazin's writings and that it is indeed much closer to a sentence of Michel Mourlet published in *Cahiers* after Bazins's death[6] However, it would be difficult to find a more succinct statement of Bazin's belief that cinema was the art which promised social emancipation in the vision that it could offer of a better world. Bazin refused the possibility of entering into the State educational system at the end of the Second World War because he believed that the educating of the tastes of working class audiences could develop the most genuinely popular art since the Renaissance so that it could become a major element in the revolutionary transformation of society. It was this belief that animated Bazin in his early work at *Travail et Culture* in the utopian years after the Liberation when he could bring his beloved films directly to working class audiences. The Cold War entailed that Bazin lost this audience as the Communist Party declared him anathema from 1948 on but, undaunted, he retired to the Café Flore where he determined that he would produce a generation of better critics, accomplishing the programme at one remove. The success of the magazine that he founded in 1951, the *Cahiers du cinema*, seemed to prove that his struggle had been anything but quixotic. Indeed it is possible that Bazin died believing his mission accomplished, for in an astonishing coincidence the day of his death was the first day of Truffaut's shooting of *Les Quatre Cent Coups*. Much more certain is that two years later after the phenomenal success of Truffaut's film and Godard's *À bout de souffle*, the young critics must have believed that Jerusalem was all but built. Disillusionment came swiftly and from both sides of the Atlantic. The cumulative effect of the break up of the studio's vertical integration and the advent of television meant that the era of classic Hollywood, the era that the young critics had themselves canonized was over. Lang's presence on the set of *Le Mépris* is visible evidence of this and there are many references which can be understood as the beginning of a work of mourning. John Shanks's essay convinces in its argument that the "let's put on a show" setting of the film and the expressive use of colour refer back to the Hollywood musical[7] but this is only one of a whole network of references which constitute a farewell to the dead. But if Hollywood is mourned the New Wave has crashed. The initial success had been followed by a string of failures – none more serious than Godard's *Les Carabiniers* that had opened in Paris with some of the lowest box office total ever recorded, as the shooting of *Le Mépris* began. Godard is impelled to begin to recount the history of the cinema in order to explain the failure of Bazin's project.[8]

The course on *Contempt* was thus an introduction both to the history of Homer's texts and their transmission and to the history of Hollywood. It should be stressed that these introductions were not in any way substantial historical lecture courses, either of which would have required much greater length than the six weeks of a Consortium core course. The course did however use the reading of *Contempt* to generate fundamental research questions and associated bibliographies. As important as these questions generated by the text was the knowledges that the students themselves bought to the class. One of the strongest founding ideas of the Consortium was that each year would form a cohort that the core courses would render a formidable intellectual network. Each year receives students from across the range of the humanities and social science, and most years see all continents and many countries represented in an intake which is designed to marry United Kingdom and overseas students in equal proportions. An example of the range and productivity of these differences can be read in the articles of Ross Adams, Alice Gavin and Anna Manubens.

In his first long article on the cinema Godard outlines a credo to which he will adhere at every stage of his filmmaking:

> "In fact, if the cinema were no more than the art of narration which some would make its proud boast, then instead of being bored, one would take pleasure in those interminable efforts which are concerned above all with exposing in meticulous detail the secret motivations of a murderer or a coquette. But there is a look, posed so afresh on things at each instant that it pierces rather than solicits them, that it seizes in them what abstraction lies in wait for... Renoir's mise-en-scene has the same quality of revealing detail without detaching it from its context".[9]

Godard's attempt to describe a look which both reveals detail without detaching that detail from its context is fundamental to his cinema and this volume contains three essays which gloss this look from very different disciplinary perspectives, that give a good idea of the range of expertises which constitute a Consortium network. Ross Adams is an architect and that formation is evident in his formulation of four fundamental categories with which to capture Godard's use of figure and ground, character and backdrop in *Le Mepris*.[10] By contrast Alice Gavin with a formation in literary criticism uses the vocabulary and analyses of free indirect discourse to capture the way in which the characters, while inhabiting their point of view, also seem, somehow, to stand just outside it so that they themselves become part of the landscape.[11] Finally Anna Manubens, drawing on psychoanalysis, uses a delicate and subtle reading of Freud's category of perversion to emphasise how Godard refuses to allow his camera to achieve any depth or penetration, determined to linger on the surface of the objects which fall into the camera's gaze.[12]

These three essays not only indicate the range of knowledges that Consortium students can draw on but also indicate the richness of the responses that Godard's film provoked. It is this richness that is the third and fundamental justification of both the course on *The Satanic Verses* and on *Contempt*. The raising of diverse research questions and the emphasis on the variety of knowledges find their justification in the value of the texts being analysed and appreciated. When the London Consortium constituted itself in 1995 one of its major distinguishing emphases was the stress that it placed on value and the processes of evaluation. At that time, possibly more than is the case today, there was a widespread rejection of questions of value. Benjamin's dictum that every work of civilization was also a work of barbarism had been understood in resolutely undialectical fashion. There can be no question of ignoring how the canons of Western culture are implicated in the exploitations and inhumanities of the societies that produced them. But for the Consortium there could be equally be no question of ignoring the value of those canons nor the importance of their revaluations. For if academics choose to ignore these questions of value they are the daily currency of aesthetic choice "Was that book or that film any good?" as they are of the political decisions about the contents of a museum, a library or a curriculum.

Of course, no one could recommend the return to the ghastly hectoring of an F.R. Leavis in which the question of value is determined by a self appointed Committee of Cultural Safety. But questions of evaluation and its procedures have been crucial to the Consortium from its beginnings. These questions gained an extra edge in the course on Godard's *Contempt* for both Laura and I had contributed to *Screen* in the mid-seventies when it distinguished itself from other similar groupings, most notably Stuart Hall's Centre for Cultural Studies at Birmingham, by its strong commitment to criteria of evaluation. These criteria were provided by a politicized aesthetic which championed texts which broke with any coherent subject position for the viewer by rupturing that coincidence of shot and narrative which marks the closure of almost all Hollywood films. Against this comfortable position of agreed knowledge between text and spectator, the valued goal was a text which clearly located the infinite creation of meaning in the spectator and his or her concrete political situation. Godard was perhaps the filmmaker who was, par excellence, the exemplar of this radical aesthetic and the goal, however ludicrous or utopian in retrospect, was nothing less that the unmasking and unmaking of the pleasures of Hollywood cinema – the abandonment of the consolations of spectacle and narrative. How far this aesthetic project was ever adopted in its entirety and, in particular, how far the cinephiliac valuation of the canon of Hollywood classics was ever genuinely abandoned is matter for more detailed historical inquiry. Thus, for example, Laura Mulvey's justly famous article on the gaze espoused this politicized aesthetic but the enduring value of the work has probably more to do with its analysis of shot and narrative and its penetrating observations on Hitchcock and Sternberg. What is certain is that by 1979, at the latest, the crusade against narrative and spectacle had revealed itself for the useless passion that it was. If questions of evaluation remained, and they were questions which fed into the formulation of the Consortium's founding concerns, they were much more complex than in the simple opposition of passive and active reading and they could certainly not find resolution in a politics whose moment had definitively passed.

The course attempted to address these questions through the work of Frank Kermode. In 1975, at the very height of *Screen*'s utopian moment, Kermode published a book *The Classic* which took issue with the key arguments that animated *Screen*'s positions. Reading Kermode's book it is more than possible to miss this confrontation. Overloaded with learning – both French and Latin quotations remain untranslated in what can only be read as an act of aggression – the first two chapters are devoted to a brilliant discussion of Medieval and Renaissance articulations of the political and cultural registers. Kermode demonstrates convincingly how each new political dispensation of Empire, from Charlemagne on, demands a renewed reading of the classics. It is this renewed reading that is the focus of Kermode's text – the paradox of the classic is that it must both preserve and alter its identity over time. The classic is a classic because it remains the text from a precious era but also because it generates fresh readings for each generation. Kermode's theme of the definition of the classic claims to find its origins in the critical writings of T.S. Eliot and the book is a record of Eliot lectures that Kermode gave at the University of Kent. However, it is only in the very last pages and in a number of glancing asides that Kermode reveals the definition of the classic that his learning has been deployed to oppose. The *Screen* position found much of its arguments in detailed analyses in the magazines *Cahiers du cinema* and *Tel Quel* but if there was one text which made the arguments in broad sweeps and for a much wider argument, it was Roland Barthes and his analysis of the Balzac novella *Sarrasine*, written in the heady days of 1968 and 1969, and published in 1970 as S/Z. In this book Barthes deploys all the advances of the previous decade's work in the structural analysis of narratives to set up an opposition between classic and modern. "Classic" is the static relation between text and reader which freezes them both in the grip of an imaginary and illusory knowledge while "modern" is the endlessly multiplying interpretations of a text which has abandoned all fixity of meaning. Kermode's learning becomes a hammer to crack the nut of Barthes's unbelievably impoverished and inaccurate definition of the classic. The classic rather than being fixed in a frozen meaning is by its very definition the source of endlessly productive re-readings. *The Classic,* which is a text as anxious as it is aggressive, does very poorly at justifying the value that it locates in the classic. However over a decade later in another series of lectures, *History and Value,* a serene and relaxed Kermode returned directly to the question of value and to much greater effect. Kermode advances two arguments as to why we cannot do without canons and classics. The first is severely practical. Confronted with the immensity of the archive, whether of books or films, we require a search engine if we are not simply to be overwhelmed with information. But this pragmatic argument, important as it is, is hardly satisfactory for, on this basis, a canon of texts selected at random would work just as well as one produced through the complicated processes of transmission. The very mutability of the classic texts, its ability to be patient of interpretation, means that an immanent account is impossible to sustain. Rather Kermode's solution lies in the very process of selection and sifting, the endless reading and re-reading which sustains a canon which is always subject to revision.

The process of the *Contempt* class in its three years, and this book itself, bear witness to the power of Kermode's solution. In an intake in which there were few students who had specialized in film, much less than half of the incoming classes had seen *Le Mépris* and many had not heard of it. We began and ended the class each year with a full screening of the film in a cinema in 35mm and Cinemascope. After the first screening many of the class were skeptical of the film's value – after six weeks of discussion almost all students had fallen under the spell of the film: had found in it matter for interpretation. The essays collected here reveal how varied these interpretations are: Stabb's meditation on production, Gross's interrogation of what a return home can mean in the modern era, Martin's reflection on the relation between thought and action, Law's consideration of the origins of representation, Gallagher's investigation of mortality, Crippa's argument about anti-theatricality. Falkof's rumination on Godard's women, Ntasouani's subtle analysis of writing and Baki's argument about quotation provide, with the other essays already discussed, strong reasons to think that *Contempt* is a film which is patient of interpretation, that warrants rememoration and transmission. We cannot know for how long European cinema of the second half of the twentieth century will be studied, but we can surmise that, as long as it is, *Contempt* will be watched and discussed. One of the features of both class and book was how our watching of the film led us back again and again from a multitude of different angles to questions of beauty and history. Indeed the film might best be summarized as history condensed into beauty. That Godard's personal history is an essential part of this condensation might be a way of explaining why *Contempt* is art rather than historiography. What cannot be denied is that once *Le Mépris* has been seen and reseen it becomes part of our own attempt to understand both past and present and has to be valued as such. Kermode's last words on the topic put it best : "Perhaps the best image for how we endow with value this or that memory is Proust's novel; out of the indeterminate, disject facts of history, a core of canonical memory out of history value".[13]

Hyderabad
September 2011

## Notes

1 William Viney, this volume, 161–169.
2 Milman Parry, *The Making of Homeric Verse: the Collected Papers of Milman Parry*, edited by Adam Parry (Oxford: Oxford University Press, 1971).
3 James Wilkes, this volume, 55–64.
4 Raphaëlle J Burns, this volume, 203–212.
5 Oliver H. Harris, this volume, 109–119.
6 "Since cinema is a gaze which is substituted for own own in order to give us a world that corresponds to our desires, it settles on faces radiant or bruised but always beautiful bodies, on this glory or devastation which testifies to the same primordial nobility, on this chosen race that we recognize as our own, the ultimate projection of life towards God", Michel Mourlet, Sur un art ignore', *Cahiers du cinéma*, August 1959, 98, p. 34.
7 John Shanks, this volume, 84–96.
8 Perhaps as important as developments in Hollywood or the poor box office of the Nouvelle Vague in 1961 and 1962 was Rossellini's pronouncements on the failure of film and his determination to abandon the cinema. See interview with Rossellini in *Cahiers du cinéma*, no. 133, July 1962, p. 6.
9 *Godard on Godard: Critical Writing by Jean-Luc Godard* (Da Capo Press, Cambridge, MA), 27.
10 Ross Exo Adams, this volume, 27–41.
11 Alice Gavin, this volume, 42–54.
12 Anna Manubens, this volume, 221–237.
13 Frank Kermode, *History and Value* (Oxford: The Clarendon Press 1988), 146.

ROSS EXO ADAMS

# Foreground, Background, Drama: The Cinematic Space of *Le Mépris*

André Bazin once wrote about cinema that '[o]ur experience of space is the structural basis for our concept of the [cinematic] universe.'[1] Criticising the contemporary cinema, he would further declare that acting itself loses all meaning if it lacks a 'living and responsive connection'[2] with the space of the film, or the décor. Precisely this relationship between décor and character – or background and figure – bears tremendous effect on plot development and, more importantly, provides a degree of freedom to the audience to participate in it. In mainstream cinema, the cinematic space as a background to the unfolding drama almost always plays a role subordinate to the action and presence of the film's central figures. In its most general sense, the scenic background provides a basic topography in which the central plot can take root and develop – a luminous surface which renders the precise texture and tension that the audience is supposed to read between characters. And much like the effect a soundtrack produces, the background often supports a singular reading of the film's drama. Yet in many of Godard's films, and quintessentially in his *Le Mépris*, he inverts this relationship, turning the background into a kind of formal device, which interacts with the drama of the film in a bizarre and unsettling way. As evidenced by *Le Mépris*, Godard's use of filmic space – the background in relation to the characters – puts into question this very coherence that we expect to see between the space of the film and the consistency of action taking place within it.

How does such an inversion appear and what is accomplished by imposing such formalism? Through a detailed examination of *Le Mépris*, I will attempt to uncover a particular *spatial facet* of Godard's aesthetic which gained clarity specifically in the making of this film. I will show how such an aesthetic device was nascent not only in his earliest films, but, to an extent, was anticipated by Bazin's critique of cinematic space years before. Suggesting a certain continuity of his use of space throughout some of the later films of his so-called 'cinematic period', I will attempt to reveal Godard's intention with such a spatial device. Yet short of remaining in continuity with Bazin's idealisation of cinematic space, I will argue that Godard's precise spatial composition in fact represented a *fundamental departure* from the notion Bazin had developed. Exactly because of this,

Godard was able to disclose a filmic surface completely new to cinema upon which he would later project his political meta-narratives, giving content to his rigorously formal cinematic realism.

## *Le Mépris*

While perhaps overshadowed by more obvious entry points into an analysis of *Le Mépris*, Godard's composition of space in this film – the hierarchy and play between figure and ground, or character and backdrop – is certainly one which merits investigation. Throughout the film he introduces very subtle, yet seemingly precise alterations to the otherwise quite standard relationship between the actors' drama and scenic background. The effect these interventions produce tends to destabilise the smooth cinematic experience, while never radically disrupting it, as in some of his later films.[3] And because it remains unclear exactly what the intention of such an aesthetic device is, it is helpful first to explore in detail the appearance of such compositional estrangement in *Le Mépris*.

Upon close inspection one can discern roughly four distinct methods of spatial composition that Godard appears to use to accomplish this estrangement. I would suggest grouping such compositional techniques in the following categories, as they tend to appear not as novel mise-en-scène configurations, but as repetitive cinematic devices that can be observed appearing at moments throughout the duration of the film. Provisionally, I will categorise them as follows: *scale shift*; *character positioning*; *obstruction*; and what I call *absorption*. It is important to note that these techniques are not mutually exclusive, as they tend at times to overlap one another to create a rich aesthetic formalism. In any case, I will try to isolate these techniques, giving exemplar cases where they appear more or less homogeneously.

The first type of spatial estrangement occurs through what I call *scale shift*. By this I mean to describe certain sequences when, by distancing the camera from the site of drama, the characters in the foreground become reduced to a point where the composition of the background suddenly competes with and overwhelms their presence. The sudden inversion makes it unclear to know on what we are supposed to focus our attention. An example of this appears early in the film, when Paul (Michel Piccoli) and the translator, Francesca (Giorgia Moll), arrive in Cinecittà to meet the producer Prokosch (Jack Palance). The camera initially captures Paul and Francesca at their first point of encounter from a fairly close-up distance, giving visual predominance to their figures. As the camera tracks, following the pair as they walk toward the large doors from which Prokosch will eventually emerge, it slowly pulls back and away from the characters. By the time Prokosch appears, Paul and Francesca are only marginally included in the shot, and Prokosch's figure on the raised platform pales in comparison to the presence of the great door behind him (see Figure 1).

**Figure 1** Scale shift, *Le Mépris*, dir. Jean-Luc Godard, 1963

From this vantage point, one is no longer able to make out the details of the characters' faces, nor their expressions, yet the monologue that Prokosch delivers seems to bear an intense emotional urgency. Instead, the background suddenly seems to be the main subject of the camera's gaze. Its composition of the large green door, the decaying concrete awning announcing itself as 'Teatro No. 6', the great wall, its pale pink, weathered paint all seem instead to bear a kind of dramatic presence over that of the characters, diminished as they are by the camera distance.

In a similar manner to his play of scale, Godard manages to marginalise the presence of the characters through a simple de-centred *positioning* of them vis-à-vis the scene, again drawing our attention away from their action and presence and toward the static space of the background. He accomplishes this by one of two ways: by either 'sidelining' the characters – placing them nearly off-camera,[4] or by imposing a sudden severely composed symmetry into the shot. In an exemplary display of the first of these techniques, in Prokosch's Roman villa, the scene of Paul's transgression with Francesca unfolds. The scene follows from Paul and Francesca's initial flirtatious encounter in the salon. As Francesca dashes off, Paul chases after her, grabbing her shoulders and stroking her hair. The two then meet Camille (Brigitte Bardot) on the landing by the door at the bottom of the stairs, where Paul pats Francesca's bottom. It is here where the camera, having followed them to this point, slowly begins a gradual retreat both backwards and to the right of the landing. Through this retreat, the tension of the encounter, Paul's fondling of Francesca having been caught by Camille, and the exchange that takes place thereafter all become slowly isolated off to the left of the screen. The camera's slow withdrawal instead begins to expose a certain overwhelming visual dominance of the set of red chairs, the baroque candelabras and the wooden staircase which diagonally bisects the screen in half (see Figure 2). This retreat of the camera definitively puts into question the hierarchy of background and figure, as

**Figure 2** Character positioning: 'sidelining', *Le Mépris*, dir. Jean-Luc Godard, 1963

even the brightly lit statue on the very edge of the screen seems to visually eclipse the presence of Paul and Camille in this shot.

In addition to 'sidelining' characters, Godard achieves a very similar effect, but through quite different means: by the imposition of symmetry. In the Naussicaa audition scene, Paul and Camille enter the theatre and take their seats opposite to one another, about the central aisle. The camera, facing them and the others as if viewed from an overly curious usher, then lulls side to side as the layered conversation unfurls. Through this sequence, a certain overwhelming sense of visual symmetry develops by the camera's swinging back and forth across the symmetry of the theatre chairs, the balanced positioning of the characters and the central focal point underscored by the aisle itself. And if the symmetrical architecture of the space is not enough, the presence of the persistent photographer marking the centre of the space with his flashbulb only confirms Godard's formal intent here (see Figure 3). Again, it is the background which presents itself not as a subordinate space of the action taking place, but in fact as a competitor to it.

Indeed as a competitor, we find the background décor often nearly jumps forward into the foreground of the scene, at times imposing an *obstruction* to the actors 'smoothly' carrying out their roles. One thinks of the comical placement of the unglazed door in the apartment, or the ladder that Camille suddenly avoids passing under as she paces about the apartment, tormenting Paul with her contempt. Or again, when Paul and Francesca first meet Prokosch in the beginning of the film and the two are accompanying him into the screening room in Cinecittà, they pause at the entrance, where Prokosch grasps the overtly low-placed green awning. As the three then turn to enter the door, they awkwardly find themselves ducking to avoid hitting their heads (see Figure 4). While such obstructions seem to play no obvious role in any scene, their precise placement appears to once again disrupt the drama of the film, momentarily inverting the standard relationship of the background to the figure.

**Figure 3** Character positioning: symmetry, *Le Mépris*, dir. Jean-Luc Godard, 1963

Lastly, through what I would call *absorption,* in an almost satirical manner, Godard again destabilises the cinematic coherence in *Le Mépris* through the subtle and momentary dominance of a deep décor. What I mean by *absorption* is the cinematographic technique whereby the background suddenly seems to project its depth forward, engulfing both the characters and foreground into a single 'fixed' composition: the figure-ground relationship becomes confounded leaving an enriched space of both figure *and* ground. Here, the importance of the individual characters is challenged by their momentary subjugation to the strangely composed visual setting they find themselves in. A particularly rich deployment of this technique occurred, once again, in the scene of the encounter between Paul and Francesca in the salon of Prokosch's Roman villa, just before Paul's transgression. As the two speak, at one point Paul gets up from the couch and the camera follows him as he walks to the other side of Francesca, revealing a highly composed arrangement of brightly coloured, ornate furniture, baroque statues, a harp and a large, feathery plant – all of which positioned in different focal planes. Following a comical stroke of the harp, Paul's figure becomes increasingly *absorbed* into this setting, as he moves gradually amongst the elaborate and colourful objects of the room, drifting from foreground to background. This loss of figure into a 'deep' background is underpinned by Francesca's static, painterly composure as she sits silently on the chair to the left of the scene (see Figure 5). In this shot, we are suddenly made aware that we can no longer distinguish the hierarchy of figure and ground. In other words, the pieces of furniture and the characters themselves are momentarily of equal visual importance to the larger affect of spatial composition that Godard intends to achieve.

While each of these examples attempts to demonstrate a particular way that Godard composed space and its effect on the cinematic relationship of figure and ground, his shooting of the extended scene in the apartment brilliantly interweaves all of these techniques into one seamlessly

**Figure 4** Obstruction, *Le Mépris*, dir. Jean-Luc Godard, 1963

choreographed performance of figure and ground. The culmination of this is captured by the camera's voyeuristic position behind a dividing wall which follows the quarrelling couple as they trade positions and insults throughout the apartment. From this position, the camera is able to use the depth of the apartment to both engulf and diminish the figures of Paul and Camille. The dividing wall and the location of the rooms on either side of it allow several shots of two to be positioned symmetrically in the lens. And from this vantage point, the bronze statue in the foreground often parodies, or simply obstructs the presence of the characters, shuffling about in the background (see Figures 6 & 7).

## Bazin

That Godard raises the background to the level of aesthetic device in his early cinematic realism should come as no surprise. The notion of cinematic space, the décor, and its relationship to the drama of the actors occupied much of the work of Godard's mentor, André Bazin. As early as 1946, Bazin, enthralled by the recent films of Orson Welles, devoted a large portion of his writing to the topic, noting specifically its contribution to the formal brilliance and originality of Welles' filming of *Citizen Kane* and *The Magnificent Ambersons*.

Inspired by such works, Bazin realised a largely overlooked potential of the cinema: that cinematic style *alone* has the capacity to constitute meaning. That is to say, through Welles' rigorous, theatrical treatment of space, he was able to produce a form of cinema that could engage the audience with the drama in a way that traditional cinema had failed to do. This accomplishment, as Bazin recognised, was due in a large part to the development of formal techniques such as the 'static shot' and his use of 'deep focus'[5]. If treated properly, the relationship between action (figures) and décor (background) creates what Bazin called a 'surplus of realism',

**Figure 5** Absorption, *Le Mépris*, dir. Jean-Luc Godard, 1963

lending the décor an 'existential density; a dramatic realism which refuses to separate actor from décor, foreground from background; a psychological realism which brings the spectator back to the real conditions of perception, a perception which is never completely determined a priori.'[6]

Bazin's defence of the spatial realism of cinema could be one of his most important contributions to film criticism. His passionate argument for an *equality* to be recognised between the film's space and the action taking place within comes across in many pieces of his writing. For Bazin, the relationship of décor and actor is one of solidity with the cinematic universe – a universe whose realism 'follows directly from its photographic nature.'[7] He proclaims: 'It is the conquest of realism – not, certainly, the realism of subject matter or realism of expression but that realism of space without which moving pictures do not constitute cinema.'[8] For example, the 'secondary' details in cinema – the sudden interruptions of elements (sounds, objects, etc.) indifferent to the action – confirm or guarantee its reality. Bazin praises Welles for his use of such 'objects, outrageously irreverent to the action yet monstrously present, [which] solicit our attention without a single camera movement conspiring to diminish their presence.'[9]

## Godard

If Bazin had championed an infallible commitment to the realism of cinematic experience, Godard's aesthetic would take the task a step further toward an expression of a cinema fixated on the realism of its own production. Stemming from the critical discourse that Godard and the other critics of the *Cahiers du Cinéma* had launched, the neo-classical uniformity and conservative nature of post-war French cinema left little room for formal experimentation. An aesthetic dominated by a dictatorial tendency to over determine the narrative, submitting its audience to formulaic, one-dimensional plot lines, the French studio of this period was increasingly

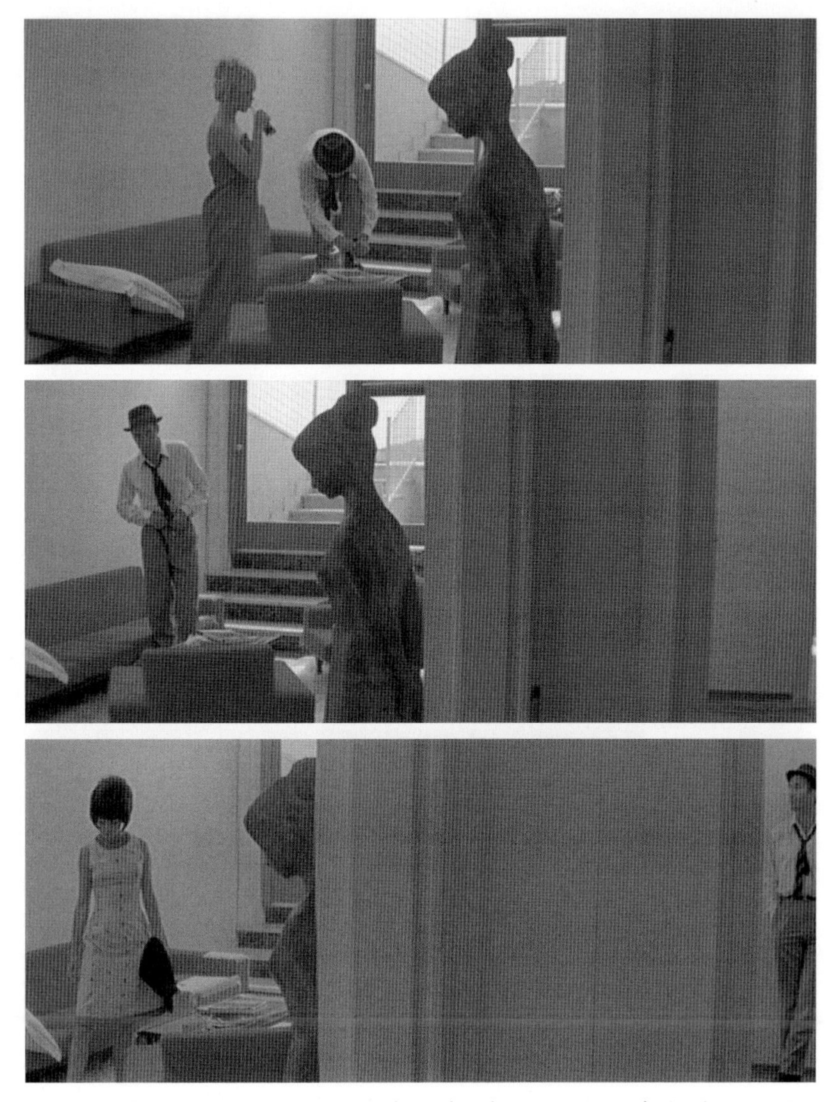

**Figure 6** The apartment scene: overlap of techniques, *Le Mépris*, dir. Jean-Luc Godard, 1963

the site of highly confining and expensive industrial film production. Moreover, because of this, the audience's expectations in terms of what cinematic form could produce were growing increasingly uniform. As a direct attack to this deadlock, Godard would develop films whose aesthetic was first and foremost a critique to these conditions. For him, this meant embarking on a formalism which could capture reality without the intervention of a consciousness or the psychological narrative of a determinist plot. It meant that his films would necessarily leave their

**Figure 7** The apartment scene: overlap of techniques, *Le Mépris*, dir. Jean-Luc Godard, 1963

audience an infinity of readings which could be made. It also meant creating a cinema which would ground its formalism in a minimalist, low-budget aesthetic. For what Godard wanted his films to show was not the technical possibilities of cinema, but the bare substance of cinema itself. Thus, Godard's films would leave the studio and take to the streets with portable cameras, tiny crews and a minimal budget. Suddenly, the filmic background would no longer rely on constructing a composed setting before shooting, but would result from and be conditioned by the contingencies of whichever location the film was to be shot. In a word, the background became a clear *aesthetic trace* of Godard's commitment to low-budget cinema.

Yet the way Godard would engage with the background or décor was not at first clear, and it indeed evolved over the course of his career. Since his first film, *Breathless* (1960), the background appeared more as a residue of his impulse to defy the studio conditions of mainstream French cinema than a consciously deliberate formal device. However, moments exist in the film when the background projects itself into the drama of the actors, interrupting the fluidity of the plot. One recalls, for example, the lengthy scene when Patricia (Jean Seberg) and Michel (Jean-Paul Belmondo) are in Patricia's apartment and the radio broadcast introduces a momentary and strangely out-of-place political layer to the film. In *Vivre sa vie* (1962), during the opening scene in the café, as Nana (Anna Karina) and her boyfriend Paul (André Labarthe) sit facing away from the camera, Godard explores a use of the background to project fragments of the characters' faces in reflections on the objects and surfaces of the café counter (see Figure 8). *Le Petit Soldat* (1960) reveals little interest in exploiting background beyond as a constant reminder of Godard's departure from the studio into the reality of the city. However, during the scene of Bruno's (Michel Subor) torture in the apartment, Godard again interjects with several sudden shots of a woman in a strangely rigid position reading texts of Lenin and Mao. The

**Figure 8** The café scene of *Vivre sa vie*, dir. Jean-Luc Godard, 1962

appearance of these shots serves to break the continuity of the scene with the introduction of seemingly incongruous elements – objects which appear to emerge from a more static background – suspending the intensity of the drama in moments of contrived estrangement.

Because Godard's formalism was so closely tied up with the conditions of production, his decisive departure in the filming of *Le Mépris* from his low-budget cinema would present significant aesthetic challenges. Indeed, *Le Mépris* proved to be a kind of testing ground in which Godard would be forced to innovate his aesthetic. By introducing the constraints of a big budget film, the demands of multiple producers and a large crew, Godard was left with little room to experiment with his typically unorthodox camera work, modes of editing or script-less acting. As well, his candid use of 'found' locations, impromptu settings and contingencies that filming within 'reality' provides, would all be eliminated by default. And perhaps more importantly, because he had deliberately chosen to adopt into film a particularly psychological novel with a strong storyline, he was forced to find new ways of positioning the cinematic experience itself above any concerns of plot development and most certainly before any kind of character identification.

Thus, how can we consider Godard's use of space – in particular his composed relationship between background and figure – to have assisted in maintaining his aesthetic authorship under such conditions? To answer this question, it is helpful to consider Godard's direction of *Le Mépris* from two distinct perspectives. On the one hand Godard's structural approach to the film worked in several key ways in terms of his treatment of adaptation of the original novel, his script writing (where he would introduce a dense layer of quotation), his choice of actors, their nationalities, the introduction of a translator, etc. All of this would serve to superimpose a certain strata of extra-narrative commentary which could be said to supplement the most basic layer of drama of the film itself, thus confirming Godard's commitment to cinematic realism. On the other hand, from a formal level, by inverting the traditional relations of background and figure he would produce a very delicate yet precise effect. In this respect, I claim Godard was able to subvert the rigidity of big-budget cinema by quietly yet constantly undermining and destabilising narrative and plot development while also undercutting the entire psychological substance of the film. Thus, by simultaneously attacking the seriousness of the storyline, Godard was able to supplement the battered drama with his own *meta-commentary,* ensuring his aesthetic dominance over dramatic, psychological or narrative expression.

How does his use of space in *Le Mépris* play such a crucial role in accomplishing this task? If we return to the initial analysis of the film, it is important to notice that Godard deploys these techniques of spatial estrangement not at random, but at very precise moments of dramatic climax. Recall, for instance, the scene of Paul's transgression. As in the equivalent scene of Movravia's novel, just when Paul is caught by Camille after having groped Francesca, it would seem to foist a dramatic fissure into the storyline. Yet exactly as we expect to be pulled into a moment of high tension, Paul and Camille's confrontation is immediately undercut by Godard's direction of the camera *away* from the two and onto the elaborate cinematic setting of furniture to the right. In so doing, Godard makes impossible our reading of the characters' facial expressions, leaving the drama suddenly flat, precisely when we expect it to explode. Instead of leading us into an emotional crescendo of the narrative, we seem suddenly to be faced with a neutral 'painting' of sorts. Similarly, in the scene of the Naussicaa audition, we are again caught between our expectations of dramatic culmination and the bizarre visual cues Godard provides for us. This scene, it seems, replaces the tempestuous dinner in Moravia's novel. Here again, our dramatic anticipations are derailed by Godard's inversion of the background over the action. The visual dominance of the symmetrical theatre, the arrangement of the characters in an uncomfortably balanced composition and the eager photographer flashing his camera's bulb at every opportunity all seem to call our attention away from the tension we expect from the storyline, leaving the drama once again flat. In fact in each one of the above examples, the same arguments applies.

His sudden visual and compositional interruptions create such strong backgrounds that the characters seem to wither away in complicity with the sudden dominance of space. Just as the temptation to fall into the psychology or narrative at particularly dramatic moments occurs, Godard abruptly removes it, reminding us that what we are watching is not the tragedy of a marriage crumbling apart, but the *essence* of cinema itself. Indeed, Godard brilliantly succeeds in producing a big-budget film while remarkably never allowing its conditions to trump his position as *auteur*.

Unquestionably influenced by Bazin, Godard's use of space, nevertheless, would bear a striking and fundamental difference from that professed by Bazin. It is true that Bazin's praise for the 'static shot' and 'deep focus' were clearly adopted into Godard's repertoire, and what Godard accomplished with his aesthetic interruptions (obstructions, etc.), Bazin had pre-empted with his notion of 'aesthetic catalysts'.[10] Yet while it is also true that both embraced realism, Bazin would remain satisfied to promote a kind of 'dramatic realism' – an ideal relation between décor and actor, which is somewhat static; a bit given over to a general *ideal state of equality* between the two. In contrast, however, Godard's development of his *cinematic realism* would reconsider this relationship in a much more specific and, moreover, strategic way. Contrary to Bazin's implicit equality of actors and décor, Godard's choreography of figures within space relied on their *inherent inequality*. In fact, for Godard's cinematic realism to take shape he would rely precisely on his calibrated interventions which sought to elevate the background *above* the actors' drama, suggesting a certain implicit hierarchical economy between the two elements. And by deploying shots of spatial estrangement only at precise moments of *Le Mépris*, he managed to put into question the entire relationship between actor and décor, or figure and background.

Godard's interpretation of cinematic space would eventually open up new possibilities for the cinema that perhaps Bazin had never anticipated. Just as his figure-ground relationship allowed him to prop his cinematic commentary on top of the storyline of *Le Mépris*, the same formal device

**Figure 9** The Parisian banlieues of *2 ou 3 choses que je sais d'elle*, dir. Jean-Luc Godard, 1967

would come to provide an entire filmic surface upon which Godard could project his own political meta-narrative. In other words, through his formal development of the background, he would discover a means by which to import *content* into his cinematic *form*. Progressing from momentary interruptions in the storyline of *Le Mépris*, Godard's figure-ground formalism would evolve beyond subtle interventions to a point where he had nearly inverted the relationship completely. This inversion would produce an effect of creating near-documentary depictions of certain realities, which, for Godard, it had become increasingly urgent to film. In perhaps its most extreme case, in his *2 ou 3 choses que je sais d'elle*, it is precisely the background itself that becomes the centre of the film, and the plot articulated by the central character, Juliette (Marina Vlady), simply justifies the documentation of the suburban landscape that 'unfolds' (see Figure 9). Colin MacCabe questions the formal clarity of this film: 'Is this a report on the urban transformations of Paris, or the fictional investigation of a woman's life?'[11]

Indeed, in such a radical inversion of figure-ground it becomes clear that Godard was not only pushing the limits of cinematic form, he was also beginning to question it altogether. For as much as his formal experimentation did create new possibilities for cinema, it also heralded his growing impatience with its core formal limitations – those which thwarted a truly political expression. MacCabe notes that 'as the political pressure of the 1960s grew more intense, and particularly the pressures of the war in Vietnam, Godard's search for a form adequate to the demands of politics which would also constitute a politics adequate to the demands of form became increasingly desperate.'[12]

In fact, shortly after his filming of *2 ou 3 choses*, Godard would abandon the cinematic form altogether, having exhausted its ability to depict the politics he could no longer avoid addressing. His eventual use of the documentary form in the Dziga Vertov films *British Sounds* and *Pravda* confirmed this. If there is one thread of continuity that can span from *Le Mépris* to his break from cinematic form, it is his impulse to destroy the dramatic coherence between background (reality) and figure (bearer of fictional narrative).

Thus what began as a formal device, questioning the relationship between figure and ground, emerged as something more connected with an inquiry into the entire construct of cinema, the necessity of plot and the significance of authorship. As this interrogation continued, it would assist in his shift from meta-commentary to meta-narrative, impregnating his formalism with a content exterior to cinema itself. And it would be this exteriority which, for Godard, would foretell his own end of cinema.

## Notes

1 André Bazin, *What is Cinema?* (Berkeley: University of California Press, 1967), 108.

2 André Bazin, *Orson Welles: A Critical View* (London: Elm Tree Books, 1978), 68.
3 For example, in *Tout va bien*, Godard often exposes the set from a distant camera as a constructed series of studio spaces, brutally undermining the drama by revealing a stark *cinematic realist* perspective of this film.
4 One will notice that this was the case for Paul and Francesca in the previously described shot.
5 André Bazin, *Orson Welles*, p. 73 (From translator's note): the 'static shot' is a shot of 'vertiginous duration' where the camera refuses to come to the aid of the viewer. Bazin's notion of 'deep focus' refers to the favoring of the mobility of actors within multiple depths of space over the portrayal of static actors captured by multiple camera angles.
6 Ibid., 80.
7 André Bazin, *What is Cinema?*, 108.
8 Ibid., 112.
9 André Bazin, *Orson Welles*, 80.
10 From Bazin, A. *What is Cinema?*, 110: aesthetic catalysts, for Bazin are those secondary details whose 'indifference' to the action' confirms the realism of the cinematic experience.
11 Colin MacCabe, *Godard: Images, Sound, Politics* (New York: Macmillan, 1980), 51.
12 Ibid., 52.

ALICE GAVIN

# Godard's Apart-ment Architectures: The Reality of Abandonment in *Le Mépris*

In Jack Palance's first appearance in *Le Mépris,* his character – Prokosch, the ruthless producer of Fritz Lang's efforts to film the *Odyssey* – emerges squinting into the Italian sun from the recesses of Cinecittà's Teatro No. 6. Given the film's Greek links, it's an entry aptly redolent of the architecture of the Attic stage, where the dramatic action took place in front of 'a façade – the *skene* or scene building – whose principle [. . .] feature was a door or set of doors' leading to a separate internal domain.[1] This was an interior territory architecturally absent from the actual theatrical space, a theatrical fiction present only in terms of its framing. In Godard's film, however, it is the *Teatro* itself that disappears. The American producer emerges into a place at once a film studio and a sort of stage, both an on-screen (Godard's film) and an 'off' (Lang's adaptation). His entry at the Cinecittà lots indexes the filmic receding in *Le Mépris* of a distinct separation between real and fictional space – a separation previously asserted in theatre by the architecture of the proscenium arch, in its turn an architecture we'll later see clinging to the wall of a reluctant participant in filmic scriptwriting, Paul. Joan Copjec, drawing on the work of Michael Fried, suggests that this 'retraction [. . .] of the proscenium stage' connotes a 'turning away from a determinate, locatable audience' in favour 'of the construction of an internally coherent space' 'in which characters [. . .] become completely "absorbed" and thus shun any acknowledgement of an extradiegetic audience'.[2] *Le Mépris* meanwhile alerts us to a further subtlety that Copjec's work also points us towards. In her refinement of the argument, the 'internally coherent space' created by the retraction of the arch is in fact actually 'semicoherent' and 'riven by a split', a splitting that is totally interior to that supposedly consistent space.[3] Godard's film of 1963 similarly has at its heart a separation, a split and a dislocation, and its architecture is constantly evocative of this – as is Curzio Malaparte's description of his villa at Capri, so crucial to *Le Mépris,* as a 'displaced slice of Greek amphitheatre'.[4]

The producer's first emergence notably occurs in a place decorated by disintegration. Shabbily signed as a *Teatro* whose interior remains unrevealed, the tall doors that frame his entry are anticipated by degenerated duplicates, iron-barred constructions that open onto nothing but brick. The filmic scenery into which Prokosch steps is, moreover, itself a vacated space – and not simply because it's being sold off to a 'five and ten cent store'. Paul, the scriptwriter upon whom Prokosch is to place the responsibility of writing 'more' for Lang's movie, has upon his arrival at Cinecittà already noted the curious de-population of the studio lots. Francesca, Prokosch's translator, tells him that 'almost everybody' has been discharged. Indeed, Prokosch initially seems to have absconded the scene himself: as Raoul Coutard's camera tracks back up the path by which it first neared us at the film's beginning, Paul and Francesca are captured peeking into corners and repeatedly calling out the producer's name (Figure 1). It is an abandoned architecture – a location emptied of its industry inhabitants; a deserted *skene* or *mise-en-scène* – that frames Prokosch's first entry.

Yet, it is exactly this aspect of abandonment that allows for the surfacing within that same *skene* of the camera that captures the remaining population of the lots, a population that includes Godard's own crew. The clearing of Italy's Cinema City reaches its limit in the appearance of Coutard's lens or *objectif*. The lots cannot be completely de-populated if Coutard's camera is to stick around to film the remaining emptiness, and so it is the emptied scene of the 'end of cinema' – as declared by Prokosch as he prowls the platform-like paving above Francesca and Paul – that makes room for the reality of *Le Mépris*.

Godard's film does not simply embrace an abandonment of the real, a straightforward desertion of descriptive or classic realism. Instead, *Le Mépris*'s inclusion of various alien or out-of-sync elements is illustrative of what we might call the reality of abandonment. The film may well involve an investigation of 'a strange and luxurious space' located 'somewhere between art and life' and inhabited by the 'liminal figure of the movie star' – a figure Brigitte Bardot's appearance in the film, in which the presence of 'B.B.' can never be completely effaced by 'Camille', might be said to signify.[5]

**Figure 1** Paul and Francesca at Cinecittà, *Le Mépris*, dir. Jean-Luc Godard, 1963

But from the discrepancies in translation performed by Francesca, to the sequence on the terrace of the Capri villa in which ten seconds of empty landscape (Figure 2) separate Paul's entry into the frame from the exact same point at which Camille left it, but in which he nevertheless neglects to locate her, the ongoing accrual of lags and dislocations in *Le Mépris* points to something much more fascinating. The film's persistent inclusion of occlusions is arguably a signal of its interest in that element of escape – a plane peripheral or additional to the image whilst being like Coutard's camera *'completely demonstrated within it'*, to draw again on the work of Copjec – that is, I will argue, directly relatable to the reality of the cinematic image itself.[6]

Speaking of the source-novel of the film, Alberto Moravia's *Il Disprezzo* (1954), Godard comments on how it 'allowed [him] to tell a classic film story, *as if movies were really like that* [my emphasis]'.[7] Like some sort of literal reading of reality's internal tripping, the 'really' of the fantasised 'as if', *Le Mépris* is the story of a parting or departure interior to reality itself. Like the appearance of Rome's recently erected apartment architectures in the periphery of the Cinecittà scenes, this is a dislocation articulated within rather than without the image. The infiltration of distance and disjuncture into both the film's form and its content amounts to a form of contact, to the formation of a form taught with fissure. 'The "right" image, Godard recalls', in a phrase that also reverberates with the parting of Paul and Camille, 'is one that establishes the correct relationship between two remote things grasped in their maximum distance'.[8] In a phrase the voice-over attributes to a key critic of the *Cahiers du Cinéma* group, André Bazin, *Le Mépris*'s credit sequence tells us that film 'substitutes a world that conforms to our desires'. For the philosopher Jacques Rancière, writing with reference to Godard's *Histoire(s) du Cinéma* (1988-1998), 'the encounter. . .of incompatible elements' – and there are a lot of incompatibilities in *Le Mépris* – 'highlights the power of a different community imposing a different measure; it establishes the absolute reality of desires and dreams'.[9]

**Figure 2** The emptied landscape at Capri, *Le Mépris*, dir. Jean-Luc Godard, 1963

So when Coutard turns his camera on the camera that captures the progress of his own *reportage*, this does not necessarily amount to a moment of textual self-reflexivity (Figure 3). It could on the contrary be said to render a parting between the *objectif* of the camera and the perspective or 'point of view' it engenders. In turning to face its own frame – in encountering its own gaze – the camera as transcendent capturer separates away from itself and a gap is inserted into the world it gathers together. The perspective Coutard's camera addresses here, the frame that frames *his* camera, cannot in fact be assimilated to any determinate source. The action of camera approaching camera – an action in which the latter lens remains invisible, its materiality increasingly, if not completely, depleted by the visible presence of Coutard's – is infringed upon by the feeling that the camera also turns on 'us'. This is in effect an 'unattributable shot', a shot that, as Copjec describes it, is 'not filmed from a space that is proximate to' or 'spatially associated with' any particular character, but which is nevertheless 'included' within the film's assemblage of perspectives.[10] Like Prokosch's initial entry, it is a shot that seems to appear out of nowhere; it represents in turn the appearance of an additional, surplus nowhere within a scenery which is itself almost emptied. These early sequences of *Le Mépris* suggest, in other words, a distancing or departure lodged wholly within reality itself: the addition of an apart-ness that, rather than referencing a beyond to what the camera can observe, is instead located entirely within the field of its frame.

Partings, departures and apartments are all crucial to *Le Mépris*. Given its hero's infamously hindered homecoming, Paul's involvement in the *Odyssey* project, alongside the seepage of the latter's images into the separate, separating story of Paul and Camille, is a further signal of the film's interest in dislocation. As Karen Bassi claims, the 'proper place in the world for both epic hero and epic poet is' in 'spatial terms' 'not at home'.[11] If one meaning of apartment is a 'separate, proper, or special

**Figure 3** Coutard's camera, *Le Mépris*, dir. Jean-Luc Godard, 1963

place of abode', a 'place appropriated to any purpose' (*OED*), then in *Le Mépris* it is at home that the film's protagonists are actually most *in*appropriate to each other, most emphatically apart. If, to adapt a phrase of Georges Perec's, the 'uninhabitable' is the 'architecture of contempt', it is on supposedly home territory that the uninhabitable aspect of their relationship is manifested.[12]

It is exactly this capturing of fracture, however, that allows Godard to make his break with traditional or classical form. (This is arguably similar to the way in which Roberto Rossellini's observation of the protagonists of *Viaggio in Italia* (1953) as obviously bored by 'empty space and time' engenders a resistance in that film to swift and busy narrative action.[13] Camille lists possible boredom as one reason for her reluctance to accompany Paul to Capri, it's worth noting.) The inclusion of Lang's *Odyssey* scenes in the narrative attended to by Godard and his crew, and the excursions of Godard and crew into the construction of Lang's movie, can be usefully described as an 'exchange of linguistic ardors', Pier Paolo Pasolini's formulation of the technique of free indirect discourse in film.[14] The architecture of *Le Mépris* is an architecture of apart-ment, an assemblage of separations and breakages; Camille's indifference to the dinner-plates she accidentally smashes and Prokosch's physical antipathy towards the film reels are instances illustrative of a theme that is also formal. Yet, this architecture remains simultaneously the locus of some kind of communion, an 'exchange of ardors'. In 'The Cinema of Poetry', Pasolini argues that Godard's form of free indirect discourse involves a 'confrontational arrangement', a 'disintegration reconstituted into unity' by exactly the kind of unattributable – or, in Pasolini's word, 'inarticulate' – perspective structured by the long take discussed above.[15]

Free indirect discourse has its roots in literature, and Pasolini's attempt to translate it to cinema is not without its difficulties. It remains, however, a useful tool for considering the architecture constructed by *Le Mépris*'s camera angles further. In Copjec's description of the filmic free indirect – Copjec's work likewise looks to Pasolini – everything occurs 'as if the characters, while fully immersed in their points of view or in their lives as such, simultaneously stood partially outside themselves, reflected in the gaze of another'.[16] This apparently external frame is not, however, inhabited by any particular persona, but instead represents the emergence of the uninhabitable within the architecture of the filmic text. The inclusion of an unrealistic element, a dialect or style not realistically assimilable to the perspective it nevertheless presents, is for Pasolini a moment of 'reanimated speech'.[17] It could moreover be suggested that the 'immersion of the filmmaker' in the point of view of a character inserts a gap or an opening into the reality that is captured: since it becomes difficult to distinguish between the point of view of the camera/filmmaker and that of the character, authority is dislodged from any transcendent location.[18] Just as Godard, *Le Mépris*'s director or 'originator', is visible in the film as Lang's assistant during the shooting of the *Odyssey* scenes at Capri, the author of the *Odyssey,* Homer, appears in Lang's film amongst the Gods of his artistic creation. Indications on the one hand of another scene, another world, these appearances take place entirely within what is available to be seen – as is emphasised by Homer's appearance in the context of a *screening*. As much a statue as his divinities, Homer moreover surfaces in terms of his creative material: his separateness has no objective consistency of its own, but is instead inserted into the tale he tells; the source of the story's construction appears in its screening as a gap in the action of its appropriate inhabitants, the Gods.

Paul and Camille's failure to settle in their apartment, a failure framed by their prolonged and incessant wandering in and out of rooms, can in this sense be seen as one instance of the many improprieties of occupation that litter *Le Mépris*. From Paul's discomfort with the role Prokosch offers him, to Ulysses' intrusion into a scene of his own story – akin to Camille when seated in the boat, Ulysses is requested to remove himself from the shot – the film's frequent accommodations of dis-occupation illustrate a breaking apart of proper or appropriate belonging. The film's dual states – the landscape of Lang's *Odyssey* and that of Godard's narrative around it – share an inhabitation of a space neither wholly nor properly theirs. Likewise, the apartment Paul and Camille inhabit is a newly moved into abode, but it might just as easily be seen as being in a state of being dismantled, taken apart. Like Anna Karina's 'place' in *Le Petit Soldat* (1960), an apartment we first witness as recently occupied but which we later see emptied and readied for removal, their apartment is a space of persistent instability, a space made-up by the breaking up of relations. It is also necessary to note, however, the possibilities of playfulness this unsteadiness sets in motion as Paul and Camille move through their apartment. In a door absconding from its frame, a mirror appearing to alternate position, and a ladder bewildering an otherwise simple passage, it is possible to decipher a kind of disconnection that holds open the possibility of creative contact, a 'clash', in Rancière's words, of 'heterogeneous elements that provides a common measure'.[19]

Certainly for Gilles Deleuze, whose work Rancière attends to in *Film Fables*, such a space is relatable to a real potentiality. Like the deserted lots of Cinecittà, spaces that seem related to the many vacated landscapes of Michelangelo Antonioni's contemporaneous *La Notte* (1961), the state of dislocation makes possible the appearance of a future form of cinema. Taking place in 'towns demolished or being reconstructed', spaces immediately inscribed by *Le Mépris*'s studio scenes, Deleuze defines such a state as an 'any-space-whatever', a space that has

> lost its homogeneity, that is, the principle of its metric relations or the connection of its own parts, so that the linkages can be made in an infinite number of ways [. . .] What in fact manifests the instability, the heterogeneity,

> the absence of link of such a space, is a richness in potentials or singularities which are, as it were, prior conditions of all actualisation, all determination.[20]

For Deleuze, the New Wave 'broke shots open' and 'obliterated their distinct spatial determination in favour of a non-totalisable space'.[21] Godard's 'unfinished apartments' are said to participate in this obliteration in their permitting of 'discordances and variations, like all the ways of passing through a door with a missing panel'.[22] The scattered, paint-tub punctuated space that is Paul and Camille's apartment is in a state of abandoning itself. But it is at the same time reminiscent both of the door-frames divorced from a portal that lop-sidedly bracket the entrance to Teatro No. 6 and the scene-painting that Paul passes on his way out of Cinecittà to catch a taxi – making it again this aspect of self-abandonment that recomposes the apartment's elements in relation to the film's alternative territories. Just as the isolated villa assembled on a 'rocky outcropping' of one of Capri's 'wildest terrains' recollects and reconstructs the scenery of Cinecittà in its repetition of iron-barred casings and regions of receding paint, so too does this brand new apartment break up into the landscapes from which it is, simultaneously, a withdrawal.[23] Its discordances are also variations on a theme.

The apartment's state of re-arrangement moreover inserts a form of apart-ness into the interior of the architecture itself: as is aptly illustrated in Camille's difficulty in passing back beneath the ladder that she initially easily passed through, this is an apartment that never seems to be quite itself. Paul's comment regarding the 'house they're building opposite', uttered as he is doubly framed by two diverging doorways, is not supported by a corresponding shot of that building-to-be. In remaining anchored within the apartment instead of revealing this point of exterior reference, the sequence has the effect of inserting that other construction-site into Paul and Camille's deconstructing *domus*. The subtraction of a shot that would corroborate Paul's point of view forces the insertion of an unseen but surplus space into the *mise-en-scène* before us.

This lack-of-a-glance-out-of-the-window makes us all the more aware of the stillness of the shot framing Paul (Figure 4). He here remains unmoved for a period of almost exactly two minutes amid the otherwise continual *chorea* of he and Camille – *chorea* being a kind of dance referred to by Homer in the *Illiad* but also, as Giorgio Agamben hints at in an essay entitled 'Gesture', the name of a neurological disorder involving involuntary, spasmodic movement 'independent of any ambulatory end'.[24] It is a shot in many ways similar to the 'unattributable' one aforementioned, the shot that takes in Coutard's approach and turn of camera.[25] On the one hand, the camera's insistence on not leaving its position, on not following the departure of Paul's thought from the apartment, seems to indicate its relationship to a determinate observer situated firmly in a particular place. On the other hand, the feeling of exceeding stillness and absence of any

**Figure 4** Paul, doubly framed, *Le Mépris*, dir. Jean-Luc Godard, 1963

subjective, empathetic identification gives the impression of a perspective that has been absconded from: the shot that watches Paul it is bare, uninhabited by any human. As with our description of the camera-to-camera above, what emerges in this sequence is the surfacing of an emptied perspective, an apartness interior to the apartment it presents.

Paul and Camille's orientation of their interior is also comparable to the action of *Une Femme est Une Femme*, Godard's film of 1961. *Une Femme est Une Femme* is a film that, like *Le Mépris*, spends a significant chunk of time pursuing its characters through a white-walled apartment – this time re-created by Godard as an exact replica of a real space that was not available for filming. *Une Femme* features a scene in which the character of Anna Karina readies herself to leave the strip joint at which she works by passing through a magic portal. Karina's character – Angela – repeats the 'trick' already demonstrated to her by a colleague, whom the doorway dresses in feathers. Her own passage is captured by an alternation in the camera's perspective. By juxtaposing two shots from opposing sides of the portal – with one corresponding to the 'before' and the other to the 'after' – Godard is able to illustrate the illusion without adding anything to the action his camera records. All that is added is in fact a subtraction: the 'intervention of [a] cut', to adapt another formulation of Copjec's.[26] The door in this sense appears as an architectural articulation of the emptiness of the incision itself.

There is certainly a sense in which this 'trick' in *Une Femme* anticipates Camille's inability to pass back beneath the ladder in *Le Mépris* (Figure 5). In addition to providing a further instance of the film's prolific framings-within-the-frame – a feature which folds into the film's reality a reference to, without quite properly resorting to, the technique of *mise-en-abyme* – the latter is an instance that seems to vibrate with something more than simply superstition on the part of Camille.

Indeed, taken together the two sequences might be seen as articulating the opposition between the long take and montage in cinema, an opposition Copjec also prompts us to consider. In the absence of the alternation of

**Figure 5** Camille and the ladder, *Le Mépris*, dir. Jean-Luc Godard, 1963

viewpoints afforded in montage – in the absence of the switch, edit or cut that facilitates the movement in *Une Femme* – Camille's passage through the ladder's frame is literally blocked. If, as Pasolini seems to suggest in his 'Observations on the Long Take' (1967), cinematic reality requires the conflation of perspectives so that an 'objectivity' divorced from any determinable location emerges from the 'dissolv[ing]' of 'various points of view', then it is this scene more than *Une Femme*'s that is the locus of an 'unseen' illusion.[27] The 'superstition' that prevents Camille from passing is, strangely enough, somehow *produced* by the nature of the camera take that frames her. It is also possible to argue, though, that this engendering of an additional if invisible obstacle to her and Paul's movements – noting as well the near-tripping of Paul as he catches his foot during his progress through the door-frame – is cinematic realism *exactement*.

For Pasolini, the intervention of montage involves a shift from cinema to film proper. For André Bazin, meanwhile, it is the long take that finds favour: for him it is in the long take that reality is really reproduced. Bazin's understanding of realism in cinema was crucial for the French New Wave; in his opinion the photographic image differs from that of other art forms in its ineffaceable reality, its object-hood. If painting only fabricates a substitute for its subject, the cinema cannot but help retain something of the reality of the thing it reproduces. As Bazin argues in 'The Ontology of the Photographic Image', 'in spite of any objections our critical spirit may offer',

> we are forced to accept as real the existence of the object reproduced, actually re-presented, set before us, that is to say, in time and space. Photography enjoys a certain advantage in virtue of this transference of reality from the thing to its reproduction.[28]

The photographic image adds, it might be said, a reality to reality. As Colin MacCabe observes in a reading of Godard's early article, 'Towards a

Political Cinema', 'the cinema is not just a representation of reality, but becomes part of the reality itself' – becomes part of reality, however, in terms of its being parted from it by what Bazin refers to as the 'nonliving' instrumentality of the *objectif*.[29] In other words, it is in terms of the addition of a certain nowhere of the lens – an inappropriate perspective in that its provenance cannot be properly occupied or reduced to any particular scene of belonging – that the cinema partakes of the real. Without adding anything substantial to the action it records, without anything more happening in terms of the action other than the presence of the inhuman lens, the cinema yields a somehow further reality situated firmly within reality itself. Though there is nothing to this further realm, it is nevertheless productive. In his series of lectures on the topic of 'Nothing', held at the Architectural Association in London in 2007, Mark Cousins related the story of Ulysses' temporary abandonment of his real name and assertion instead of 'Mr. Nobody' as his appellation, so that the Cyclops thereby accuses 'Nobody' of attacking him. The story is neatly illustrative of the way in which such an insertion of nothingness, the assertion of an empty place, adds to reality a hiatus that is also the space of a potential change or alteration. As Bazin writes, 'all the arts are based on the presence of man'; 'only photography derives its advantage from his absence'.[30]

Such an absconding is not to be mistaken for a hidden, inaccessible depth – although this of course is exactly the error made by Paul in his reading of Camille. Indeed, Paul's mistake is precisely his attempt to read into Camille and her loss of love for him – he would be better off simply watching her properly, like a movie camera. As Godard remarks with respect to his own interiority, 'there is no difference between my own inside life and my outside life which is there in the picture, with the help of what I see, for I'm not capable of inventing anything'.[31] *Le Mépris*'s treatment of Camille is particularly interesting in light of this. During the scenes at Prokosch's villa situated at the periphery of Rome, we are suddenly confronted with a swiftly-cut series of additional images of Camille (Figure 6). These do not seem to amount to revelations of a perspective intrinsically hers – they do not necessarily tell us any more about her private, interior life. Instead, they just seem to be further proliferations of her face. Interspersed with images of her initial meeting with Prokosch and an otherwise consistent background scenery – apparently a balcony of the recently arrived at villa – the sequence resists any sort of depiction of Camille's ulterior motive, of a hidden interior refused to Paul. It simply renders a scattering of Camille across the surface of the film, a scattering that is articulated in an extremely small space of time. Interrupted by shots that seem on the one hand to associate with Lang's perspective on Camille and Prokosch as he approached them at the car, the frank – remembering Paul's use of this word in his descriptions of Camille – frontal images reveal no particular, confirmable viewpoint.

**Figure 6** Images of Camille, *Le Mépris*, dir. Jean-Luc Godard, 1963

Malaparte saw his villa at Capri as capturing a 'displaced' segment of a Greek amphitheatre. In the opinion of one connoisseur of montage, Sergei Eisenstein, the 'Greeks have', in their architecture, 'left us the most perfect examples of shot design, change of shot, and shot length (that is, the duration of particular impression)'.[32] The Acropolis of Athens has 'an equal

**Figure 7** Ferdinand Pierrot scales the abandoned seaside house, *Pierrot le Fou*, dir. Jean-Luc Godard, 1965

right to be called the perfect example of one of the most ancient films'.[33] For Eisenstein, montage quite literally begins with buildings. Orientating the Acropolis is equivalent to the experience of reality afforded by montage. The traversing of structures is certainly key to *Le Mépris*. There is a sense in which Paul's calling after Camille as he navigates the edges of the terrace at Capri – in a scene that follows the ten seconds of empty landscape aforementioned (Figure 2) – relates not only to Ferdinand-Pierrot's scaling of the abandoned seaside house he has been living in with Marianne in *Pierrot le Fou* (1965) (Figure 7), but also to the kind of positions assumed by Godard's cameras themselves: the characters' navigation of Godard's chosen architectures amounts to yet another choreographing and emphasising of the frame.

This recurrent traversal of edges, boundaries and peripheries is moreover another articulation of the possibility of making space, of undoing its co-ordinates and re-forming them. If this necessitates the inclusion of a perspective not born by any body in particular, it also makes possible its harnessing: as Bazin observes in a comment that seems directly relevant to the landscapes of *Le Mépris* 'photography actually contributes something to the order of natural creation instead of providing a substitute'.[34]

## Notes

1 Karen Bassi, '*Nostos, Domos,* and the Architecture of the Ancient Stage', *South Atlantic Quarterly*, 98 (1999), 415–49 (416).
2 Joan Copjec, *Imagine There's No Woman: Ethics and Sublimation* (Cambridge: MIT Press, 2002), 220; 221.
3 Ibid., 221.
4 Quoted in Michael McDonough, 'Malaparte: A House Like Me', in *Malaparte: A House Like Me*, ed. by Michael McDonough (New York: Clarkson Potter, 1999), 8–37 (8).

5 Simon Dixon, 'Ambiguous Ecologies: Stardom's Domestic Mise-En-Scene', *Cinema Journal*, 42 (2003), 81–100 (81).
6 Joan Copjec, *Read My Desire: Lacan Against The Historicists* (Cambridge: MIT Press, 1994), 178.
7 Quoted in Nicholas Paige, 'Bardot and Godard in 1963 (Historicizing the Postmodern Image)', *Representations*, 88 (2004), 1–25 (2).
8 Jacques Rancière, *The Future of the Image* (London: Verso, 2007), 58.
9 Rancière, *The Future of the Image*, 56.
10 Copjec, *Imagine There's No Woman*, 201.
11 Bassi, '*Nostos, Domos*, and the Architecture of the Ancient Stage', 416.
12 Georges Perec, *Species of Space and Other Places* (London: Penguin Classics, 2008), 89.
13 Laura Mulvey, *Death 24x a Second: Stillness and the Moving Image* (London: Reaktion Books, 2006), 112.
14 Pier Paolo Pasolini, 'Comments on Free Indirect Discourse', in *Heretical Empiricism*, ed. by Louise K. Barnett, trans. by Ben Lawton and Louise K. Barnett (Bloomington and Indianapolis: Indiana University Press, 1988), 87.
15 Pier Paolo Pasolini, 'The Cinema of Poetry', in *Heretical Empiricism*, 182.
16 Copjec, *Imagine There's No Woman*, 215.
17 Pasolini, 'The Cinema of Poetry', 175.
18 Ibid., 181.
19 Rancière, *The Future of the Image*, 55.
20 Gilles Deleuze, *Cinema 1: The Movement Image*, trans. by Hugh Tomlinson and Barbara Habberjam, 3rd edn (London and New York: The Athlone Press, 2005), 113.
21 Ibid., 124.
22 Ibid., 124.
23 Curzio Malaparte, quoted in McDonough, 'Malaparte: A House Like Me', 8.
24 Giorgio Agamben, 'Notes on Gesture', in *Means Without End: Notes on Politics*, trans. by Vincenzo Binetti and Cesare Casarino (Minneapolis and London: University of Minneapolis Press, 2000), 51.
25 Ibid., 51.
26 Copjec, *Imagine There's No Woman*, 199.
27 Pier Paolo Pasolini, 'Observations on the Long Take', trans. by Norman MacAfee, and Craig Owens, *October*, 13 (1980), 3–6 (5).
28 André Bazin, 'The Ontology of the Photographic Image', trans. by Hugh Gray, *Film Quarterly*, 13 (1960), 4–9 (8).
29 Colin MacCabe, *Godard: A Portrait of the Artist at Seventy* (London: Bloomsbury, 2004), 72; Bazin, 'The Ontology of the Photographic Image', 7.
30 Bazin, 'The Ontology of the Photographic Image', 7.
31 Quoted in Colin MacCabe, *Godard: A Portrait of the Artist at Seventy*, 404.
32 Eisenstein, Sergei, 'Montage and Architecture', trans. by Michael Glenny, *Assemblage* 10 (1989), 110–31, 117.
33 Ibid., 117.
34 Bazin, 'The Ontology of the Photographic Image', 8.

JAMES WILKES

# *'O gods . . .'* Hidden Homeric Deities in Godard's *Le Mépris*

This article aims to explore some ways in which the Homeric gods appear in disguise in Jean-Luc Godard's *Le Mépris*. The object of this is not to reduce the unfolding of the film's plot to a series of divine interventions or godly appearances, but rather to add further layers of complexity to the already complex readings this work demands. Like any search this process will, I hope, throw up tangential discoveries which may prove just as interesting as the ostensible object. And like any explorer making their way through unfamiliar territory, I have relied upon knowledgeable guides, most notably Jenny Strauss Clay, whose book *The Wrath of Athena* provides an excellent account of the *Odyssey*'s theology.[1]

The first question we must ask concerns the nature of the Homeric gods, as there will be little point in attempting to track their appearances in *Le Mépris* unless we know what we are looking for. The ontological status of these divinities was a difficult question even for ancient interpreters of the *Iliad* and *Odyssey*: as early as the Sixth Century BC, Xenophanes was criticising the amoral and anthropomorphic aspects of Homer's gods.[2] This can be seen as an early foray in the centuries-long attempt to idealise, allegorise or rationalise away the Homeric deities; indeed, it is a project that continues to this day, with critics such as E.R. Dodds suggesting that the gods might be projections of internal psychological processes for which Homer's society had neither concepts nor language.[3]

But as Clay observes, such readings differ little in principle from the allegorical interpretations offered by ancient commentators like Eustathius,[4] quite apart from the fact that they ignore passages where gods impart concrete information otherwise unavailable to mortals (as when Athena warns Telemachus of the exact location where the suitors are lying in ambush for him at the start of Book 15 of the *Odyssey*.) The overall effect, as Clay puts it, is to minimise and rationalise the divine in Homer.[5]

Naturally, if a defining quality of classic texts is their 'openness to accommodation' which 'keeps them alive under endlessly varying dispositions', as Frank Kermode writes,[6] one should expect reinterpretation and revision to accompany a book such as the *Odyssey* down the ages. Yet sensitive criticism relies on another kind of openness too, one which attempts to approach a text in its own terms, quixotic task though that may be – and in that spirit, there is much to be said for taking the Homeric gods as they are, or at least as they appear to be from the evidence we have before us. This does not mean attempting an impossible re-creation of the world of Homer, as the Fritz Lang of *Le Mépris* would do, but rather in accepting that in any text, even a classic, there are certain aspects that we cannot assimilate to our own desire of how the world should be.

With that preamble out of the way, let us make a first attempt to understand the nature of the Homeric gods by contrasting two epic appearances of Athena – the first in the first pages of the *Odyssey*, and the second in Apollonius of Rhodes' *Argonautika*, written some four hundred years later, and in a world of Hellenistic expansion and scholarship where, to paraphrase Peter Green, *logos* had grown fat at the expense of *mythos*.[7] For Homer, Athena flashes down from the heights of Olympus, and appears to Telemachus disguised as a stranger. When she comes to take her leave, she does so equally lightly, 'vanishing like a bird through a hole in the roof', in E.V. Rieu's translation.[8] Appolonius's Athena though, as translated by Green, has size and bulk: she mounts a 'light cloud/that would bear her onwards at once, huge though she was',[9] and on this divine escalator she descends to help the crew of the Argo trapped between the clashing rocks. The description of her intervention in Jason's fate reinforces this imposing image: 'Then Athena, left hand jammed against a massive/rock, with her right thrust *Argo* through and onward,/and the vessel sped, airborne, like a swift-winged arrow'.[10] The image of Athena as a tree-trunk thighed figure of majesty such as Rubens might have painted is a wild contrast to the Homeric grey-eyed goddess of wiles, whose interventions work more subtly to render things *alloeidea*, to 'change the look of a thing or to make it invisible, and yet to leave its nature intact', as Clay explains.[11]

Whilst we will return to examine the nature of Homer's gods in closer detail, it should be possible even now to sketch in broad strokes what we should be looking for, if we are to find such deities in Godard's film: we should expect gods appearing in disguise to effect subtle changes, gods who do not announce their presence; and yet gods who should be taken literally, and not rationalised away as allegory or morality tale. In short, it should be clear that the painted statues that represent the gods in Lang's film-within-the-film, which appear only after many other elements have been established, do not provide an exhaustive index of the gods' presence.

Indeed, I would like to suggest that the gods make their presence felt in *Le Mépris* at exactly the same point as they do in the *Odyssey*, that is to say, in the first words of the proem or prologue. The famous opening line of the *Odyssey*, 'Tell me of the man, O Muse . . .', is an invocation of a divine power beyond the human, both a giving over and a founding of Homer's authority as singer of truth, with the poem in its entirety testifying to the prayer's success. As Clay writes, 'the prayer of invocation involves nothing extraneous to itself. Without reference to past or future favors, invocation becomes, in a sense, pure prayer in which the medium of words is sufficient unto itself'[12]. Such a purity of prayer is surely also the effect of Godard's extraordinary prologue, in which Coutard's slow-moving camera arrives above the extra-diegetic camera, revolves through ninety degrees, and then lowers its gaze to stare straight at the viewer. Immediately before this, Godard says in voice-over: 'Le cinéma, disait André Bazin, substitue à notre régard un monde en plus accord de nos désires. *Le Mépris* est l'histoire de ce monde.'[13] When, in the next moment, the medium of cinema asserts its sufficiency unto itself, the effect is less a declaration than a plea – a plea that cinema will not betray its Bazinian promise.

It may perhaps seem a banal point to state that for Godard the camera takes the role of Homer's Muse, but a complex web of associations between gods, gazes and cameras can be derived from such a starting point. For the Greeks, to see and to know were intimately linked; in fact, the word *oida* meant both 'I have seen' and 'I know'.[14] Thus, one of the central attributes of the gods is that they possess superior 'knowledge through sight', or *eidenai*, and Zeus himself owes his pre-eminence amongst the gods to his 'wide-gazing' vision.[15] The poet, notwithstanding his proverbial blindness, is also endowed with superior sight by the Muse, allowing him to identify the gods in spite of their disguises, and to offer more precision than the typical mortal claim that 'some god' must have intervened in the action.

Although Godard's camera cannot offer an Olympian perspective, and indeed uses its limited vision to great creative effect in the cramped confines of Paul and Camille's apartment, it nevertheless seems to know more than the hapless protagonists. The best example of this *eidenai* comes when Paul arrives at Jerry's villa, having sent Camille on ahead with the producer. We cut from a shot of Paul walking from the taxi to a view which seems to be Paul's, as he walks towards Jerry and Camille. The impression that we are seeing through Paul's eyes is maintained as Jerry first greets the camera and then directs a comment to it, 'Fix you a drink, Paul?' But the camera ignores him, and focuses its gaze on Camille for several long moments, patiently waiting for her to take up position centre shot, head turned away and eyes downcast. The next cut reveals we have been misdirected: these were not Paul's eyes at all; Paul is over to the left, taking a drink from Jerry and lighting a cigarette. Paul is oblivious to the depth of betrayal that Camille feels; only the camera has seen it and known it.

Another characteristic of the Homeric gods is that their ability to transform things is figured as a superior technical skill. Indeed, Athena's transformation of Odysseus for the benefit of Nausicaa is explicitly compared to the human *techne* of metal-working:

> As when a skilful man pours gold over silver,
> one whom Hephaestus and Pallas Athena have instructed
> in every facet of his art, and he completes graceful works;
> just so, she poured grace over his head and shoulders.[16]

The ability to intervene in the world in this way is dependent upon the gods' knowledge of the *physis*, or nature, of things. This is exemplified by the one use of the word in the *Odyssey*, when Hermes appears to Odysseus to show him the *physis* of the herb that will protect him from Circe's spells. This is not a divine plant – Hermes has plucked it from the ground in front of him – but it has a black root which is dangerous for mortal men to dig up.[17] Thus only the gods can know its true nature. As Clay argues, '*physis* unites two components, the one visible to all, the other hidden, the root of things. The gods' knowledge comprehends the whole and allows them to transform and manipulate the appearance of things'.[18]

This duo of interlocking attributes – superior *techne* and superior knowledge of the nature of things – suggests that the Homeric gods might share something in common with the constructivist vision of the cinematic eye as a superhuman eye. For Russian film-makers of the revolutionary and post-revolutionary periods such as Dziga Vertov, this technological advantage was to be put to work to transform consciousness and make possible the 'communist decoding of the world'.[19] As he wrote in 'The Birth of Kino-Eye' (1924):

> Kino-eye is understood as "that which the eye doesn't see," [. . .]
> as the possibility of seeing without limits and distances [. . .]
> Kino-eye as the possibility of making the invisible visible, the unclear clear, the hidden manifest, the disguised overt, the acted nonacted; making falsehood into truth.[20]

The cinema-eye might hold superhuman potential, but crucial to its effective use was radical editing. Indeed, the film-maker should use 'every possible means in montage, comparing and linking all points of the universe in any temporal order, breaking, when necessary, all the laws and conventions of film construction', as Vertov put it in 1929.[21] However, despite the fact that Godard later formed a film-making group named after Vertov,[22] we should not necessarily impute this particular complex of revolutionary ideals and technical injunctions to Godard himself in 1963: even a cursory reading makes it clear that *Le Mépris* is the product of a very different aesthetics, politics and mode of production to *Man with a Movie Camera*, for example.

*Le Mépris*'s position on montage is in fact far closer to the one advocated by Bazin, who insisted on respect for the spatial unity of the event and militated against montage as 'the literary and anticinematic process *par excellence*.' 'Essential cinema', he continued, 'is to be found in straightforward photographic respect for the unity of space'.[23] Most of the film's camerawork manifests such a Bazinian respect for spatial unity: the long tracking shots during Paul and Camille's argument in their apartment, or the dispute between Jerry and Paul in the Villa Malaparte epitomise this. There are, it is true, a few notable montage sequences which break up the long takes, such as the 'flashback' episodes and the images of the gods from Lang's film-within-the-film, but the overall impression, especially as the scene of the action moves to Capri, is of solid, expansive spaces filling the camera.

Despite these different approaches to editing, both Vertov's writing and Godard's filming place an emphasis on the camera as an instrument which is not subservient to the demands of narrative. Harun Farocki has commented that Godard's camera is a piece of machinery that 'does not subordinate itself to what it films, but insists on its own autonomy',[24] and indeed it regularly frustrates our expectations as viewers, cutting away from characters in the middle of their speeches, or refusing to shoot the object of their attention, dictated by its own rhythms and its own interests. We could perhaps reach back tentatively towards the Ancient Greeks here, and draw parallels between these last few observations and certain wilful objects that exert a pull on the structure of the *Odyssey*. Homer makes use of objects encoded with time, which prove just as insistently autonomous as Godard's camera: when Eurycleia touches the scar on Odysseus's knee, for example, this action pulls the narrative back to his childhood hunting accident, and then further back to his naming by his grandfather. It is only when the scar's narrative boxes have been fully unpacked that the loop closes and the main narrative continues.

As a last point on this topic, and lest the connections between camera-eyes and gods seem too abstracted from *Le Mépris* itself, it is worth exploring a few simple, visual associations between gods and cameras which appear in the very fabric of the film. This requires us to focus on the scene in the projection room, when Lang shows Jerry, Paul and Francesca his rushes. One shot shows a rush of the statue of Ulysses, the eyes painted a sky blue; the next is a reverse shot into the projectionist's booth. He is adjusting the focus on one of two projectors, the eye of which glows with the same bright blue. The next shot shows a bust of Athena (going by the name of Minerva) with her eyes painted red, but the crucial point here is her movement: the statue swivels smoothly ninety degrees to the left and then back, in an inescapable echo of Coutard's camera in the prologue. The next god to be shown, Neptune, is also blue-eyed. Both colour and movement create a clear analogy between the statues of the gods and heroes and the eyes of cameras and projectors.

'I like gods. I like them very much. I know exactly how they feel.' These lines, spoken by Jerry (Jack Palance) as he watches the rushes of Lang's film, intimate that certain characters in *Le Mépris* are indeed closer to the gods than others. Given that Palance's character is so utterly without redeeming qualities, and is even described by Lang as 'un dictateur', it seems counter-intuitive at first to give his claim any credence. If anyone is going to be accorded this status, it should surely be the wise, cosmopolitan figure of Lang himself. In *The Wrath of Athena* however, Clay makes a persuasive argument for the paradoxical closeness of the races of the Cyclopes and the

Phaecians, and exploring their proximity might allow us a new perspective on the relation between the seemingly equally opposed roles of director and producer in *Le Mépris*.

The Cyclopes and the Phaecians would appear to share nothing in common: the former are brutal, without knowledge of the arts of shipbuilding or agriculture, and without respect for the laws of hospitality towards strangers. The latter meanwhile are hyper-civilised, and generous to a fault, providing passage home to any traveller who comes to their city. And yet, Clay contends, both are united by a mysterious bond. The clearest indication of this comes when Alcinous, the king of the Phaecians, claims that the gods do not hide themselves from his people, 'since we are near them,/just as the Cyclopes and the wild race of giants'.[25] This 'near them' has a genealogical sense, in that Poseidon is both Alcinous's grandfather and Polyphemus's father, but also carries a sense of a privileged position vis-à-vis the gods. Whilst the Phaecians enjoy divine technologies such as magic ships, watchdogs and fertile orchards, the Cyclopes are also divinely favoured, for 'all the crops they require spring up unsown and untilled, wheat and barley and vines with generous clusters that swell with the rain from heaven', as Rieu's translation puts it.[26] What is more, they have the gods' ears: Poseidon acts immediately on the curse Polyphemus brings down on Odysseus. Clay summarises it as follows: 'the Phaecians live like the gods; the Cyclopes act the way the gods sometimes do'.[27]

Having established that certain Homeric beings can be close to the gods without being civilised, it is worth teasing out a few of the possibilities that interpreting both Prokosch and Lang as such borderline mortals might release. In the Homeric world, it is the gods who know better, and who pass their knowledge onto seers, such as Chalcas in the *Iliad*, who knows 'those things that are, those things that will be, and those things which were before'.[28] At various points in *Le Mépris*, Prokosch demonstrates such a prophetic ability, suggesting for example, 'I have a theory about the Odyssey. I think Penelope has been unfaithful. . .' He says nothing more before Lang interrupts him with a quote from Dante, but his cryptic statement is enough to prefigure, or even precipitate, the coming catastrophe of Paul and Camille's relationship.

Indeed, even Lang's interruption is worth examining as a prophetic statement, one containing deep knowledge about those things that are and will be. Encrypted in his quotation of a few lines from the *Inferno* is Dante's alternative characterisation of Odysseus/Ulysses: not as a man destined for home, but as an eternal wanderer destined to travel ever onwards. Dante's Ulysses is overcome with a desire to explore, and on leaving Circe he travels not back to Penelope, but to the utter ends of the earth, where the sea swallows him and his crew. Here, as W.B. Stanford writes, we see in Ulysses a 'scorner of religious and social ties, a man overpowered by one great passion, the characteristically Greek desire to know'.[29] Urging his men onward with the words that Lang delivers as 'vous n'avez pas été fait pour *être,* mais pour connaître la science et la virtue', Ulysses encourages them to a Christianised doom. And buried within Lang's version of Dante's Ulysses we also see Paul: a man who cannot simply be, but whose desire to know what founds Camille's love will, by the end of the film, have finished by confounding it. Paul's error is fundamentally one of misinterpreting the oracle: he reads the Dante quotation as a simple expression of melancholy, completing it with a highly selective abridgement: 'already the night looked upon the stars ... and our joy quickly turned to tears ... until the sea had closed over us.' To read the classic as pure elegy, in other words as totally detached from the present – this is Paul's first mistake.

This mistake forms one note in a symphony which declares, throughout the film, that no story or life stands alone, and is always tied into a complex web of influences that reach deep into the past and future. The fact that Lang, Palance and Georgia Moll bring with them the histories of Hollywood and German and Italian cinema adds to the sense that the characters they play – in Lang's case, himself – are somehow on the fringes of the human. As Jacques Aumont writes, they are all 'living quotations [. . .] survivors of a vanished world', which Godard uses to evoke a 'distant, already heroized and mythicized past'.[30] Once again, Homer is a shadow's breadth away: his races of giants and magic sailors, inhabiting the 'remote edges of the Epic', as Clay puts it, are also a last reminder of the golden age in which gods communed directly with mortals.[31]

The heroic characters may be close to the gods but they are still susceptible to error. Perhaps the greatest feint, the biggest piece of misdirection in our search for the hidden traces of the gods, comes when Fritz Lang characterises Minerva as Odysseus's protectoress and Poseidon as his mortal enemy, as their images appear on screen before and after a shot of Paul's face. From that moment on, we will associate the appearance of Poseidon with critical moments in the film which are under this god's malign influence. This association bears examination, to a point: Paul's arriving late in a taxi and his urging Camille into Jerry's speedboat are two decisive moments where her contempt for him could plausibly blossom. But the statue of Minerva-Athena interposes itself at one crucial point as well: between Paul and Camille leaving Jerry's Roman villa, and arriving at their own apartment. This could be understood as Athena extending her aegis to protect their homecoming; but what if, far from being a protectoress, the goddess is secretly wrathful? Such an argument forms the central premise of Clay's book, which rather than assuming the 'man of many turns' was simply a favourite of the goddess, suggests a more ambivalent relationship between Odysseus and Athena. Indeed, Odysseus's very name suggest he will suffer *odium* from both gods and men, and this lack of favour finds expression in his complaint to the goddess in Book 13:

> You were gracious to me in the old days so long as we Achaeans were campaigning at Troy. Yet when we had sacked Priam's lofty citadel and gone

> on board our ships, and a god had scattered the Achaean fleet, I did not notice you then, Daughter of Zeus, nor did you set foot on my ship to save me from any of my ordeals. No; I was left to wander through the world with a stricken heart.[32]

As Clay points out, all heroes risk transgressing the invisible line dividing men from gods and thereby bringing divine wrath upon themselves.[33] Yet there are certain faults common to both Odysseus and Paul that might tempt divine anger; and there are further faults which are Paul's alone. One fault they both share is disrespect. For Odysseus, this involved stealing the Palladion, the sacred statue of Athena that kept Troy safe. Paul enacts an equivalent disrespect when he raps the breasts and genitals of the bronze statue in his apartment (as Silverman and Farocki point out, this statue 'cannot help but signify something like "household god"');[34] shortly after this he slaps Camille in the face, in a genuinely shocking moment of violence. And yet beyond this disrespect, Paul shows he is no Odysseus through his inability to do what Odysseus does so well: to accept the double-edged gifts of the gods in silence. Reticence is one of Odysseus's greatest resources, allowing him to escape from the Cyclops's cave by withholding his name, and to hold off from denouncing the suitors until the moment for reprisal is ripe. But it is Paul's relentless questioning in the apartment scene, under the sign of Athena's contemptuous gaze, that finally drives Camille to pronounce her own contempt for him. It is during their protracted argument, no less than in the betrayals in Cinecittà and Capri, that Paul and Camille's relationship turns to ashes.

There is of course one simple objection to all this, which is a variation of the accusation Jerry throws at Paul, through the creative translation of Francesca: 'You're wrong. You dream of a world like Homer's. You want it to exist but it doesn't.' It is one thing to take the gods as real phenomena in Homer; it is another to treat them as such in Godard's work, which exists in a completely different time and society.

One response to this might be to invoke Jean-Pierre Vernant's claim that 'the Greek gods are powers, not persons'.[35] By this, he means that any particular god is less an individual than an accretion of diverse attributes, which are not merely restricted to the natural world, but are also 'at work in human activities and social relations'.[36] If the pantheon is understood as a set of forces within rather than external to the world, working on mortals but also susceptible to their influence ('man has created gods', as Lang says), then the gods become as effective as any other structuring system which appears to span the natural, the cultural, and the social. As Vernant puts it, the Greek gods seem to form a kind of language and 'continue, when we listen to them, to mean something to us'.[37] Understood in this way, the gods of Homer simply provide another resource to draw upon in our attempts to better understand *Le Mépris*, no more or less appropriate in principle than a reading which analyses the film through economic relations or psychoanalytic thought. As long as the interpreter of a text bears in mind the potential for distortion that all interpretations carry, and is honest enough to admit where their analysis falls short, it should still be possible for Homer's gods to form one more language amongst the many that come together to form *Le Mépris*.

## Notes

1 Jenny Strauss Clay, *The Wrath of Athena* (Princeton: Princeton University Press, 1983).
2 Peter Green, *The Argonautika* (Berkeley and Los Angeles: University of California Press, 1997), 14.
3 E.R. Dodds, *The Greeks and the Irrational* (Berkeley and Los Angeles: University of California Press, 1951).
4 Clay, *Wrath of Athena*, 136.
5 Ibid., 138.
6 Frank Kermode, *The Classic: Literary Images of Permanence and Change* (London: Faber and Faber, 1975), 44.
7 Green, *Argonautika*, 16.
8 Homer, *The Odyssey*, trans. E.V. Rieu, revised trans. D.C.H. Rieu (London: Penguin Books, 2003), 11.
9 Green, *Argonautika*, 93.
10 Ibid., 94.
11 Clay, *Wrath of Athena*, 167.
12 Ibid., 10.
13 *Le Mépris*, dir. Jean-Luc Godard (France/Italy, 1963). All quotations from the film are transcribed by the author.
14 Clay, *Wrath of Athena*, 12.
15 Ibid., 12–13.
16 Ibid., 162.
17 Homer, *The Odyssey*, trans. Rieu, 133.
18 Clay, *Wrath of Athena*, 159.
19 *Kino-Eye: The Writings of Dziga Vertov*, trans. Kevin O'Brien, ed. Annette Michelson (Berkeley and Los Angeles: University of California Press, 1984), 50.
20 Ibid., 41.
21 Ibid., 88.
22 Kaja Silverman and Harun Farocki, *Speaking About Godard* (New York and London: New York University Press, 1998), 112.
23 André Bazin, 'The Virtues and Limitations of Montage' in *What is Cinema?*, trans. and ed. Hugh Gray (Berkeley and Los Angeles: University of California Press, 2004), 46.
24 Silverman and Farocki, *Speaking About Godard*, 49.
25 Clay, *Wrath of Athena*, 130.
26 Homer, *The Odyssey*, trans. Rieu, 113.
27 Clay, *Wrath of Athena*, 132.
28 Ibid., 149.
29 W.B. Stanford, *The Ulysses Theme* (Oxford: Basil Blackwell, 1954), 181.

30 Jacques Aumont, 'The Fall of the Gods: Jean-Luc Godard's *Le Mépris* (1963)', trans. Peter Graham, in *French Film: Texts and Contexts*, ed. Susan Hayward and Ginette Vincendeau (London and New York: Routledge, 2000), 176.
31 Clay, *Wrath of Athena*, 172.
32 Homer, *The Odyssey*, trans. Rieu, 177.
33 Clay, *Wrath of Athena*, 182.
34 Silverman and Farocki, *Speaking About Godard*, 44.
35 Jean-Pierre Vernant, *Myth and Society in Ancient Greece*, trans. Janet Lloyd (New York: Zone Books, 1996), 108.
36 Ibid., 106.
37 Ibid., 119.

NICKY FALKOF

# Godard's Women

*Le Mépris* (*Contempt*) inspires a multiplicity of readings. Its combination of Homeric narrative, compelling star power in the form of Bardot, visual splendour, awareness of cinematic history and complex formal games has combined to ensure it a vaunted position in Godard's filmography. Some critics, like Richard Roud and Colin MacCabe, situate it within the *Cahiers* critique of cinema. More important than the marital breakdown that centres the narrative, says Roud, 'Godard has actually made ... a documentary on film-making in Italy', while MacCabe calls it 'almost a remake of *Viaggio in Italia*'.[1] According to Wheeler Winston Dixon, however, the film-within-the-film of *The Odyssey* and its director-within-the-film Fritz Lang '[seem] almost peripheral to Godard's central interest ... exactly how, and why ... two people cease to love each other'.[2] Ginette Vincendeau, meanwhile, describes *Le Mépris* as both 'explicitly about Bardot as a star' and as 'about artistic production'.[3] Leo Bersani and Ulysse Dutoit are interested in the notion of contempt itself, but point out that most other writers interpret the film as a tragic tale of the breakdown of a marriage.[4]

This profusion of opinions diverges wildly from the critical response to Godard's cheeriest film, the 1961 'musical comedy' *Une Femme est Une Femme*, starring the luminous Anna Karina as stripper-with-a-heart-of-gold Angela. We cannot, says Roud, 'take very seriously' the affair between the two central characters.[5] Peter Harcourt calls it 'pleasing nonsense'.[6] Dixon says it is 'generally considered lightweight'.[7] Unlike the chapters, essays and analyses that have been devoted to *Le Mépris, Une Femme est Une Femme* is often dismissed as a bit of fluff, entertaining but unimportant.

*Une Femme est Une Femme* 'can be seen as a rehearsal for *Le Mépris*' in its use of CinemaScope and colour, Dixon suggests.[8] There are, however, more links between these films than the technical. This essay uses the two as a means of examining Godard's doubly polarised portrayal of women, considering narrativity, content, film style, star persona and representations of the body.

## Two women: textual echoes

There is a plethora of similarities between *Une Femme est Une Femme* and *Le Mépris* on the narrative, formal and stylistic levels. Both feature a romantic triangle and the possible dissolution of a couple. Both showcase a lengthy central scene in the couple's apartment in which they attempt to work their way through their personal dramas while followed around the space by Raoul Coutard's probing camera. Both revolve around bookish men attached to beautiful women of low culture: Angela in *Une femme* is a stripper and her lover Émile (Jean-Claude Brialy) works in a bookshop. *Le Mépris'* Camille (Bardot) is a typist and her husband Paul (Michel Piccoli) a writer. Both couples communicate through books. Émile and Angela, during a whimsical bedtime argument, use the words on the covers of books scattered around their flat to silently trade insults. The book of pornographic classical artwork that was a gift from Prokosch becomes a third player in an argument between Paul and Camille, echoing the sheet-toga he wears and the statues that decorate the flat as well as the images of Odyssean statuary that are an enduring visual conceit. During one of Angela and Émile's arguments, she even throws at him the crushing verdict that will eventually separate Camille and Paul: 'I despise you.'

Visually and audibly, too, the pair collide. The coloured gels that illuminate Angela's face as she sings her song in the Zodiac strip club recall the lighting used to display Camille's supine body in the opening scene of *Le Mépris*, while the cutting of background noise and music when Angela sings each phrase is a precursor to the soundtrack dropping in and out when Paul and Camille are in the cinema. The films are intertwined; *Le Mépris* is the dark twin of *Une femme*.

## Portrait of the artist as a young man

From its title and narrative to much of its dialogue, *Une femme* is deeply concerned with questions of the feminine. Whether we believe that *Le Mépris* is essentially about Homer, about filmmaking, about death or about the impossibility of lasting love, this film too deals at least in part with the problem of woman, in the form of woman who cannot be understood by the male protagonist-auteur.

It is, of course, impossible for the viewer to know precisely what motivates an artist. Nonetheless it is clear that Godard's portrayal of the feminine changed radically from 1961 to 1963, from Angela-Karina's endearingly exuberant wilfulness to Camille-Bardot's capricious un-readability. MacCabe writes, 'It is tempting to interpret [*Le Mépris*] as a representation of Godard's relationship with Karina,' especially since some of Camille's dialogue comes directly from Karina herself and Godard dates the end of their relationship from the end of the filming process of *Le Mépris*.[9]

*Une femme*, meanwhile, was made in the full flush of the couple's romance, with Karina becoming pregnant during the shooting of this story about a woman who wants a baby. Rather than Camille, it is the radiant Angela who seems somehow an anomaly in Godard's pantheon of beautiful women.[10] Themes of prostitution and feminine betrayal have been present in Godard's work from as early as 1955; in this case, however, it is Émile who visits a prostitute, betraying Angela as much as she betrays him by going to bed with Alfred.[11] Characteristic female duplicity is modulated and neutralised by equally destructive masculine behaviour. Karina is at her most innocent here, neither the petulant child of *Bande à part*, the cold automaton of *Alphaville* or the amoral betrayer of *Pierrot le Fou*. If *Le Mépris* can be seen as the filmmaker's farewell to his wife then *Une femme* is perhaps his love letter. Whatever Godard's intentions, it is clear that the films mark two very different, though related, depictions of the feminine.

## Categorical disparities: consumption, action, dialogue, setting

The original choice to play Camille in *Le Mépris* was Kim Novak, a Hitchcock blonde fresh from 1958's *Vertigo* whose persona suggested the dual entities of girl next door and *femme fatale*. This feminine duality is characteristic of Godard: 'Woman is divided into an appearance that can be enjoyed and an essence that is only knowable at risk, deceptive and dangerous', or 'woman as enigma and mystery [and] woman as consumer'.[12] This is extended into, broadly, available against unavailable, safe against perilous, compliant against wilful. Within the diegesis of *Le Mépris*, these roles could be filled by Camille-Bardot as dangerous, unruly and fickle against the multilingual translator Francesca (Giorgia Moll) as unthreatening and agreeable. They map just as neatly, however, onto Camille and Angela.

If, as MacCabe suggests, one of the roles of the Godardian woman is as typical modern shopper, embodied by Juliette's prostitution to pay for consumer goods in 1967's *Deux ou trois choses que je sais d'elle*, then Camille's willingness to walk away from Paul in Capri, jeopardising her comfortable bourgeois home, marks her as the risky opposite to that consumer, in contrast to the female character in Alberto Moravia's novel *Il Disprezzo*, on which the film is based. With her blank expression, unreadable desires and refusal to elaborate on the source of her contempt, Camille is entirely unpredictable. Angela, meanwhile, lives in a small flat, strips for money and seems to have no greater aspirations, but the commodity she fetishises, for which she prostitutes herself, is a baby. Godard himself says the film deals with her desire for a child, 'the most natural thing in the world', in an 'absurd manner'; absurd perhaps, but also indulgent and largely free of moral judgement.[13] This suggests that the duality of the feminine, while fundamental to Godard's work, is temporarily altered by events in his personal history, mediated by his moment of homely happiness with Karina at the start of the 1960s. Godard depicts not only women but Woman, seen through the eyes of a man in love; or not. How, then, can the intimations of these two forms of womanhood be pinpointed within the texts in question?

The films' conflicting depictions of femininity throw up an unexpected paradox. Sphinx-like and played by the most celebrated beauty of her time,

Camille seems to embody the eternal feminine, her recalcitrance positioning her as one of those mysterious creatures of whom Freud asked his baffling question about what women want. Angela, on the other hand, is flighty, adorable, beautiful, but in a girlish way: the pigtails she wears in her hair before going to bed signify a childlike nature very different to Bardot's sexualised youthfulness. There is no Freudian mystery here. We know exactly what Angela wants: for Émile to give her a baby. But nonetheless Angela is constantly referred to as 'woman', which suggests that she functions as a signifier. From the film's title to her witty final line, untranslatable with its pun intact – 'Non, non je suis pas *infame*, je suis *une* femme' – constant references are made to Woman as a category with Angela its representative. Both Émile and his love rival Alfred (Jean-Paul Belmondo) launch into descriptions of what is wrong with women and the film is littered with conversations about what women do, how they behave and what that behaviour means, from the discussions about crying to Angela's assertion that she, as a woman, is permitted to evade questions and Émile's cry, 'All women to the stake.'

The dialogue of *Le Mépris*, by contrast, never explicitly refers to this universalised conception of Woman despite its constant visual invocation. Camille stands alone, unique, individual. It is as if the repetitive references to Angela as evocative of womanhood are required to make her such, as if she needs to be positioned in her role because her lovable girl-next-door persona could not accomplish it alone. Camille, on the other hand, naturally embodies an image of womanhood that requires no clarification. Her strut, her pout, her refusal to explain herself, her devastating effect on Paul, her appeal to Prokosch, are sufficient to align her with a particular version of the cinematic feminine archetype.

This emphasis on Camille as Woman is visually accentuated by the paucity of people in *Le Mépris*. *Une femme* features many other characters: the denizens of the strip club, the women in the bar with Alfred, the women whom Alfred and Émile chat up at Marcel's, the men who light their cigarettes off Alfred's as he waits for Angela's signal, and most spectacularly the many craggy, characterful Parisian faces that are the camera's close-up focus while the audio track follows the conversation between Angela and her friend as they walk from the apartment to the Zodiac. This is a Paris full of people. *Le Mépris*, however, has minimal extra faces; other than the scene in the cinema, where a few audience members and the onstage players appear, we only see the central characters and the crew and actors attached to the film-within-a-film.

This lack of outside action serves to highlight Camille's unbreakable exterior, the sense Godard creates that she is like the statues that populate Lang's film: mythical, unmoving, separated from the bluster of everyday life. Where Angela dances, fidgets and is in constant motion, Camille moves slowly and stately, with balletic turns on the heel and suspended pauses. When she sits she sits still, composed and appealing to the eye. This is in marked contrast to many of Bardot's films, often characterised by whirling, vibrant, frenetic dancing, most notably the mambo scene in her breakthrough role in Roger Vadim's *Et Dieu... créa la femme* (1956). Here her dance is 'an expression of her charisma, which arguably 'resists' her objectification'.[14] Her stillness in *Le Mépris* performs the same resistance. She is poised, immobile, especially when compared to Francesca's versatile quickness. In the scene in the Villa Malaparte when Paul outlines his reasons for wanting to quit the film, it is almost startling when Camille finally moves, so steady has she been. Godard allows us to gaze at the famous film star but in so over-determined a fashion that the act of looking cannot remain neutral. He provides us with what we *really* want from Bardot: a posed pin-up lacking all agency, who will not move or surprise us or make us consider the nature of our gaze. But he does this within the context of cinema, where the mobile body is the norm and the static body is unexpected. This makes our looking awkward, unsustainable, disconnected, and resists the casual pleasure of staring at the screen goddess unfettered.

The contrasting populations of these films suggest, too, something about the way love functions in Godard's world. For Angela and Émile, the happy couple (and they are happy, despite the misunderstandings), the outside world is unthreatening, a teeming backdrop to their own pleasant days. For Paul and Camille, the world has vanished. Outside the unhappy couple, Godard seems to suggest, there is nothing. The absence of background humanity, like the looks they share of contempt, love and bemusement, 'reduce the entire relational field to the structure of the intimately conjoined couple'.[15]

Another visual association between Angela and Camille, which also highlights the disparity between them, is the blazon, a form of praise that involves a 'male anatomization of a woman's charms [that] could be territorializing in effect'.[16] This form is used by Émile during the long apartment scene when Angela questions his love and he responds, 'I love no one but you. Your eyes, your neck, your shoulders, your waist.' He anatomises her and lays his claim to this body, interpellated in logical fashion from the top downwards as something knowable, understandable, ownable. In *Le Mépris*, though, it is Camille who performs the blazon. She divides her own body up in an 'ironic' reprisal of the way the camera's eye usually eroticises Bardot.[17] In keeping with the opposition between the two women, this permits Camille a degree of ownership of her own body, accentuated by her starting from the feet and moving upwards. Unlike Angela's, hers is a body that is difficult to understand and equally difficult to possess. Whereas the camera during Émile's blazon remains on his face, emphasising the him-ness of this statement of possession, Camille's self-blazon is accompanied by slow movement up the span of her remarkable form, with Paul largely kept from our field of vision, reduced to agreeing with her assertions and forming part of her backdrop. She retains an agency, withheld from the more compliant Angela, that is concomitant with her status as mythic evocation of Woman, impossible to know and possess.

## The 'bride' stripped bare

Roland Barthes, in his hugely influential *Mythologies*, discusses the nature of Parisian striptease, how the slow removal of items of clothing designed to titillate actually de-eroticises the female body, and how a succession of other layers – of exoticism, props, luxury – appears to distance the voyeuristic viewer further from the 'truth' of the body: 'Woman is desexualised at the very moment when she is stripped naked.'[18] This understanding of the nature of striptease can be applied to both Angela and Camille, and is clearly in evidence in *Une femme*. The emphasis for most of the Zodiac's strippers is on costume. Angela dons a sailor's outfit to sing her song and proceeds to remove it, item by item, until she is left only in a basque. This is the selfsame item we saw her wearing during the opening credits in her dressing room; she is no more naked there than she was on stage, the removal of clothing serving as a theatrical act rather than a reveal. In a characteristically alienating technique she sings her flirtatious song directly to the camera. The viewer is not even permitted the pleasure of thoughtless voyeurism, since Angela's engaged gaze and awareness of the camera's presence negate the audience's opportunity to escape self-awareness within the cinematic spectacle.

The only time we see Angela engaged in anything that promises a more erotic reveal is in the shower, when the static camera frames her from behind as she pulls her nightdress over her head. The white fabric breaches her shoulders and stays perched on her head, a tantalising promise of things to come, when the 'striptease' is halted by a phone call that comes for Angela in the neighbour's flat. Her pause, re-assumption of clothing and swift exit of the bathroom remain coquettish, a teasing refusal to let us see what she was, ostensibly but never actually, showing off at the Zodiac.

In a later scene one of the other strippers parades in a wildly excessive Indian Chief outfit, her feather-topped head drawing far more visual attention than her exposed breasts. The camera's movement distracts from what would usually operate as a visual spectacle: rather than lingering on the displayed woman it pans between Angela and Émile, with the stripper serving as background. Similarly, when Dominique performs towards the end of the film we see her disrobe in a series of sharp cuts, from fully clothed down to topless with arms aloft, each edit minus one article of clothing with no movement from her; she is like a statue, cold, unbending, available for admiration but lacking in erotic charge. Godard foregrounds the striptease event as explained by Barthes, where woman's nakedness is denatured by the application of layers of flamboyant, exotic costume or the addition of a less tangible layer of covering: in Dominique's case, her unnatural stillness.

With the raising of the question of bodies, and specifically naked female bodies, we must take account of the slippage that occurs between the character Camille and the actress Brigitte Bardot, that 'icon of rebellious youth, sexiness and of French womanhood'.[19] The opening scene of *Le Mépris* was famously inserted on the insistence of Godard's American producer Joe Levine, who protested at the relatively low nudity levels of this most famously sensual actress. How does this compare to Karina's striptease in *Une femme*? At first glance both seem like uncomplicated examples of female display. However, my understanding of stripping in *Une femme* as a de-eroticising act would initially suggest that they function in almost oppositional ways, with Camille's body actually revealed in contrast to Angela's evasive undressing. But once we consider the additional factor of Bardot as a star the naked scene in *Le Mépris* acquires a more complex set of responses. Bardot's body actually works to *hide* her nakedness, just like the costumes and exotic poses of the Parisian stripper. Godard has 'given Levine Bardot with a vengeance – not simply the erotically luscious Bardot but the visual icon that drew millions of desiring gazes to her body'.[20] The character Camille is subjugated to the image of the star and the star is cloaked in her fame. We are not seeing a naked woman revealed; rather we are seeing another example of this much-viewed, paraded, remarked on and photographed body. There is nothing here that the viewer has not seen before and as such there is *nothing to reveal*, nothing hidden that her nakedness brings to light.

While this striptease does not utilise the 'time taken in shedding clothes' that Barthes calls its 'mystifying spectacle', it has its own techniques of mystification, consequent upon the collusion of actress and director.[21] Godard's use of the coloured gels is a distanciation technique that detaches the viewer from an uncomplicated enjoyment of the erotic spectacle of Bardot naked. During her aforementioned blazon the camera pans slowly, almost lasciviously, up her body. It does not, however, picture the body part she names when she names it, preferring a disconcerting disjuncture between vocal and visual that further complicates the possibility of immersion in the spectacle. The use of sound performs the same function. As the camera moves along her body Bardot's voice fades from the soundtrack. We are still listening to her but her voice is no longer prominent. This enforces the fragmentation between visual enjoyment of the pictured body and audience awareness of the mechanisms of production, the 'filmicness' of this film. The scene creates an 'aura of otherworldiness', its unnatural radiance making Bardot 'erotically [unavailable] to the spectator ... [protected] against the overtures of strangers'.[22] The star, exposed unclothed to the eyes of her public, is nonetheless protected by her own unnatural celebrity and by Godard's cinematically conscious style.

## 'A ballad by poor B.B.'

As I mentioned at the start, there is a strain of critical discourse about *Le Mépris* that argues about the *meaning* of the film, whether it follows Paul's or

Camille's perspectives, what the source of her contempt is. In the main these critics are writing years, and more often decades, after the film was made; they are divorced from the hysterical affect that surrounded Bardot in her heyday. Unlike the whimsical Angela, who enjoys a degree of fictional life within her milieu, Camille as a character *does not exist*; she is only Bardot. Richard Dyer writes, 'Audience foreknowledge, the star's name and her/his appearance ... all already signify that condensation of attitudes and values which is the star's image'.[23] Like Charlton Heston, who Dyer uses to illustrate his ideas, Bardot 'means' Bardot no matter what the film is attempting to do with her.[24] The characters she plays are inscribed with her persona, so discussing Camille's compliance with or disgust at Prokosch's advances is irrelevant to this understanding of the film. Bardot's public promiscuity was, according to Vincendeau, 'a strong intertext to the expression of her sexual desire on screen'.[25] This is an extra-diegetic reference to the appeal of the star herself: Camille's response to Prokosch is fed through the audience's awareness of gossip about Bardot's own lifestyle. Character and star echo each other, adding a level of narrative detail that is never explicit but nonetheless seamlessly informs the audience's reading of the action. The presence of the cinema siren moves the contemporary viewer always-already a step away from the Homeric narrative and the characters that populate it. Like Penelope, her uncanny metatextual double, Camille is mythical, infused with the power of Bardot's aura.

The opening quote of this section, 'A ballad by poor B.B.,' refers to a comment made by the director Lang to Paul when the couple are at the cinema. Godard's inclusion of this inter-textual in-joke, permitting the audience to 'confuse' Brecht with Bardot, illustrates his awareness of the effects of his leading lady's star persona and of the doubling that must occur between Camille and Bardot. Brecht himself wrote, 'The actor appears onstage in a double role, as Laughton and as Galileo ... the showman Laughton does not disappear in the Galileo whom he is showing ... the tangible, matter-of-fact process is no longer hidden behind a veil.'[26] Bardot embodies that very Brechtian device of alienation. She is both actor and character, her perfect and perfectly blank visage added to the repertoire of techniques that disallow the viewer from losing herself, inculcating a constant awareness of the film *qua* film. Bardot is the perfect screen on which to project these cinematic concerns in this most cinematic of films. Angela, with her constant motion, conversation with the camera and generic flourishes, contrarily but aptly emphasises the theatricality, the element of performance, that is at the heart of *Une femme*.

***

Godard and his contemporaries, says MacCabe, dreamed 'of their star – the woman who would come alive before their camera and fall in love not with money or worldly power but with the genius of their art'.[27] In Karina, Godard had found his; and come alive before his camera she duly did, even winning Best Actress in Venice for *Une femme*. But by the time of the making of *Le Mépris* Godard replaced *his* star with *the* star, the iconic sex kitten with her promiscuous past, the twisted apotheosis of the romantic dream of the Nouvelle Vague's young Turks, impossible to possess, understand or impress. From the endearing love object who seduces the camera with her winks, flirtations, songs and sighs to the statuesque impenetrable beauty, these two films mark the opposite poles of the range of the Godardian woman. It is true that 'Godard's practice seems to be out of sync with feminist arguments on the representation of women'; it is true that his conflation of woman with her sexuality is ideologically problematic for a feminist viewer.[28] But is also true that Bardot represents more than an iconography of the feminine. The star is also a metonym for cinema, Godard's other loved object. Just as *Le Mépris* concerns the caprice and unknowability of women so it reveals a detached and less affectionate exposure of the mechanisms of cinema, that heartless mistress. His films are, Godard says, 'the only way to go, to recount, to take account myself, that I have a history in myself . . . If there were no cinema, I wouldn't know that I had a history'.[29] Between Bardot and Karina, between Camille and Angela, we can read the preoccupations of the filmmaker himself, the man revealed in his representation of woman: in the final analysis his own, eternal object.

## Notes

1 Richard Roud, *Godard* (London: Secker & Warburg, 1976), 64; Colin MacCabe, *Godard: Portrait of the Artist at 70* (London: Bloomsbury, 2004), 162.
2 Wheeler Winston Dixon, *The Films of Jean-Luc Godard* (Albany: State University of New York Press, 1997), 41.
3 Ginette Vincendeau, *Stars and Stardom in French Cinema* (London: Continuum, 2000), 105.
4 Leo Bersani & Ulysse Dutoit, *Forms of Being: Cinema, Aesthetics, Subjectivity* (London: BFI Publishing, 2004), 19.
5 Roud, *Godard*, 25.
6 Peter Harcourt, *Six European Directors: Essays on the Meaning of Film Style* (Harmondsworth: Penguin Books, 1974), 223.
7 Dixon, *The Films of Jean-Luc Godard*, 28.
8 MacCabe, *Godard: Portrait of the Artist*, 28.
9 Ibid., 162, 169.
10 Ibid., 135.
11 Ibid., 84.
12 Colin MacCabe & Laura Mulvey, 'Images of Women, Images of Sexuality', in Colin MacCabe (ed) *Godard: Images, Sounds, Politics* (London: BFI, 1980), 85 & 102.
13 Jean-Luc Godard, *Godard on Godard: Critical Writings by Jean-Luc Godard*, eds Jean Narboni & Tom Milne (London: Secker & Warburg, 1972), 182.
14 Vincendeau, *Stars and Stardom*, 95.

15 Bersani & Dutoit, *Forms of Being*, 21.
16 Kaja Silverman & Harun Farocki, *Speaking About Godard* (New York: New York University Press, 1998) 34.
17 Vincendeau, *Stars and Stardom*, 95.
18 Roland Barthes, *Mythologies* (London: Vintage), 84.
19 Vincendeau, *Stars and Stardom*, 82.
20 Bersani & Dutoit, *Forms of Being*, 36.
21 Barthes, *Mythologies*, 84.
22 Silverman & Farocki, *Speaking About Godard*, 34.
23 Richard Dyer, *Stars* (London: BFI Publishing, 1986), 142.
24 Ibid., 148.
25 Vincendeau, *Stars and Stardom*, 96.
26 Bertolt Brecht, 'A Short Organum for the Theatre', in John Willett (ed), *Brecht on Theatre: The Development of an Aesthetic* (London: Methuen Drama, 1964), 194.
27 MacCabe, *Portrait of the Artist*, 124.
28 MacCabe & Mulvey, 'Images of Women', 84.
29 Kaja Silverman, 'The Dream of the 19th Century', *Camera Obscura* 17.3 (2002), 15.

**JAKE REEDER**

# The Signature of the French New Wave (Godard's *Le Mépris*)

Once an artistic movement is established, it is easy to forget the complex conjunction of elements that ministered to its birth. At this point, its final configuration is still uncertain not yet associated with the fully articulated aesthetic characteristics (such as 'the Baroque' or 'Impressionism') that would later define it. The process through which a certain force, driven by a desire to make manifest something new, comes into being at the moment of a movement's formation may be usefully considered through the term 'paradigm shift'. Although Thomas Kuhn originally developed the concept in the context of science, in this essay I want to apply it to aesthetics: the cinematic transformation associated with the French New Wave. I will then examine Giorgio Agamben's concept of authorial signature in order to focus on the singular, or the example, in the coming into being of a movement. Also following Agamben, I will highlight the importance of the contribution made, as within every new movement, by writing in the formation of the French New Wave. I will then discuss these ideas through *Le Mépris* (*Contempt*) 1963 by Jean-Luc Godard as an exemplary site where this strange new aesthetic force has left its signature.

I will begin by highlighting the problems of a retrospective analysis of a movement's birth if a rule driven interpretation overdetermines its initial uncertainty. In Michel Marie's important study of the French New Wave, he argues that the films made by the group of young French filmmakers from 1958–1964 demonstrated from the very beginning a coherence of critical thought and of cinematic style. For Marie, the arrival of the New Wave was marked by: "a body of basic critical doctrine ... an aesthetic program ... some strategy, an ensemble of artists, [and] finally, adversaries ..."[1] He goes on to point out that, even though these elements were not present in every New Wave film, their "co-presence" in general constituted the New Wave as "one of the most definite and most coherent schools in film history."[2] He cites, as evidence of critical thought, the manifestos written by Alexandre Astruc ("The Birth of a New Avant-Garde: La Caméra Stylo", 1948) and Francois Truffaut[3] ("On a Certain Tendency of French Cinema", 1954), while the adversarial position taken by the left-wing magazine *Positif*, contributed to establishing a 'New Wave' identity. Furthermore, Marie suggests that innovative production strategies and aesthetic principles unified New Wave cinema. It is here that he seems to over determine the movement's origins by imposing a dominating list of rules. A contrast to this may be found in Jean-Luc Godard's advocacy of spontaneity and play in this letter to his fellow filmmakers:

> I play
> You play
> We play
> At cinema
> You think there are
> Rules for the game
> Because you are a child
> Who does not yet know
> What is a game and what is
> Reserved for grownups
> Which you already are
> Because you have forgotten
> That it is a child's game . . .[4]

Godard's flippant dismissal of 'rules' undercuts Marie's endeavor to classify the aesthetic sensibility of the New Wave and draws attention to the dialectic between the birth of a new paradigm and the rules that later represent it. In its every aspect (the adversaries, the manifestos, and the production techniques) Marie's approach imposes rules on this new paradigm of film, of which, I will argue, each movie serves as an example.

Giorgio Agamben uses the term 'example' to address the question of a paradigm, as first proposed by Thomas Kuhn and Michel Foucault. He illustrates the complexity of the question by distinguishing between Kuhn's two definitions of the word:

> The first meaning of 'paradigm'. . . designates the common possessions of the members of a certain scientific community, namely, the set of techniques, models, and values to which the group members more or less consciously adhere. The second meaning refers to a single element within the set, such as Isaac Newton's *Principio* or Ptolemy's *Almagest* that serves as a common example and thus replaces explicit rules and permits the formulation of a specific and coherent tradition of inquiry.[5]

The second meaning emphasises that, in order to grasp the elusive moment in which a new aesthetic paradigm is formed (such as the French New Wave), it is important to return to the artist and the artwork. Marie's study, on the other hand, rather than treating each film as the site of the paradigm's production, takes each as proof that the presumed 'agenda' of the movement has been realised. His interpretation of the New Wave suggests that a paradigm is defined in the very constitution of its new values and new models (manifestoes, aesthetic criteria).

1. The *auteur* director is also the scenarist for the film.
2. The director does not follow a strict, pre-established shooting script, leaving instead much of the filming to improvisation in the conception of sequences, dialogue, and acting.
3. The director privileges shooting in natural locations and avoids building artificial sets in the studio.
4. The director uses a small crew of only a few people.
5. The director opts for "direct sound" recording during filming rather than relying too much on post-synchronization ...
7. The director employs non-professionals as actors.
8. If the director has access to professionals, newer actors will be chosen and directed in a freer manner than conventional productions allow.[6]

In order to prove the existence of this agenda, Marie cites films and their directors that illustrate his own list of characteristic New Wave aesthetic 'choices'. For instance: "It would be Rouch who was the most faithful to this approach throughout the 1960s, with films like *The Human Pyramid* (1961) and *Lion Hunt* (1965)."[7] Rather than understanding a movement to be fully formed and rule driven in its origins, Kuhn's second definition emphasises that: "... a paradigm is simply an example ..."[8] While Marie establishes the framework for the New Wave's revolution, he is at risk of losing sight of the *lawlessness* that must enact any shift in paradigm. As such, it is only via 'analogical logic' that "the universal logic of the law is replaced by the specific and singular logic of the example."[9]

Agamben then develops Foucault's definition of a paradigm (close to Kuhn's second one): the analogical logic of the example is one where, "a singular case is isolated from its context insofar as, by exhibiting its own singularity, it makes intelligible a new ensemble, whose homogeneity it itself constitutes."[10] The analogue's path forward leads towards a break with tradition or rules and opens a space for the appearance of the new, displacing the question of definition and the presence or absence of the New Wave as such.[11] It is here that Agamben develops his own theory of the paradigm by referring to the tradition of the signature (this is not to be confused with the signature that Foucault describes in *The Order of Things*). He begins by looking at Book 9 of Paracelsus' *De natura rerum*, titled "Concerning the Signature of Natural Things": "The original core of the Paracelsian episteme is the idea that all things bear a sign that manifests and reveals their invisible qualities ... *signatura* is the science by which everything hidden is found ..."[12] Agamben adds that there must also exist a 'signatory art' or a paradigm in order for each signature to be revealed.[13] That is to say, the signature and the paradigm interact dialectically. This 'paradigm of the signature' can be rephrased as the art movement and its artists or the New Wave and its *auteurs*.

As Marie fails to analyse individual films, sacrificing the singular for the general,[14] his approach cannot take into account the way that each signature film of the New Wave is able to generate the paradigm of the New Wave itself. He thus establishes what a New Wave film *ought to have been*, but loses sight of the element within the film itself that presents this artistic paradigm. To clarify: Godard's *Le Mépris* still functions as a signature of the New Wave, although it departs from many of the aesthetic values that Marie lists.[15] The film had contemporary Europe's most famous actress as its lead, it had an American producer who afforded Godard a larger budget than was usual for New Wave films, and its script was adapted from a popular novel. Yet, Godard's film *Le Mépris* is *nothing* if not New Wave. In this film in particular, which does not share the youthfulness of *Breathless*, Godard is self-referential enough to sign the New Wave's aesthetic while calling it into question at the same time.

Agamben's view that language has a privileged relation to the paradigm and the signature draws attention to the importance of the written word as a means to proclaim the task and establish the logic of innovation. In the case of the French New Wave, the new paradigm emerged on the threshold between the practice of film criticism and film making. Godard had been part of the team of film critics who wrote during the 1950s for *Cahiers du cinéma*, (founded and edited, until his death in 1958, by André Bazin) and whose radical approach to film criticism earned them the name 'young Turks'. As early as 1948, Alexandre Astruc wrote the article "The Birth of a New Avant-Garde: La Caméra-Stylo" for *L'Écran français*. His fiery words all but scream out for this elusive site of the signature to herald the new. "The cinema of today is getting a new face."[16] And beneath this face, "there is always an avant-garde where something new takes place ..." There is always a signature. For Astruc, this newness is achieved at the moment when cinema finally understands the specificity of its own language. This new freedom, he continues, makes it possible, "to write ideas directly on film without even having to resort to those heavy associations of images that were the delight of the silent cinema";[17] cinema, in the 'new wave' of film to come, will be free of the "tyranny of what is visual." At last, cinema does not have to bow its head to literature and overemphasise its visual constraints; finally, cinema can be the signature of its own language. Jean-Luc Godard takes this statement further by declaring that cinema is the only medium that can affirm itself by its signature alone: "In short, to assert its own existence as its justification ..."[18] Movies that are beautiful, "can reveal or conceal the secret of a world of which they are the sole repository and also the fascinating reflection. Truth is their truth. They secrete it deep within themselves ..."[19] Rhetoric aside, Godard clearly envisions this new cinema to be one whose possibility is realised in its own enactment.

In 1954, Francois Truffaut wrote the article "A Certain Tendency of the French Cinema", for *Cahiers du cinéma*, criticising the type of literary adaptations made by those like Pierre Bost and Jean Aurenche who worked in 'The Tradition of Quality.' His use of irony strips the tried and true rules of cinema of their authority. Truffaut argues that Bost and Aurenche in their attempt to create an equivalence between the work of literature and its film adaptation do nothing more than produce 'an insipid' reproduction of the former. As Truffaut emphasises that an *auteur's* adaptation allows the language of cinema to transcend the literary, he not only draws attention to the specificity of film language but also includes the figure of a *signator*.

In analysing his concept of the signature Agamben asks, "What does the signature *Titianus fecit* add to the sign "Annunciation" that we have before our eyes?"[20] Distinguishing between the sign and the signature, he says. "The sign itself is inert and mute, and must, in order to effect knowledge, be animated and qualified in a signature . . ."[21] However, it is clear that if the signature was removed, the painting would not change either in its materiality or its quality.[22] Although Agamben is, at this point, rather vague, he compares the signature of Titian to the seal on a coin; that is, the signature determines the value of the sign. However, the idea of the signature, as in the example of Titian, should not be taken literally: a signature, for Agamben, is the analogical activity that brings value to an object through the appearance of its authority. The first *signator* was God and his signature was Nature. The exemplary nature of this relationship makes it impossible to think that God came before his signature; on the contrary, the signature is the very coming into presence of the *signator*. In this case, Nature itself is the manifestation of God.

The importance of a *signator* held great weight for the critics and soon to be filmmakers at the *Cahiers du cinéma*. One of the founding principles of the *politique des auteurs* was to identify those directors who made films which "'by definition [did] not conform to the vague norms fixed by the tradition of dark cinemas.'"[23] At the time, Hollywood films were in general critically dismissed as industrial productions for escapist mass consumption. However, the *Cahiers du cinéma* critics declared directors such as Hawks, Ford and Hitchcock, by the very quality of their signature, to be authors who transcended these constrictions and clichés. As they 'adopted' these and other directors, including Renoir and Rossellini, the *Cahiers* critics were already marking out a paradigm, tracing the outline of a tradition that had yet to be articulated cinematically. More generally, as I will discuss below in relation to film quotation, each new aesthetic infuses old tropes with new character. Another example of pre-figuration of this kind, can be found in André Breton's *Manifesto of Surrealism;* he lists a number of literary figures who were Surrealists before the Surrealist movement existed:

> Swift is Surealist in malice,
> Sade is Surrealist in sadism.
> Hugo is Surrealist when he isn't stupid.
> Poe is Surrealist in adventure.
> Baudelaire is Surrealist in morality.
> Rimbaud is Surrealist in the way he lived and elsewhere . . .[24]

Breton went on to say that these men could not function systematically as Surrealists because they had yet to hear the call from the Surrealist movement itself.[25] Similarly the *politique des auteurs* brought forth from Hollywood cinema of the 1950s (and earlier) the directors who would unwittingly father the New Wave to come.

Although in his essay "La Politique des Auteurs" André Bazin disassociates himself from some extremes of auteurism, he is convinced that in other arts the name or signature of a great artist is perceived as a sign of mastery. He recognises, however, that problems of authorship are intrinsic to film production, with its diverse creative collaborators and subordinated to particular economic and technical demands. Furthermore, the cinema was a new art form. Thus, Bazin championed the *politique des auteurs* as a way of raising the cinema to the level of other fine arts, where the presence of a *signator* is already a 'paradigm'. His very loose analogies indicate how difficult it is to describe the process at stake in Agamben's concept of signature. Bazin writes, "Genius is an H-bomb ... But a sun cannot be born from the disintegration of an individual alone unless this disintegration has repercussions on the art that surrounds it."[26] The effect of the *auteur* is at the same time the coming into being of the *auteur.*

Basing his argument on Thomas Aquinas' definition of "sacramental character" in his *Summa theologiae*, Agamben uses the term to develop the concept of a "sign that exceeds the sign ... In the efficacious sign of the sacrament, character is what marks the irreducible excess of efficacy over signification."[27] For Agamben, the two concepts are identical: in both cases the sign that manifests the signature or the sacrament (a seal on a coin, or a baptism) does so with an excess agency or with *character.* In other words, to be successful, a signature or a sacrament must possess a force that transcends, or exceeds, the habitual or the normal, thus enabling renewal. Adapting this argument, I would suggest that *Le Mépris* inhabits the norms of the cinematic medium (the sacrament of cinema), but simultaneously transforms them. As this excess goes beyond the sign, it initiates the paradigm within which a signature can function. Thus, rather than maintaining an isolated perfection within his own work, the auteur creates a new space for cinematic possibility at the moment that his signature exceeds his own existence.

*Le Mépris*, produced towards the end of the French New Wave era, is exemplary of the way that Godard both confronts and fulfills the *analogic* of the New Wave paradigm. This is precisely because the film does not conform to each sign (rule) of New Wave film production and aesthetics. However, Godard, begins the film by loosely quoting André Bazin, thus locating the film within the historical space of *Cahiers du cinéma*. After the credits, a title reads "The cinema substitutes for our gaze a world more in harmony with our desires"[28] to which Godard himself then adds, in voice over, "*Le Mépris* is a story of that world." The cameraman then turns the camera lens to look directly at the viewer. With this gesture Godard intrudes a sign from the old New Wave paradigm into the 'world more in harmony with our desires', signified by its big movie stars (Brigitte Bardot and Jack Palance) and the aspirations of its American producer. Godard produces the New Wave by adding new character, the excess of character, to the old signs or sacraments of cinematic integrity.

To reduce *Le Mépris* to its stylistic continuity within the New Wave and to its formal similarity to other Godard films (for instance, his refusal to use shot/countershot[29], and his concern for depth-in-scene) obscures the dialectical site of the signature's efficacy. The stylistic elements of the New Wave (the handheld camera, the long shots, the improvised dialogue and so on) are the characteristics realised by way of signature: its excess and its verification. The formal rules of the new paradigm, and the action of signing it, remain separate from each other. Godard's achievement lies in his ability to maintain his identification with the New Wave, as a school of cinema, while simultaneously maintaining an ambiguous relation to the rules that characterised it. That is, the self-awareness and self-reflexivity of Godard's cinema signs the ability of the cinema itself to produce new paradigms. In the process of this negotiation, quotation is one key Godardian device that allows the dialectic to seep joyfully into the screen.

In his essay "Death of the Author," Roland Barthes challenges the significance of authorship by pointing out, "The text is a tissue of quotations drawn from the innumerable centres of culture."[30] He says, "To give a text an Author is to impose a limit on that text, to furnish it with a final signified, to close the writing." Godard, on the contrary, makes the most of quotation in his films, ensuring that they serve as material for a new production of meaning. While Barthes' intention is to question the longstanding paradigm of literary *authority*, for Godard, in agreement with Bazin, an author enables quotation to resonate anew, as quotations without signature would simply be empty signs. Thus each successful signature or sacrament amounts to a declaration linking the past to the present: here is what was once the paradigm but, as excess overwhelms tradition, it becomes entirely other and new. And when the opening scene of *Le Mépris* suggests that the film lies in a continuum with the values of the past, it inscribes into each moment an allegory derived from the new paradigm: here is what was once the dream of cinema. That is not to say that if this first scene were removed this consciousness of this allegory would no longer be present. Each moment of *Le Mépris* repeats the allegory stated bluntly at the beginning of the movie.

Bertolt Brecht's theory of Epic Theater, which had a particular influence on Godard, illuminates the duality of this allegory and the 'distance' it brings with it. For Brecht, an actor in Epic Theater performs the division between himself and the character he plays: "... The actor put[s] himself at a distance from the role he play[s] ... He behaves naturally as demonstrator and he lets the person demonstrated behave naturally."[31] Godard takes this rubric further and extends it across the cinema, using each of its elements (music, framing, camera movement and so on) to perform this type of demonstration or distanciation. If Brecht's Epic Theater prescribes a method of acting that watches itself, Godard's *Epic Cinema* extends this method to each aspect of the cinematic world.

Godard, who once said that all you need to make a movie is a gun and a girl, draws on both old and new cinematic conventions, which are then filtered through his Brechtian, distanciating lens. The signatory character of quotation exceeds cinematic convention, particularly due to its close relation to language, which Agamben has described as "the archetype of the signature, the signatory art *par excellence*."[32] However, the question of language also, necessarily, returns to the cinema itself: by signing its own language, cinema becomes its own language. Where can this language, in a medium that borrows from music, writing, and the visual arts, be located? The *Cahiers du cinéma* used the concept of *mise-en-scène* to convey the cinematic moment in which all moral and political requirements are stripped from the screen, where the camera lens, the actors, and the landscape all gleam with an excess of character, and every choice "[is] akin to a writer's pen or a painter's brush."[33]

For me personally, one sequence and its *mise-en-scène* from *Le Mépris* encapsulate these ideas perfectly. After the movie has shifted to Capri, Brigitte Bardot, as Camille, walks idly atop the roof of the Villa Malaparte and waves to someone off scene, the rich blue sea behind her; receiving no response, she walks with her head down back to the edge of the roof. The shot conveys a distance that Colin MacCabe identifies as: "a refusal of 'mastered space' whether that mastery is understood visually or psychologically."[34] The most *un-refusable* woman in European cinema is refused by something unknowable beyond the presented scene (a person, but even more the lens itself). As she turns away from the camera, after trying to light it up, I believe that, in the failure of her gesture, I can feel the shot as a quotation, as the impression of a new seal onto an old one. This is an exemplary moment in which I become conscious of the very inscribing of Godard's signature. Bardot the beautiful is reduced to one more sign of a new cinema. No rules can prescribe the vitality of this scene, and there are many more examples to be found or cited. This intangible quality, that Aquinas called 'character', highlights the importance of witnessing an artistic movement from within the space of its own innovation, a space rife with all the paradoxes of creation.

## Notes

1 Michel Marie, *The French New Wave: An Artistic School*, trans. Richard Neupert (Oxford: Blackwell Publishing, 2003), 28.

2 Ibid., 29.

3 Francois Truffaut, 'A Certain Tendency in French Cinema', In *The French New Wave: Critical Landmarks*, ed. Peter Graham and Ginette Vincendeau (London: Palgrave Macmillan, 2009).
4 Jean-Luc Godard, *Godard on Godard*, ed. and trans. Tom Milne (London: Da Capo Press, 1972), 242-243.
5 Giorgio Agamben, *The Signature of All Things: On Method*, trans. Luca D'Isanto and Kevin Attell (New York: Zone Books, 2009), 11.
6 Marie, *The French New Wave*, 70-71.
7 Ibid., 71.
8 Agamben, *The Signature of All Things*, 11.
9 Ibid.
10 Ibid., 18.
11 Ibid., 19–20.
12 Ibid., 33.
13 Ibid., 35.
14 Marie, *The French New Wave*, 3.
15 "... This was a film which saw a radical break in production methods, a break which Godard neither enjoyed nor repeated." C. MacCabe, *Godard: A Portrait of The Artist at Seventy* (London: The Bloomsbury Press, 2003), 147.
16 Alexandre Astruc, "The Birth of a New Avant-Garde: La Caméra-Stylo" in *The French New Wave: Critical Landmarks*, ed. Peter Graham and Ginette Vincendeau (London: Palgrave Macmillan, 2009), 31.
17 Ibid.
18 Godard, *Godard on Godard*, 76.
19 Ibid., 75.
20 Agamben, *The Signature of All Things*, 39.
21 Ibid., 42.
22 Ibid., 40.
23 Jim Hillier, *Cahiers du Cinéma: The 1960s, New Wave, New Cinema, Reevaluation Hollywood*, ed. Jim Hillier (Boston: Harvard University Press, 1992), 168.
24 André Breton, *Manifestoes of Surrealism*, trans. Richard Seaver and Helen R. Lane (Ann Arbor: University of Michigan Press, 1974), 26-27.
25 Ibid., 27.
26 Ibid., 137.
27 Ibid., 50.
28 *Le Mépris*, dir. J.L. Godard, Les Films Concordia, 1963.
29 MacCabe, *Godard*, 154.
30 Roland Barthes, "The Death of the Author" in *Image, Music, Text*, trans. Stephen Heath (New York: Noonday Press, 1977), 146.
31 Bertolt Brecht, "A Model for Epic Theater", *The Sewanee Review*, Vol. 57, No. 4 (1949), 425, 432.
32 Agamben, *The Signature of All Things*, 36.
33 Ginette Vincendeau, "Introduction: Fifty Years of the French New Wave: From Hysteria to Nostalgia", in *The French New Wave: Critical Landmarks*, ed. Peter Graham and Ginette Vincendeau (London: Palgrave Macmillan, 2009), 4.
34 Colin MacCabe, *Godard*, 155.

JOHN SHANKS

# *Le Mépris* and the Hollywood musical

Just two years before *Le Mépris*, Godard made *Une Femme est Une Femme* (1961), a film which has been described as 'a light-hearted homage to the Hollywood musical'.[1] Over the previous ten years, Godard and his colleagues of the Nouvelle Vague, in numerous reviews of Hollywood musicals published in *Cahiers du cinéma*, had demonstrated themselves to be enthusiastic viewers and astute critics of a genre which they evidently regarded as embodying many of the desirable elements of authentic cinema. I propose that *Le Mépris* shares a number of important features with the Hollywood musical, that the reviews of Hollywood musicals in *Cahiers du cinéma* by Godard and his colleagues between 1951 and 1960 suggest that this is no accident and that *Une Femme est Une Femme* (1961) stands as a bridging work between the Hollywood musical and *Le Mépris*.

I shall consider, firstly, the opinions of Godard and his contemporaries on Hollywood musicals, expressed in *Cahiers du cinéma* between its first edition in 1951 and the release of *Une Femme est Une Femme* in 1961, particularly Godard's own review of the Doris Day musical *The Pajama Game* (George Abbott/Stanley Donen, USA, 1957)[2] and the review by Jean Domarchi of *Brigadoon* (Vincente Minelli, USA, 1954).[3] I believe that the opinions of Godard and other *Cahiers* colleagues on the merits of the Hollywood musical which find their way onto the screen in light-hearted ironic fashion in 1961 in *Une Femme est Une Femme* re-emerge in a darker, bleaker key in 1963 in *Le Mépris*.

## *Cahiers du cinéma* and the Hollywood musical 1951–1961

*Cahiers du cinéma* in its first ten years played a key role in expressing and forming the shared opinions and positions of the Nouvelle Vague in relation to Hollywood. It therefore seems appropriate to seek in the pages of *Cahiers* the considered views of the Nouvelle Vague on that most typically Hollywood product, the movie musical, since, as Feuer reminds us: 'The musical is Hollywood writ large'.[4]

The early enthusiasm of the French New Wave for Hollywood has been well documented but is more often associated with genres such as the Western, *film noir*, detective stories, gangster films or B-movies. The heavy-weight intellectual analysis favoured by writers and readers of *Cahiers* would not immediately seem to suggest interest in a cinematic genre such as the movie musical, often regarded as banal and merely decorative, a prejudice noted and dismissed more than once in the pages of *Cahiers* itself. [5,6] In fact, *Cahiers* ran more than 25 articles on the Hollywood musical in the first ten years of the journal's existence (see Appendix A). A Hollywood musical featured in the lists of The Ten Best Films of the Year in two of the six years of the decade 1951–1961 in which *Cahiers* produced such a ranking (*It's Always Fair Weather* in 1955 and *Les Girls* in 1958) while *Singin' in the Rain* (Stanley Donen/Gene Kelly, USA, 1952) was in the list "Ten Best American Sound Films" drawn up by Godard himself.[7] Gene Kelly was the subject of two extended pieces, one a review of his work, the other an interview, the only director other than Hitchcock to be distinguished with such extensive coverage during this period.[8,9] The champion swimmer turned aquatic musical star, Esther Williams, was subject to a profound analysis in one of the very first numbers of *Cahiers*.[10]

Contemporary foreign critics who commented on the unusual preferences and innovative approach to criticism of the *Cahiers* team noted their predilection for Westerns and *film noir* but either missed or thought unworthy of comment the place of musical films and directors in the *Cahiers* pantheon. [11,12] More recent reviews of French film criticism of Hollywood continue this oversight, for example attributing critical interest in the Hollywood musical to 'surrealist groups' rather than *Cahiers* critics[13] or omitting any reviews of musicals or interviews with directors of musicals in translated compilations of *Cahiers*.[14,15]

A *Cahiers* review of a Hollywood musical was rarely limited to comments on that specific movie but often provided the opportunity for an extended reflection on the nature of the musical genre as a whole and its more general relation to the evolution of cinema.[16,17] Godard described the movie musical as 'in a sense, the idealisation of cinema'[18] while Eric Rohmer declared: 'the musical is the cinema because, quite simply, the cinema is the musical.'[19] A glance at the selection of musicals reviewed by *Cahiers* writers suggests preferences which are largely confirmed by the content of the relevant reviews. Gene Kelly, for example, was accorded almost godlike status as *homme-orchestre* who combined the talents of a noted performer, a choreographer and director who was named auteur in the title of the very first article to feature his work[20] which cited his perceived personal vision and determination to create a new type of dance movie. Cyd Charisse '*La divine*' attracted universal praise and favourable comment even in movies judged disappointing. [21,22]

Some of the interest of the musical genre for *Cahiers* reviewers concerned cinematic techniques which were more frequently deployed in spectacular Hollywood musical productions. The use of colour for expressive rather than purely realistic ends was remarked on by a number of reviewers who discussed the different colour qualities of competing systems such as Technicolor, Ansocolor and Warnercolor.[23,24] The various widescreen techniques such as Cinemascope, Todd-AO, Cinerama and VistaVision evidently fascinated the New Wave: Eric Rohmer claimed widescreen as a

French invention, sold by Henri Chrétien to 20th Century Fox, and declared: 'in this year of 1954 . . . the avant-garde . . . is Cinemascope'[25] while the first musical version of *A Star is Born* (George Cukor, USA, 1954) was reviewed under the title 'Birth of Cinemascope'.[26] The use of deliberately non-realistic, fantastical scenery and settings was rare in most genres of movie but a feature of a number of 1950s Hollywood musicals including *Moulin Rouge* (John Huston, USA, 1952) and *An American in Paris* (Vincente Minelli, USA, 1951), which incorporate painted backdrops in the style of French Impressionist and Cubist artists, and *Brigadoon*, which emphasises the fairy-story quality of its narrative through artificial settings which create a stylised Scotland of romantic colour contrasts.

Movement was apparently of more interest to *Cahiers* than music; the dance movies of Gene Kelly and Stanley Donen were especially favoured as were, later on, musicals with the innovative modern choreography of Bob Fosse which incorporated elements from burlesque, vaudeville and gymnastics alongside the more familiar ballet and tap routines. And it wasn't just the movement of the dance routines themselves which was of interest but the camerawork and technical adjustments necessary to capture a three-dimensional art on the flat plane of the cinema screen.[27] Godard himself undertook the review of *The Pajama Game*,[28] Claude Chabrol reviewed *Singin' in the Rain* [29] and Eric Rohmer reviewed both *Les Girls* (George Cukor, USA, 1957) and *South Pacific* (Joshua Logan USA 1958).[30,31] By contrast, the singing often went completely unremarked or was mentioned as an afterthought in the final few lines of a review. One senses the continuing influence of André Bazin's pronounced preference for "directors who put their faith in the image".[32]

## Jean Domarchi and *Brigadoon*

The erudite and intellectual *Cahiers* writer Jean Domarchi, a professor at the University of Dijon, was a close collaborator with Godard from the outset and made a brief appearance playing a drunk in Godard's first feature film *À bout de souffle*. Domarchi became an enthusiastic champion of the musical genre, particularly of the movies of Vincente Minnelli. Initial reviews of Minnelli's films in *Cahiers* were dismissive of the director, attributing more to Gene Kelly and Leslie Caron the admitted merits of *An American in Paris*, for example.[33] In his consideration of the evolution of the musical, Domarchi credits Minnelli with a decisive influence in shaping the post-war era of musicals, refers to him as 'a great surrealist' and identifies Minnelli's *The Band Wagon* (1953) as being a turning point for the musical genre.[34] Domarchi's review of *Brigadoon* in *Cahiers* of October 1956 was the clearest statement of his campaign to have Minnelli recognised as an auteur.[35] The title 'Minnelli the magnificent' makes the reviewer's intention clear from the outset and the opening sentence of the review throws all Domarchi's personal authority behind that opinion: 'I should say at the outset that I find it impossible to express the slightest reservation about *Brigadoon*, a film as ravishing as it is profound'. Domarchi specifically rebalances the superior importance which earlier reviewers had attached to the contribution of Gene Kelly; he declares Kelly's dancing and choreography as correct, but repetitive of earlier musicals, and pronounces Minnelli inherently more at ease in the musical genre. The reviewer's praise is lavished on Minnelli's mastery of those elements so important to *Cahiers*: the use of colour, camerawork and mise-en-scène. I reproduce at Appendix B an abridged translation of the review which, as far as I am aware, has not previously been included in any compilations or translations of *Cahiers* criticism. A lengthy and admiring interview with Minnelli appeared in *Cahiers* the following year and further developed the same critical themes.[36] By 1959, when Minnelli's *Gigi* turned out to be disappointing, his standing was sufficiently secure that *Cahiers* blamed the failure of *Gigi* on the clichéd performances of the French artists Leslie Caron and Maurice Chevalier and on the fact that there was too much singing and not enough dancing in the movie. The review largely exonerated Minnelli himself by concluding that he could not seriously believe in *Gigi* and that his future career would probably take him away from the musical towards more serious drama.[37]

## Godard and *The Pajama Game*

Godard's comments in his review for *Cahiers* of *The Pajama Game* are of particular interest and I reproduce an edited extract here:

"Stanley Donen is the master of the musical and this is his best film. It is better than *Seven Brides for Seven Brothers* because it is more securely founded on crazy comedy. Doris Day is far better than *Sabrina* and the movie has fewer weak moments than *Funny Face*. This is the first left-wing operetta. The presence of a choreographer of the calibre of Robert Fosse gives the director wings. Harry Stradling extracts the maximum effect from the austere Warnercolor process, playing with the red of lips, the blue of jeans, the green of grass, the yellow of waving pennants, the white of underskirts ... the most ravishing kaleidoscope. It's a curious fact that while classical dance does not transfer well to the screen, modern ballet is in its element in the cinema because it is the stylisation of realistic everyday gestures. Classical dance seeks the stillness within movement, which is, by definition, the opposite of cinema. This is especially true in musical comedy which is, in a sense, the idealisation of cinema. Hurrah for Robert Fosse and Stanley Donen! – the grace of their movements is that of something caught on the wing, absent from the purely mathematical choreography of a Michael Kidd. Perhaps the best way to describe it is to say that, here, the actor who dances does not turn into a dancer doing a number, he's not a dancer playing a role (cf Gene Kelly) but rather he remains the same character, suddenly seized with the desire and need to dance ... A couple of songs by Doris Day ... nicely rounds things off."[38]

Godard's characterisation of the movie as "the first left-wing operetta" was presumably based on the workers-versus-management plotline which has Doris Day cast as the trade union shop steward in a pyjama factory who falls in love with the boss. The music itself is mentioned only fleetingly at the very end of the review; the points which strike Godard as especially noteworthy are the movement of camera and individuals and the use of colour, a range of interests shared by other *Cahiers* reviewers of musicals and which, I suggest, were to find a place in *Le Mépris* five years later.

## Godard and the meta-musical

The movie *Une Femme est Une Femme* (1961) stands alongside the scenario of the same name which Godard published two years previously in *Cahiers*.[39] This was Godard's second film, his first to use colour, widescreen and directly-recorded sound. The plot of the film turns around a triangular relationship between three young adults: Angela (Anna Karina), a performer in a striptease club and Émile (Jean-Claude Brialy), a bookseller, who live together plus Alfred (Jean-Paul Belmondo) who is a friend of both and a secret admirer of Angela. When Angela decides she wants a baby right away, Émile refuses but Alfred obliges. Faced with a *fait accompli*, Émile finally complies with Angela's wishes and prepares for fatherhood. Is Godard's movie actually a musical? The opening credit titles in red, white or blue capitals which fill the screen include the word "MUSICAL". It has musical numbers – Angela sings a saucy little song as she strips in the club where she works, which is reprised at the end of the movie. The Charles Aznavour song "You've Let yourself Go", in which a husband affectionately insults his slatternly wife, is briefly heard at the beginning of the movie and appears again in a more extended form towards the end. Michel Legrand composed some of the sound track music. The movie has a backstage setting for part of the narrative and special effects in a visual gag of a costume-changing machine. It also has elements of dance: Alfred leaps balletically into the frame to pursue Angela, Angela herself dances a few jazzy steps, they both strike identical dance-like poses in a sequence of rapid edits. But there are some distinctly odd features to this 'musical': the piano accompaniment cuts out each time Angela starts a line of her song and the dance-like movements of Angela and Alfred are static.

One of the fundamental features proposed as a definition of a Hollywood musical, as opposed to a film which simply has some songs in it, is that, in a musical, a substantial proportion of the musical numbers should be "impossible" from the standpoint of the realistic discourse of the narrative; characters may burst into choreographed song and dance walking down the street or segue into a show-stopping performance with full orchestral backing from a setting which starts as an improvised try-out with a rehearsal piano.[40] Godard's impossibility is of a different sort; he makes Angela's song more plausible diegetically by setting it in the realistic ambience of an entertainment venue, a device used in backstage musicals, but then fragments the musical line by cutting the sound between the piano and the voice. He repeatedly uses Legrand's soundtrack score to propose the sweeping introduction to a song but no song materialises to follow it up. Jane Feuer draws attention to a number of formal features which the Hollywood musical shares with Godard's films – an inherently self-reflective nature as an entertainment which comments on entertainment[41] and the use of direct address to the viewer.[42] The Hollywood musical resolves the resulting tension by bringing together at the end of the movie the strands of the realistic and the musical narrative and by re-concealing any revealed apparatus of film-making. In contrast, Godard leaves unresolved the enigmatic effect of his disruptive techniques. The film's intertitles comment on the action in the style of silent movies, consign part of the narrative to the written medium and constitute another form of direct address to the audience. Like a musical, the pleasures of Godard's film are principally sensory – the product of music, dancing, colours, gags and the attractive performers – but the overall mood is ironic rather than the utopian optimism of the Hollywood product.[43,44] Godard gives us the musical transformed like the refraction of an image through a prismatic lens.

The scenario for *Une Femme est Une Femme* published in *Cahiers* in 1959 contains broadly the same plot line as the movie; Josette, Emile and Paul become in the film Angela, Emile and Alfred.[45] The screenplay makes no mention of the piece as a musical with dancing. One of the three movie stills which illustrates the published scenario is, however, from a minor Hollywood musical, *Glory Alley* (Raoul Walsh, USA, 1952). It pictures Leslie Caron in a revealing showgirl costume on the stage of the seedy club in New Orleans where she sings and dances; the caption relates her to Godard's character: 'Josette takes her performing seriously'. The other two movie stills in the scenario highlight other aspects of Josette's situation. Two old men drinking at a café table are captioned 'Old people make a big impression on Josette'. The image is taken from *L'opéra Mouffe* (Agnès Varda, France, 1958) a short film which depicts vignettes of daily life in the rue Mouffetard in the Latin Quarter of Paris including derelicts drinking and a weary pregnant woman shopping. Godard's screenplay tells us that Josette's longing for a baby leads her to stare at old people, imagining herself in later life. The third still is from *Et Dieu... créa la femme* (Roger Vadim, France, 1956) and shows Brigitte Bardot lying awake in bed. The character is torn between two brothers. She marries one but loves the other. Her reputation is scandalous – *infâme*). The caption reads '*Josette n'est pas infâme. Elle est une femme*' (Josette is not disgraceful. She is just a woman), a pun which becomes the final line of dialogue in *Une Femme est Une Femme*, spoken in the first person by Angela.

Godard cut a long-playing record of his commentary on *Une Femme est Une Femme* but it was never released. In a transcription from the disc, he refers to Angela's housework as paying homage to "*My Sister Vera Ellen*", [46] a reference which conflates Bob Fosse's first choreographed musical *My Sister Eileen* (Richard Quine, USA, 1955) with a sequence featuring the actress Vera Ellen in *On the Town* (Stanley Donen/Gene Kelly, USA, 1949) in which she dances as she irons the laundry, an image reproduced in a *Cahiers* review on the evolution of the musical. [47]

The overall effect of these multiple, fleeting and transformed references to earlier works evokes what one commentator described as 'a sort of meta-citation, a reference to cinema as a medium for telling stories rather than a detailed reference to any specific film'.[48]

How does this compare to *Le Mépris*? The triangular relationship between two men and a woman recurs, as, of course, does Bardot. There are no musical numbers as such, though the score by Georges Delerue is certainly lush enough for a musical. *Le Mépris* does, however, deploy the *mise-en-abyme* typical of countless Hollywood musicals in that it is a movie about "putting on a show". Just like that most classic of Hollywood musicals, *Singin' in the Rain*, *Le Mépris* has a back-screen location, on a movie set, with the lights, camera and other apparatus of movie-making intermittently visible and some in-jokes about the artistic compromises imposed by the commercial pressures of movie-making. Like the biggest movie musicals of the 1950s, *Le Mépris* is in wide-screen CinemaScope, a format whose arrival had been enthusiastically commended via a *Cahiers* review of the first musical version of *A Star is Born* (George Cukor, 1955, USA).[49] In common with many classic musicals, *Le Mépris* is in Technicolor, at times obtrusively and eye-poppingly so. Colour in *Le Mépris* is almost always used for expressive rather than realistic effects[50] a practice commended in Domarchi's review of *Brigadoon*.[51] The famous sequences of the naked Bardot are tinted and the artifice is emphasised as such by an abrupt shift to a quite different colour palette in mid-sequence. The colour red, emblematic of early Technicolor through the luminous saturated reds of the first movies shot in this system, reappears as a visual motif for the emotion named in the title of *Le Mépris*: it is the colour of Jerry's Alfa Romeo in which he first symbolically separates Camille from Paul, it is the colour of the bathrobe in which Camille wraps herself when she first recognises the contempt that she feels for Paul, and it is the colour of the blood which we see when she and Jerry die in the fatal accident in his red sports car. A similar deliberately obtrusive form of sound editing occurs in both *Une Femme est Une Femme* and *Le Mépris*: the piano accompaniment cuts out each time Angela starts her song in *Une Femme est Une Femme* just as in the variety scene of *Le Mépris* the song is arbitrarily cut in mid-flow.[52] A sequence in which Camille and Paul sit either side of a table with a central lamp while the camera repeatedly tracks back and forth between them makes camera movement itself the most striking feature of the scene. Regarding *Une Femme est Une Femme*, Godard explained it as 'it is not a musical, but the idea of a musical. The musical is dead ... That's what my film refers to . . . it is nostalgia for the musical . . . '.[53] In *Le Mépris*, the charm of nostalgia has given way to something bleaker. It is not just the musical which is dead and must be mourned but classic big-budget Hollywood-style cinema itself which has now passed into myth.[54] In *Le Mépris*, Cinecittà stands for Hollywood; Godard later explained that he considered the movie to be as much a meditation on the fate of cinema as on the destiny of the central couple of characters and noted that he would have shot and set the movie in Hollywood itself had it been practically possible.[55]

The progression of ideas from *Une Femme est Une Femme* to *Le Mépris* and beyond has already been noted by others; Brenez points out that *Une Femme est Une Femme* was the very first scenario written by Godard, that some of the same ideas would resurface almost thirty years later in *Une histoire seule* (1989) which forms Chapter 1(b) of Godard's mammoth video project *Histoire(s) du cinéma* (1988–1998) and that *Le Mépris* itself can be considered as part of the conduit between Godard's ideas in his screenplay of 1959 and those of 1989.[56]

Both in *Une Femme est Une Femme* and in *Le Mépris* there are echoes of the 'epic theatre' of Bertolt Brecht. The making strange and new of the familiar subject, the lack of connection between succeeding scenes, the distancing effect of music which is at odds with the apparent action and inconsequential dialogue which illuminates the characters rather than the plot, all provoke the viewer into speculation and judgement, a process which Brecht regarded as a necessary component of bringing about change.[57,58] Sontag detects the influence of Brecht in the formal devices which Godard uses to counteract ordinary plot development and complicate the emotional involvement of the audience,[59] devices amongst those which MacCabe has identified as "strategies of subversion" of the otherwise dominant tendency of mainstream cinema to adopt the conventions of the classic realist literary text.[60] In *Le Mépris*, not only are Brecht's techniques deployed but the script draws our attention to the source by direct quotation and attribution:

> *Fritz Lang*: Each morning, to earn my daily bread, I go to the market where lies are for sale and stand hopefully beside a seller.
>
> *Camille*: What's that?
>
> *Fritz Lang*: Hollywood. An excerpt from a ballad by poor BB.
>
> *Paul*: Bertolt Brecht?

If in Godard's references to the musical there is deference, there is also difference. The Hollywood musical has been described as a genre which employs unconventional techniques to conventional ends, namely the encouragement of viewer identification with the characters and the widest possible appeal to a mass-market audience.[61] When Godard employs some of the same cinematic techniques as the Hollywood musical, he has a quite different end in view. His use of expressive colour, unrealistic sound, visual gags and direct address to the viewer, for example, seems calculated towards that provocative distancing of the audience which Brecht recommended as a precondition for producing change.

*Le Mépris*, even more clearly than *Une Femme est Une Femme*, is not a Hollywood musical, nor even a Nouvelle Vague version of one. The features which it shares with the Hollywood musical – expressive and non-realistic use of colour, sound and camera movement – can also be found in other non-musical movies. But I would suggest that they are features which were first and most fully developed in the genre of the Hollywood musical. From the *Cahiers* reviews it is evident that Godard and his colleagues found much to admire in the movie musicals' use of these techniques. In this sense, *Une Femme est Une Femme* stands as the first New Wave homage to the Hollywood musical and *Le Mépris* as the most radical. It would be impossible to imagine incorporating Gene Kelly into either *Une Femme est Une Femme* or *Le Mépris* in the way that Demy and Varda later did in their *Les Demoiselles de Rochefort* (Jacques Demy/Agnès Varda, France, 1967). The difference, I would suggest, turns on something of the distinction between a pastiche and a palimpsest. Godard has reused the ancient manuscript of the Hollywood musical for a completely new type of work, leaving only traces of the older text visible on close inspection. It is ultimately unsurprising that the most rigorously cinematic of directors should have found creative possibilities in the most cinematic of Hollywood genres at an early stage in his career. More intriguing is the extent to which the inspiration of the musical genre continued to show its effects in more mature Godard works such as *Le Mépris* (1963) and his great video project *Histoire(s) du cinéma* (1988–1998).

## Appendix A: Articles in *Cahiers du cinéma* about Hollywood musicals 1951–1960

| *Year* | *No.* | *Subject of article* | *Director of film reviewed* | *Reviewer* |
|---|---|---|---|---|
| 1951 | | Esther Williams | | Pierre Kast |
| 1952 | 14 | *An American in Paris* | Vincente Minelli | Frédéric Laclos |
| | 14 | Gene Kelly, auteur | Gene Kelly | Jean Myrsine |
| 1953 | 28 | *Singin' in the Rain* | Stanley Donen/ Gene Kelly | Claude Chabrol |
| 1954 | 38 | *The Band Wagon* | Vincente Minelli | Philippe Demonsablon |
| | 31 | *Moulin Rouge* | John Huston | |
| | 31 | *Lili* | Charles Walters | Jacque Doniol-Valcroze Phillipe Demonsablon |
| 1955 | 48 | *A Star is Born* | George Cukor | Charles Bitsch |
| | 45 | *Sabrina* | Billy Wilder | Jacques Doniol-Valcroze |
| | 54 | Evolution of the musical | | Jean Domarchi |
| 1956 | 64 | *Invitation to the Dance* | Gene Kelly | Claude de Givray |
| | 59 | *Love Me Or Leave Me* | Charles Vidor | Jean Domarchi |
| | 62 | *It's Always Fair Weather* | Stanley Donen/ Gene Kelly | Charles Bitsch |
| | 63 | *Brigadoon* | Vincente Minelli | Jean Domarchi |
| 1957 | 67 | *Guys and Dolls* | Joseph Mankiewicz | Louis Marcorelles |
| | 68 | *The King and I* | Walter Lang | Louis Marcorelles |
| | 74 | Vincente Minelli interview | Vincente Minelli | Jean Domarchi |
| 1958 | 79 | *Funny Face* | Stanley Donen | Jean Domarchi |
| | 80 | *Silk Stockings* | Rouben Mamoulian | Jean Domarchi |
| | 83 | *Les Girls* | George Cukor | Eric Rohmer |
| | 85 | Gene Kelly interview | Gene Kelly | Charles Bitsch/Jacques Rivette |
| | 85 | *The Pajama Game* | George Abott/ Stanley Donen | Jean-Luc Godard |
| 1959 | 92 | *South Pacific* | Joshua Logan | Eric Rohmer |
| | 94 | *Gigi* | Vincente Minelli | Louis Marcorelles |
| 1960 | | *Deep in My Heart* | Stanley Donen | Jean Domarchi |

## Appendix B: Review of Brigadoon by Jean-Domarchi from Cahier 63 (1956)

Let me declare at the outset that I find it impossible to express even the slightest reservations about *Brigadoon*: this is a film as ravishing as it is profound. I found myself even more impressed when I watched it again. Some may say that I am prejudiced in favour of Minnelli and that this leads me to exaggerate the importance of the film or to allow its strengths to blind me to its weaknesses. I sincerely do not believe this to be so. In my opinion, *Brigadoon* is a wonderful film, even if it is not perfect, and I will attempt to set out here the basis for a judgement which I am aware many may consider rash. . . ..*Brigadoon* represents the triumphant return to the screen of the fairy story and marks an important stage in the evolution of cinema. This is not only because Minnelli is a man of refinement and taste and a great director. In this film, perhaps more than any other of his, he has achieved a synthesis of the painterly and the cinematic. Could anything be more enchanting than the fluid, dancing camerawork as day breaks over the little Scottish village? There is a wonderful interplay between the use of the camera, the colours and the deployment of light and shade as a purely decorative element. Minnelli has an incomparable understanding of the language of cinema: his entirely personal use of colour on the screen recalls the great painters of the Northern Renaissance. Formally speaking, *Brigadoon* now stands as the third triumph of Cinemascope (the two others being *A Star is Born* and *Rebel Without a Cause*). What other director could have captured the flickering torchlight on the ferns or the brilliant red of Cyd Charisse's gown against the verdant night landscape of the Scottish countryside? I hope I may have been able to give an idea of the charm of this film as something which is specific to the films of Minnelli. In my view, the contribution of Gene Kelly is a lesser one. Kelly's choreography is entirely correct; his own dance number is an exact repetition of similar numbers which I found delightful in *Singin in the Rain* and *It's Always Fair Weather*. For all the richness of his invention, Kelly is infinitely less at ease that Minnelli in the difficult genre of the movie musical.

*Brigadoon* is a film infused by a deep melancholy, despite its happy ending. In this sense it recalls the endings of movies by Aldrich, Mankiewicz or Hawks. It subscribes to an aesthetic of refusal. The divine, irreplaceable Cyd Charisse is entirely captivating. I confess that I had previously considered Minnelli to be the latest representative of what historians regard as a form of mannerism: a slightly limp perfection not entirely free of eclecticism. I now unreservedly withdraw that charge: Minnelli is a great European artist to whom we owe the survival of the best elements of the painterly style from the past and present and to whom the cinema will remain indebted for two or three truly great films.

## Notes

1 Canal+Image International, *Une Femme est Une Femme*, VHS, Warner Home Video, 2000.

2 Jean-Luc Godard, 'Voyez comme on danse *The Pajama Game*' *Cahiers du cinéma* 85 (1958), 49–51.
3 Jean Minelli Domarchi, 'Le magnifique' *Cahiers du Cinéma*, 63, (1956), 44–47.
4 Jane Feuer, *The Hollywood Musical*. London: British Film Institute and Macmillan, (1982). vii-viii.
5 Jean Myrsine, 'Gene Kelly: auteur de films et homme-orchestre' *Cahiers du cinéma* 14 (1952), 35–37.
6 Eric Rohmer, 'La quintessence du genre *Les Girls*' *Cahiers du cinéma* 83 (1958), 46–50
7 Jean-Luc Godard, *Godard on Godard*, translated by Tom Milne, edited by Jean Narboni and Tom Milne (London: Secker & Warburg, 1972), 204.
8 Jean Myrsine, Gene Kelly: auteur de films et homme-orchestre *Cahiers du cinéma* 14 (1952), 35–37.
9 Charles Bitsch and Jacques and Rivette, 'Rencontre avec Gene Kelly' *Cahiers du cinéma* 85 (1958), 24–33.
10 Pierre Kast, Une Stakhanoviste de l'erotisme de choc: Esther Williams *Cahiers du cinéma* (1951), 38–39.
11 Richard Roud, 'The French Line' *Sight and Sound* 29: 4 (1960), 169.
12 Andrew Sarris, *Cahiers du cinéma in English*. Number 1. (New York: Flashback Edition, Cahiers Publishing Company, 1966).
13 Thomas, Elsaesser, 'Two Decades in Another Country. Hollywood and the Cinephile' in Thomas Elsaesser. *European Cinema. Face to Face with Hollywood* (Amsterdam: Amsterdam University Press, 2005), 240.
14 Jim Hillier, (ed.) *Cahiers du cinéma. The 1950s, Neo-Realism, Hollywood and the New Wave* (Cambridge: Harvard University Press, 1985).
15 John Flowers, (ed.) *Cahiers du cinéma Presents: The Hollywood Interviews* (Oxford and New York: Berg, 2006).
16 Jean Minelli Domarchi, 44–47.
17 Eric Rohmer, La quintessence du genre '*Les Girls*' *Cahiers du cinéma* 83 (1958), 46–50.
18 Jean-Luc Godard, Voyez comme on danse '*The Pajama Game*' *Cahiers du cinéma*, 85 (1958), 49–51.
19 Rohmer, 46–50.
20 Jean Myrsine, 35–37.
21 Domarchi, 44–47.
22 Philippe Demonsablon, 'The Band Wagon' *Cahiers du cinéma*, 38 (1954).
23 Jean-Luc Godard, 49–51.
24 Domarchi, 44–47.
25 'The Cardinal Virtues of Cinemascope' [from *Cahiers du cinéma* January 1954] in Jim Hillier (editor) *Cahiers du cinéma. The 1950s, Neo-Realism, Hollywood and the New Wave* (Cambridge: Harvard University Press, 1985), 280.
26 Bitsch, A Star is Born *Cahiers du cinema* (1955), 48.
27 Bitsch and Rivette, 24–33.
28 Godard, 49–51.
29 Claude Chabrol, 'Que ma joie demeure'. '*Singin' in the Rain*' *Cahiers du cinéma*, 28 (1953), 55–57.
30 Rohmer, 46–50.
31 Rohmer, South Pacific, *Cahiers du cinema* (1959), 92.

32 André Bazin 'The Evolution of the Language of Cinema' in André Bazin *What is cinema?* Essays selected and translated by Hugh Gray (Berkeley and London: University of California Press, 2005), 24.
33 Frédéric Laclos, 'An American in Paris', *Cahiers du cinema* 14 (1952), 51–52.
34 Domarchi, Évolution du film musical, *Cahiers du cinema* 54 (1955), 34–383.
35 Domarchi, 44–47.
36 Domarchi, 'Entretien avec Vincente Minelli', *Cahiers du cinema* (1957), 74 .
37 Louis Marcorelles, 'Amérique, Année zero', *Cahiers du cinéma* (1957), 49–50.
38 Godard, 49–51.
39 Godard, '*Une Femme est Une Femme*. Scenario de Jean-Luc Godard, d'après une idée de Geneviève Cluny', *Cahiers du cinéma* (1959), 46–51.
40 Steven Cohan (ed), *Hollywood Musicals, the Film Reader* (London and New York: Routledge, 2002), 2.
41 Feuer, 'The Hollywood Musical: An Annotated Bibliography', in Rick Altman (ed). *Genre: The Musical.* (London, Boston and Henley: Routledge and Kegan Paul, 1981), 208–215.
42 Feuer, *The Hollywood* musical (London: British Film Institute and Macmillan, 1982), vii-viii.
43 Ben Lacker, Godard's Ironic Erotics in *Une femme est une femme* http://www.nyu.edu/cas/eup/lackergodard05.pdf. 2005 Accessed: 12.05.2009, 210.
44 Richard Dyer, 'Entertainment and Utopia' in Stevan Cohan (ed) *Hollywood Musicals, the Film Reader* (London and New York: Routledge, 2002), 19.
45 Jean-Luc Godard, *Une Femme est Une Femme*, 46–51.
46 Godard, *Godard on Godard*, 167.
47 Domarchi, Évolution du film musical, *Cahiers du cinema* 54 (1955), 34–383.
48 Gilles Delavaud, Jean-Pierre Esquenazi, and Marie-France Grange, *Godard et le metier d'artiste* (Paris: Harmattan, 2001), 37–38.
49 Bitsch, A Star is Born, *Cahiers du cinema* (1955), 48.
50 Aumont, 'The Fall of the Gods. Jean-Luc Godard's *Le Mépris* (1963)', In: Susan Hayward and Ginette Vincendeau (eds) *French film: texts and context*, (London: Routledge, 1989), 184.
51 Domarchi, Le magnifique (1956), 63, 44–47.
52 Aumont, 'The Fall of the Gods'. 180.
53 Delavaud, Esquenazi and Grange, *Godard et le metier d'artiste* 37–38.
54 Aumont, 'The Fall of the Gods'. 174–6.
55 *L'Avant-Scène cinema, Le.* Double issue numbers 412/413. May/June 1992, 97.
56 Nicole Brenez, Cinematographie du figuratif in *L'Avant-Scene cinem., Le Mépris.* May/June 1992 double issue numbers 412/413, 2.
57 Anatoly C Biomechanics and Epic Theatre. http://filmplus.org/biomx/epic.html Accessed: 25.05.2009.
58 Bertolt Brecht, 'On Film Music' Unpublished typescript [1942] sent to Hans Eisler for his book on composing music for film. In *Brecht on Film and Radio*, translated and edited by Marc Silberman, (London: Methuen, 2001), 11–14.
59 Susan Sontag, Going to the Movies, Godard, *Partisan Review* 2 (1968), 294–5.
60 Colin MacCabe, Realism and the Cinema: Notes on Some Brechtian Theories *Screen* (1974), 15, 2, 19.
61 Feuer, 'The Self-Reflective Musical and the Myth of Entertainment' in Rick Altman (ed). *Genre: The Musical.* (London, Boston and Henley: Routledge and Kegan Paul, 1981), 159.

ELIA NTAOUSANI

# The written and the writing Or how Godard's film functions textually

> If one had to name a filmmaker for whom, through the last 50 years, every form of writing is organically and systematically present in (and around) the *image*, it would have to be Jean-Luc Godard.
> – Philippe Dubois, 'The Written Screen: JLG and Writing as the Accursed Share'

> [. . .] Godard meticulously constructs a richly layered *aural* palimpsest – one could even say a mystic writing pad. [. . .] One is continually confronted by the work of reading, listening, viewing, deciphering, and searching.
> – Nora Alter, 'Mourning, Sound, and Vision: Jean-Luc Godard's *JLG/JLG*'

> Godard's film asserts itself as writing inasmuch as it practices dismantling writing while drawing its resources from it.
> – Marie-Claire Ropars-Wuilleumier, 'The Graphic in Film Writing: À bout de souffle or The Erratic Alphabet'

This essay draws on the concept of *écriture* to analyse the writing in Godard's films and how that use of writing enables us to understand the process of the Godardian production of meaning. Introduced by Barthes and developed by Derrida, in which the French word for handwriting (*écriture*) was used to designate the way in which writing itself is a pragmatic process constantly exceeding the control of the conscious subject. This concept has been developed in relation to cinema in order to emphasise, according to Joanna Paul, 'the cinematic product *as text*, focusing on the 'literary' elements of narrative and dialogue, referring to the visual aspects of editing, camerawork and so on, as "film grammar"'.[1] David Rodowick, Thierry Kuntzel and Marie-Claire Ropars-Wuilleumier, for instance, are, among others, raising the question of 'writing' in relation to cinematic signification, adaptation and translation. My own focus however is not on the more general questions of *cinécriture* or, better, those general questions are only raised by the very specific question of how writing itself, in its most material senses, functions in Godard's films.

The essay uses for this purpose examples not only from *Le Mépris* (1963)[2] but also from Godard's *Á bout du souffle* (1959)[3] and from McBride's American remake *Breathless* (1983),[4] to demonstrate first how differently

Hollywood and the French New Wave treat writing in the image and, second, to further examine that difference.

In 1992 Raymond Bellour, taking his cue from Godard's opinion that writers are more 'condemned' than painters or musicians to analyse the world and themselves, proposed a methodology suitable for analysing Godard's film-making. Bellour's scheme has four modes 'that link text and speech to image, but also divide them';[5] it examines the impact not only of the text on the image – and vice versa – but also of the written text as image on speech and that of speech on image.

Specifically, Bellour's first mode concerns shots of *books as physical objects*. The second mode refers to quotation, where the book itself is absent from the screen but the reference exercises the spectators' memory or incites a physical movement in the film or ultimately veils the image, by imposing the influence of the past on the present. The third mode focuses on *text over image* in a myriad of forms – not just the letter of some specific character filling the frame but all the ready-made texts like ads, signs and graffiti. Fourth and finally, there are *'all the voices*: those of the book and of quotation, and those of all the characters'; voices that share 'the singularity of always addressing the spectator at least somewhat – even when talking to a partner, whether on- or offscreen'.[6]

Despite dealing with both written and spoken text, Bellour's method provides us with inspiring ideas about how a film might be approached analytically without reducing the analysis of the filmic language to a merely literary register. For the proposed modes do not only avoid what Nora Alter would call a category mistake, namely the scholarly temptation of exhaustively decoding and unproductively identifying 'every single reference, allusion, and "image" (visual or auditory) in Godard's videos and films';[7] they actually manage to group different processes of signification in order to analyse the plurality and intermediality of the cinematic text overall. This plurality and intermediality is a result of the fact that the cinematic text, according to Rodowick, 'resists characterisation as an univocal sign because it conjoins five distinct matters of expression – phonetic sound, music, noise or sound effects, written inscriptions, photographic registration'.[8]

For this essay, however, special focus will be given to the written and what in Godard's use of the written reveals the more 'writerly' qualities of his films. The methodology will follow Bellour's template of modes, while at the same time reinventing the respective categorisations in relation to their specific application in Godard's work. So the first two modes become one: text over image includes not only letters, ads and graffiti, but also shots of books, libraries or any other material symbol of the written.

'Godard has succeeded in using (some might say "over-using") "all" the possible ways of presenting written text in and through images', as Dubois insightfully points out;[9] and yet, writing on screen is definitely not the only recurring gesture of Godard's work. At least two other modes of literal and literary textuality emerge: *écriture* as spoken quotation, so the pre-written *text over sound* on one hand, and the *écriture* as dialectic/dialogic process involving both image and sound, so the *text in its becoming*, on the other. Unlike the two first modes that separate functions and examine an already existent written, the final mode looks at words that are performed (or interrupted) in such a way that they become *écriture* on the screen; what is fixed dialogue in the script becomes in the image a poem that stands alone and actively rewrites itself.

## *Écriture* over image

> The film doesn't just say "I am a film, I am an object-in-construction being presented to you as a self-constituted commodity," it also says: "I am a series of images within images, sounds within sound, subject to constant recontextualisation [...]; thus I am always graphic in two senses, that of the pictorial and that of the written."
>
> – David Wills, 'The French Remark: Breathless and Cinematic Citationality'

At the beginning of his essay *The Figure and the Text*, Rodowick refers to a 'complication of our notion of reading as a "writerly" activity. In fact,' he underlines, 'reading becomes a form of writing, the actualization of Text'.[10] There is no such thing as a self-existent identity of the written, I would add, and therefore, just like each book is steadily gaining and changing its substance through the eyes of the reader, every spectator decodes and actualises the cinematic text (*cinécriture*) as if he were its original – or any other – author. Except that 'to a certain extent at least, the *auteur* is', according to André Bazin, 'a subject to himself; whatever the scenario, he always tells the same story, or, in case the word "story" is confusing, let's say he has the same attitude and passes the same moral judgements on the action and on the characters'.[11] In other words, the *politique des auteurs* consists of a personal factor in artistic creation that moves on from one film to the next. Seen from this angle, the *politique des spectateurs*, if anything, shall then be marked by an equally personal view in understanding or interpreting, one that keeps consistency throughout the different films watched. Whatever the story the author is telling, whatever the message to be passed on, the reader always uses the same moral filters, composes the same attitude and ultimately reads the same personal story.

With these remarks in mind, this section explores at least two ways of representing the written text and the act of reading as a 'writerly' quality on screen. First, we will consider the impact of a textual image both in terms of audience reaction and plot development by analysing close ups of handwritten, painted or typewritten letters. Second, we will examine the role of the shots of physical books or book titles.

The most powerful shot in *Le Mépris* of a text in the image comes undoubtedly at the moment of death. After a short stop at a gas station,

Camille (Brigitte Bardot) gets back in Jeremy Prokosch's (Jack Palance) car only to crash a few moments later. Instead of seeing the fatal scene the spectators are only hearing the sounds of the accident as they read the last words of Camille's letter to her husband and playwright Paul Javal (Michel Piccoli): *Je t'embrasse. Adieu. Camille* (With *love. Goodbye. Camille*). We already know the entire content of the letter, yet not in its written form but through Camille as she voices her last goodbye to Paul. When the letter's last line appears on screen, the spectator not only recognises the source of the now silent words but also recalls the exact moment of their writing, actualised under the form of an entirely auditory activity: that of their reading.

Although the text is treated as an image on screen, the shot consists of a slow-moving close-up; one that interrupts the plot's action visually, while overlapping the car accident acoustically – crash and then silence. By subverting any conventional order, the stillness is therefore not associated with the interposed handwriting; it is instead referred to the very next shot, which zooms in on Camille's and Prokosch's dead bodies and holds for eleven seconds as if it were a single static frame, reminiscent of a photograph.

Godard seems to have succeeded not only in decoding death as both a process and an irreversible state but also in presenting its critical moment (and ever-elusive momentum) through the deconstruction of this very representation within the film; and yet, there are several other levels of ambiguity that linger in the *écriture* scene itself. On one hand, the words *Je t'embrasse. Adieu* sound like a response to the pun that Camille is making at the gas station stop. While having his car filled up with gas, Prokosch actually asks Camille *Qu'est-ce que tu penses...moi?* (*What do you think of me?*) for her only to answer *Montez dans votre Alfa, Romeo. On verra ça après* (*Get in your Alfa, Romeo. We'll see about that later*). Except that there is no later moment: the Alfa Romeo is not merely metaphorically decomposed in Alfa (first class car) and Romeo (Prokosch), a reference to the romantic hero who dies in Shakespeare's famous play, but gets literally and entirely smashed on the highway.

On the other hand, the screen image of the heroine's handwriting consists in a certain re-enactment of the same letter that was written and read in the past. When Camille's last paper-kiss to her lover at last acquires visual presence and gets here re-contextualised, we cannot help but doubt as to whether her unspoken words are indeed re-addressed to Paul, her husband, or rather waving at this point goodbye to any implicit intimacy with Prokosch. The close-up of the particular text constitutes after all a double gesture both at a very pragmatic and at a conceptual level. For, like her pun referring to the *Romeo and Juliet* tragedy, Camille's pre-written *Adieu* ironically forebodes at once the couple's death (Prokosch and Camille) and the decisive end of any affair.

In any event, regardless of whether we read the impact of the image of the letter as favouring an emotional regression to the dead-ends of the past or a contribution towards a deadly ending, the most striking feature of *écriture* in this case is the unusual way Godard chooses to insert the written text into his film. Interrupted abruptly, yet only visually in the first place, with *Je t'embrasse* shown full-screen, the gas station scene is succeeded by some seconds of almost static action: Camille and Prokosch in the car ready to depart. When *Adieu* appears as a screened image, depriving the spectator of the view of the car, the sound is still on; it shortly disappears a moment or two after the crash-bang, that is, after the camera reaches *Camille*'s name – a signature of deathly silence. As memory, presage or even representation of fate, the *écriture* intervenes therefore multiplicatively into the plot, whereas the dramatic alteration of shots escalates the emotions and infuses the accident scene with an enigmatic density of metaphysical signification. Godard is invariably pushing the audience towards a 'writerly' way of 'reading' underneath the scenario lines – as Jim Hillier points out, the *auteur* film is engaging the spectator in a more active apprehension of reality, staying thereby in a kind of oppositional tension with Hollywood conventions.[12]

In McBride's *Breathless* (1983), for instance, the shots of the comic *Silver Surfer* are treated in an entirely different way: not only do they flow with the story but they also follow the narrative's sequential linearity and rather serve to illustrate any slight shift in the plot. While in *Le Mépris* the interpolated text is memorable because it marks once and forever the ultimate denouement, in the *Breathless* remake the pages of the comic book are shown repeatedly throughout, especially every time that Jesse reads or quotes its hero. Let us take as an example the crucial moment, when Jesse (Richard Gere) needs to decide whether to leave the town or to stay endangered because of his love for Monica (Valerie Kaprisky). He goes into a bookshop, opens an issue of his favourite comic and – ta-dah! – *Silver Surfer* helps him to make up his mind. As he reads, the camera alternates between a shot of Jesse moving around and holding the book and a still close-up of the written text; *if such be my destiny . . . willingly do I accept it* or *love is the power supreme* are emblematic phrases that visually precede the at-the-time spoken words.

Compared to McBride who freezes *écriture* and conventionally represents action by motion (of the camera), Godard seems to inventively emphasise the written screen as moving image, whilst producing a photographic quality within the film. Besides, in *Breathless* the *Silver Surfer* is visible both as part and as a whole, as a close-up of a particular comic strip and as a shot of the entire book, yet further doubled in sound and image inasmuch as every quotation is read aloud by the actor and also silently by the audience. In *Le Mépris* on the other hand, there is no need to show any overview of the physical paper in order for the audience to recognise Camille's letter as the source of the words on screen. For even in the very unlikely event of not matching the two instances and not merging them into one another, the spectator would anyway 'read' the strikingly inserted handwriting as a farewell to love and to life. In brief, whereas text over image in McBride's film repeats a single message, by multiplying only its expressions, *écriture* in Godard produces a plurality, and hence ambiguity, of meaning.

## *Écriture* over sound

> People in life quote as they please, so we have the right to quote as we please. Therefore I show people quoting, merely making sure that they quote what pleases me. In the notes I make of anything that might be of use for a film, I will add a quote from Dostoevsky if I like it. Why not? If you want to say something, there is only one solution: say it.
>
> – Jean-Luc Godard, '"From Critic to Film-Maker": Godard in Interview ("Entretien", *Cahiers du Cinéma* 138, December 1962)'

In his essay *"A form that thinks": Godard, Blanchot, Citation*, Leslie Hill remarks that 'quotation always serves at least two masters, which is a way of saying that it is always liable to take orders from either'.[13] There is the realm of the original location, the first creation on one hand, and, on the other, the re-contextualisation of its fragments. Except that 'the self-identity of any quotation is essentially problematic', Hill goes on. 'When is a quotation a quotation and when is not? How to tell where a quotation begins or ends?'[14]

People in their everyday lives as well as writers or film-makers often use quotations not only without being able to supply the name of the original speaker but sometimes without even realising that they are actually quoting. In the final analysis, it does not matter if one is able to indicate the source or if one quotes at all, as the contextualization process changes the meaning 'always already'. The case of a film remake is a characteristic example: 'it necessarily both covers and fails to cover the discontinuities or incoherencies that structure it', as David Wills explains; 'it can only ever repeat itself as difference and inscribe those differences in the process of its writing'.[15] Taking things further, the film, just like any other piece of art (poem, musical composition, architectural design and so on), is then never a seamless and self-contained whole of quotations, but rather an auto-poetic text in constant recreation and connection. 'For in writing itself and in automatically being rewritten,' Wills unfolds his thought, 'the film translates itself, [. . .] recontextualizes itself to a foreign place within itself'.[16]

*Le Mépris* provides a perfect example of this iterability of quotation as both repetition and difference. Godard is preeminent as the filmmaker who celebrates and decomposes quotation, not by just over-using it but by equally over-exposing it. While priding himself on the fact that 'not a single line of the dialogue in *Détective* or in *Soigne ta droite* was written by him,' the recognised master of the quotational genre, as Jacques Aumont puts it, uses literary quotes in *Le Mépris* really and truly as citations – 'i.e. spoken, in quotes, by one character to another, instead of being an integral part of the movie'.[17] It is precisely from this perspective, after all, that quotation might be considered as *écriture* over sound.

There are a number of scenes in *Le Mépris*, where a spoken quotation enables this very quality of producing a certain ambiguity or controversy of meaning. Jeremy Prokosch, for instance, reduces his giant figure of the handsome and powerful producer as he appears to derive wisdom from a little red book that he carries in his pocket: *To know that one does not know is the gift of the superior spirit. Not to know and to think that one does know is a mistake.*[18] According to Leslie Hill, quotations like this one 'have a lapidary quality that not only allows them to be repeated from one context to the next but also gives them the status of so many mysterious incitements or provocations to thought'.[19]

In fact, later in the movie, Prokosch reads from the same tiny book that *The wise man does not oppress others with his superiority. He does not try to humiliate them for their impotence.*[20] Although these words clearly mark the end of a dialogue with Paul about a vision of the *Odyssey* as a return to the cinema of Griffith and Chaplin, it is nevertheless unclear whether Prokosch is addressing Paul's stiffness and seeking to dispute his superior spirit as a playwright or whether he is indicating his own material superiority as movie investor, whilst also demonstrating his supposed wisdom as a free-going spirit and an open-minded man. Besides, the quotation indirectly refers both to the great days of United Artists and to an earlier scene, in which Bardot submissively affirms in front of Prokosch that her husband is the one who makes the decisions for her (*c'est mon mari qui decide*). A sarcastic comment on the husband's lack of will-power, on the playwright's radical idealism or on the producer's superiority, the quotation hovers over all the characters and demonstrates its potential for rewriting or being decoded in as many different ways as there are points of view.

Pompously pulling a book out of one's pocket and so pausing the action to utter a quotation is, however, by no means the only possible mode of *écriture* over sound. To avoid answering Paul's question as to whether she still loves him, Camille chooses to read aloud an abstract from a book about Fritz Lang while lying in the bath: *Le problème, selon moi, ce ramène à la façon que nous avons de concevoir le monde; conception positive ou négative...* (*The problem, as I see it, comes down to the way we look at the world; whether we have a positive or a negative conception*).[21] Suddenly the written text, when spoken, fits so well in the new context of the couple's dialogue that the conversation, instead of reaching a dead end, is actually taken further, to another level of complexity. The quotation undergoes at once a dual movement of de- and re-contextualisation, and yet in opposite directions. On the one hand, it serves as an insightful, generic and elaborate answer from Camille's side to Paul's polar question and, on the other, it makes of this particular mundane affair a metaphor of a philosophical world apprehension.

Although *écriture* over sound plays a decisive role in Godard's films, either by bridging references of past and future scenes or by offering different levels of signification, this does not seem to be so much the case in American mainstream cinema, where the spoken quotation is rather taken as illustration of a single meaning. In the example of McBride's *Breathless* remake, Monica is curious to know what Jesse is reading while she is getting dressed. As Jesse tells her about the story of *Silver Surfer* and the problems that the latter has with his girlfriend, Monica comes closer in order to have a look at the page by herself. Embracing, Jesse and Monica ostentatiously enact the characters by alternatively reciting their words, which are literally visualised, thus repeated, through their actual appearance as comic strips on screen. Besides, after the self-dramatising quotation *I have seen the birth of planets and the death of worlds. I have seen galaxies crumble and new suns aborning. But in every star, in every sun, I see her face!*,[22] Jesse looks up at Monica's image reflected in the mirror, as if the connection between the comic and the movie characters had to be further underlined.

Godardian quotation is contrariwise not always marked as in Prokosch's red book. Whether identifiable or not, the spoken quotation can also be well-hidden within the characters' flow of words. In other instances, it may equally be the character herself who hides behind the curtains of *écriture*, as with Camille in *Le Mépris*' bathroom scene - her face staying literally invisible behind the book she reads about Lang. The primary role is here given to the quotation by subtly keeping the actual character further in the background. Except that, incarnated in the actor's voice, the quotation is in practice *becoming* the character - the two are merging into one another within the new context provided, that of the film scenario – an *écriture* in its writing. Despite the many different ways of dealing with the written over sound, Godard is drawing attention to his staging of quotation and the reinventing of its possible meanings rather than upon its use as an already given and fixed secondary material simply sustaining or justifying the characters' decisions and actions within the plot.

## *Écriture* in becoming

> I read in *Sight and Sound* that I improvised Actors' Studio fashion, with actors to whom one says 'You are so-and-so; take it from there.' But Belmondo never invented his own dialogue. It was written. But the actors didn't learn it: the film was shot silent, and I cued the lines.
>
> – Jean-Luc Godard, '"From Critic to Film-Maker": Godard in interview ("Entretien", *Cahiers du Cinéma* 138, December 1962)'

The last aspect of textuality into which the present essay wishes to delve deeper considers *écriture* as a dialogic process or, alternatively, dialogue as a text that is written through its performance on screen. Rather than getting involved with either the *auteur*'s understanding of the script writing process, as André Bazin does in *La politique des auteurs* (1957), or with the *Odyssey* script that Paul is writing in *Le Mépris*, my *écriture in (its) becoming* refers to dialogue as an auto-poetic modality of the written and the writing within the film. The goal is to explore dialogue as a visible and audible motion inscribed in space and time, and not as lines awaiting their interpretation by the actors.

To paraphrase Hill, when speaking about the process of quoting: *to write a text is to do so here and now; and to write a text here and now is to write a different text from the one I wrote a moment ago.*[23] Regardless of whether they derive from a given script or not, the words exchanged between the characters in front of the camera can sometimes reveal a 'writerly' quality in Godard's films. The lines actively rewrite themselves as they come alive on screen, and ultimately acquire a life of their own. Depending on whether the performance is a dialectic or a dialogic one, that is, whether point and counterpoint (thesis and antithesis) merge into a certain state of compromise and agreement (synthesis) or whether various approaches coexist in their interaction, the resulting *écriture* may be either a monolithic poem or a chiasmatic (reversible) structure of separate monologues.

My emphasis here is on the dialogic case and a characteristic example of a comparatively relativistic interaction of viewpoints leading to chiasmus can be found in *À bout de souffle*. The plan 446, sequence 14 in particular, shows Patricia (Jean Seberg) explaining to her lover Michel (Jean-Paul Belmondo) the reasons why she has denounced him to the police. An efficient way of analysing the ingredients of the performance model of *écriture* over both image and sound is to juxtapose at this point Godard's dialogue with McBride's version in *Breathless*.

There are indeed obvious differences. In *À bout de souffle* the camera faithfully stays with Patricia as she delineates, according to Michel Marie, an orbit of one hundred steps in randomly circular movement within Michel's studio.[24] This *plan sequence* which unifies time, space and action,[25] has a duration of two minutes and ten seconds, whereas in *Breathless* the corresponding incident consists not of a single shot but of twenty-one different shots: for a period of two minutes and forty seconds the camera either follows the dialogue by separately focusing on Monica's and Jesse's faces or alternates in quick succession between long action shots and portrait close-ups.

However, the audience is invited to 'see' beyond the moving or placing of the camera, that is to say, beyond the mode of an exclusively visual *cinécriture*, to the textual dimension of the script's performance. More explicitly, the spectator is encouraged to 'listen' attentively to the words that get articulated by the protagonists and thus to explore the diversity of meanings produced. For although the plan 446 of *À bout de souffle* is meant to be a dialogue between Patricia and Michel, the characters are not always really and truly interacting; rather than responding to one another, their phrases are often treated as fragments of separate monologues in a quite sophisticated way.

On a more practical level, the chiasmatic impression has been made possible thanks to Godard's audiovisual manipulation of the scene. While the camera, and therefore the spectator's eye, continuously keeps track on Patricia's movement in space, not everything she utters remains clearly audible: some of her words are overlapping with or even temporally interrupting those of her lover, others are fading in the background – and the same goes for Michel as well. There are moments when it becomes almost impossible to identify who said what, with both voices merging into one single text and at the same time separately performing a sort of dual voiced monologue. Except that the 'writerly' quality of the performed speech or of the eloquent performance is only partly based on this multiple functioning; whether a dialogue or a combination of monologues, the lines in Godard's film have an inherent reflexivity that is largely content-based and not exclusively context-dependent.

> Patricia: Michel, j'ai téléphoné à la police. (Michel, I called the police.) J'ai dit que tu étais ici. (I said you were here.)
> Michel: T'es cinglée? (Are you crazy?) Ça ne va pas, non?
> P: Si, ça va très bien. (No, I'm fine.) Non, ça ne ma va pas. (No, I'm not). Je n'ai plus envie de partir avec toi. (I don't want to go with you.)
> M : Oui, je le savais. (I knew it.)
> P : Je ne sais pas. (I don't know.)
> M : Quand on parlait, je parlais de moi, et toi, de toi. (I just talked about myself, and you, yourself.)
> P: Je trouve que je suis idiote. (I'm so stupid.)
> M : Alors, tu aurais du parler de moi, et moi, de toi. (You should've talked about me, and me, about you.)
> P: Je ne veux pas être amoureuse de toi. (I don't want to be in love with you.) J'ai téléphoné à la police pour ça. (That's why I called the police). Je suis restée avec toi parce que je voulais être sure que j'étais amoureuse de toi. (I stayed with you to see if I was in love with you.) Ou que je n'étais pas amoureuse de toi. (Or if I wasn't.) Et puisque je suis méchante avec toi, (And since I'm being cruel to you,) c'est la preuve que je ne suis pas amoureuse de toi. (it proves I'm not in love with you.)
> M : Quoi dis-le (Say that again!)
> P: Et puisque je suis méchante avec toi, (And since I'm being cruel to you,) c'est la preuve que je ne suis pas amoureuse de toi. (it proves I'm not in love with you.)
> M : On dit qu'il n'y a pas d'amour heureux . . . (They say there's no happy love.)
> P: Si je t'aimais (If I loved you . . .) / M: . . . mais c'est le contraire. D'ici une pensée simple / P : oh, c'est trop compliqué (It's too complicated!)
> M : Au contraire, il n'y a pas d'amour malheureux. (On the contrary, there's no unhappy love.)
> P: Je veux que les gens ne s'occupent pas de moi. (I want people to let me be.) / Moi je ne crois pas d'être indépendent.
> M: . . . mais je suis indépendent (I'm independent.)
> P : Peut-être que tu m'aimes. (Maybe you love me.)
> M : Toi tu y crois (You think you are.) et tu l'es pas. (You're not.)
> P : C'est pour ça je t'ai denoncé. (That's why I denounced you.)
> M: Je te suis superieur. (I'm better than you are.)
> P: Maintenant tu es forcé de partir. (Now you have no choice but to go.)
> M: Tu es cinglée! (You're nuts!) C'est lamentable comme raisonnement! (That's a rotten way of thinking!)[26]

On a metaphorical level, the words in *À bout de souffle* are driving circles around each character. In the *Breathless* remake on the contrary, the words are unfolding linearly, marked as they are by both an emphatically repetitive tone and an entirely sequential rationale:

> Monica: I called the police. I told them you were here.
> Jesse: What the fuck for? Ah? It don't (sic) make any sense!
> M: It makes sense! No, it doesn't.
> J: Monica, you love me.
> M: I don't want to love you! I don't want to go with you. Just now when I went down the hill, I wanted to keep going on. I was not gonna come back.
> J: You love me. You say it!
> M: I was not going to come back! But I knew you would come after me and I knew you wouldn't stop coming after me!
> J: But you love me! Now say it!
> M: It doesn't matter if I . . .
> J: Say it!
> M: It doesn't matter if I love you! It's wrong for us. You don't see, but I can't stop you, Jesse.
> J: You're damn right you can't stop me.
> M: That's why I called the police – so that you would have to go! Go, Jesse, please! Quickly!
> J: All right. You say you don't love me. Then I'll go. You gotta say it. Say it and I'll go. It's easy. Go on. Say it. You can't say it, can you?
> M: I don't love you.[27]

While Monica and Jesse are expressing their tension by dramatically shouting to each other, the words of Godard's couple in *À bout de souffle* are almost half-spoken, almost simultaneously uttered, even lost in translation to such an extent that it becomes impossible for the spectator to distinguish the sounds, let alone to perceive each monologue as autonomous or the dialogue as a criss-cross structure. Through the interactive perplexity of vision and hearing, a kind of cinematographic delirium emerges; one that infuses the actors' interpretation with a 'writerly' mode, where the script's lines get literally exchanged, psychologically reflected, intellectually processed, sensually experienced and actively reinvented. At the end of the day, it is all . . . à bout du souffle; it is all about a text still unwritten and an *écriture* always already *in becoming*.

## Notes

1 Joanna Paul, 'Homer and Cinema: Translation and Adaptation in *Le Mépris*', in *Translation & the Classic: Identity as Change in the History of Culture*, eds Alexandra Lianeri and Vanda Zajko (New York: Oxford University Press, 2008), 154.
2 *Le Mépris*. Based on the novel *Il disprezzo* by Alberto Moravia. Dir. Jean-Luc Godard. Perfs Brigitte Bardot, Michel Piccoli, Jack Palance, Giorgia Moll, Fritz Lang (Compagnia Cinematografica Champion, 1963). DVD: Momentum Pictures World Cinema Collection, 2003.
3 *À bout de souffle*. Screenplay by Jean-Luc Godard, story by François Truffaut. Dir. Jean-Luc Godard. Perfs Jean-Paul Belmondo, Jean Seberg (Les Productions Georges de Beauregard, 1959). DVD: Optimum Releasing, 2000.

4 *Breathless*. Screenplay by L.M. Kit Karson & Jim McBride, based on the story *À bout de souffle* by François Truffaut and on the screenplay *À bout de souffle* by Jean-Luc Godard. Dir. Jim McBride. Perfs Richard Gere, Valerie Kaprisky (Company Breathless Associates, 1983). DVD: MGM Home entertainment, 2001.
5 Raymond Bellour, '(Not) Just an Other Filmmaker', *Son+Image* (1992), 219.
6 Ibid., 220.
7 Nora M. Alter, 'Mourning, Sound, and Vision: Jean-Luc Godard's *JLG/JLG*', In: *Camera Obscura* 44, 15:2, (Durham: Duke University Press, 2000), 85.
8 David N. Rodowick, 'The Figure and the Text', *Diacritics*, 15:1 (Baltimore: The John Hopkins University Press, 1985), 35.
9 Philippe Dubois, 'The written screen: JLG and writing as the accursed share', in *For ever Godard*, eds Michael Temple, James S. Williams and Michael Witt (London: Black Dog, 2004), 232.
10 Rodowick, 'The Figure and the Text', 34.
11 André Bazin, 'La politique des auteurs (*Cahiers du Cinéma* 70, 1957)', in *The New Wave*, ed. Peter Graham (London: Secker & Warbung in association with the British Film Institute, 1968), 150–1.
12 Jim Hillier, 'Introduction: Re-thinking American Cinema', in *Cahiers du Cinéma 1960-68: New Wave, New Cinema, Reevaluating Hollywood*, ed. Jim Hiller (Cambridge: Harvard University Press, 1992), 168.
13 Leslie Hill, '"A form that thinks": Godard, Blanchot, Citation', in *For ever Godard*, 399.
14 Ibid., 400.
15 David Wills, 'The French Remark: Breathless and Cinematic Citationality', in *Play it Again, Sam: Retakes on Remakes*, eds Andrew Horton and Stuart Y. McDougal (Los Angeles; London: University of California Press, 1998), 150-1.
16 Ibid., 149.
17 Jacques Aumont, 'The Fall of Gods: Jean-Luc Godard's *À bout de souffle* (1959)', in *French Film: Texts and Contexts*, eds Susan Hayward and Ginette Vincedeau (New York; London: Routledge, 2000), 177.
18 *Le Mépris*. Chapter 3, 0:08:03.
19 Leslie Hill, '"A Form that Thinks": Godard, Blanchot, Citation', 399.
20 *Le Mépris*. Chapter 3, 0:33:13.
21 Ibid., Chapter 10, 0:50:25.
22 *Breathless*. 0:53:25.
23 Leslie Hill, '"A form that thinks": Godard, Blanchot, Citation', 400.
24 Michel Marie, *À bout de souffle: Jean-Luc Godard* (Paris: Nathan, Series title: Synopsis, 1999), 76.
25 Ibid., 74.
26 *À bout de souffle*. Chapter 9, 1:19:16–1:22:46
27 *Breathless*. Chapter 15, 1:29:12–1:31:53.

OLIVER H. HARRIS

# Pure Cinema? Blanchot, Godard, *Le Mépris*

What fascinates us robs us of our power to give sense.
– Maurice Blanchot, *L'Espace littéraire*

The enigmatic French critic, novelist and philosopher Maurice Blanchot lurks in *Le Mépris* (1963), as he lurks in Godard's career. In the film he is unnamed, and the use of his writings unreferenced but when, in the screening room of Cinecittà, Fritz Lang begins discussing Hölderlin, it is not just the German poet that he quotes, but a passage of Blanchot's. Lang begins with four lines from Hölderlin's *The Poet's Vocation*:

But when it is necessary man remains without fear
Before God, simplicity protects him,
And he needs neither arms nor guile
As long as God does not fail him.

Lang comments: 'The last verse is very odd. Hölderlin first wrote "so long as God does not fail him", then "so long as God's *absence* does not fail him."' Lang concludes: 'It is not the presence but the absence of God which reassures man.'

In September 1963, the writer Jean Collet questioned Godard about this moment. Godard conceded: 'Yes, it is a very odd text of Hölderlin because it is incomprehensible.'[1] Asked why he included it, Godard replies:

'Because it is a text called 'The Poet's Vocation' and in *Le Mépris* Lang symbolises the poet, artist, creator. Thus, it was right that he speaks poetically about the 'poet's vocation'... I chose Hölderlin because Lang is German and also because Hölderlin wrote many poems about Greece ... But the poem needs to be taken as a poem. One doesn't ask Beethoven what his music means.[2]

Godard provides three reasons (Lang's symbolism within the film, his nationality, and the relevance of a Greek setting), and then suggests that it is a mistake to seek meaning at all. But nowhere does he mention that the four lines of Hölderlin, their change in later drafts, and the discussion of God's absence are all drawn from Blanchot's 'L'itinéraire de Hölderlin', the concluding essay of his 1955 collection, *L'Espace littéraire*.[3]

Blanchot is a deep and often unacknowledged influence on Godard, although the director has been open about his influence more recently. In his 1995 documentary film, *JLG/JLG: autoportrait de décembre*, Godard states that his original aim in cinema had been 'to make a movie like the books I happened to read when I was growing up, by Blanchot, or Bataille'.[4] Indeed, by the 1990s it seems he was more involved with the writings of Blanchot than ever, producing a cluster of citations that have been studied by Leslie Hill.[5] Dialogue over the closing credits of *Hélas pour moi* (1993) is taken from Blanchot's novel, *Au moment voulu* (1951). In *For Ever Mozart* (1996), Godard borrows a discussion of philosophy and history from Blanchot's tribute to Emmanuel Levinas, 'Notre compagne clandestine' (in *Textes pour Emmanuel Lévinas*, 1980). Tellingly, in a later interview Godard attributes the quote to Levinas himself.[6]

In this paper I ask what the figure of Blanchot means for Godard, what his texts allow the filmmaker to explore in his work, and how this relates to the themes of *Le Mépris*. Lang's brief allusion disguises how important Blanchot's thoughts are for the film, in particular for Godard's reflections on cinema itself and the medium's distinct promise. This is a question at the heart of *Le Mépris* and the oppositions it establishes: literature and film, classical and modern, sentimental and objective, corrupt art and pure.

## Between Nature and the Gods

In a 1963 article in *Cahiers du Cinéma*, Godard is explicit about the geographical symbolism of *Le Mépris*: 'Rome is the modern world, the West; Capri, the ancient world, nature before civilisation and its neuroses.'[7] This lament over the divide between nature and modernity recurs frequently in Godard's statements about the film. 'Paul Javal ... is a bad offspring of civilisation .... in *Le Mépris*, the catastrophe comes from the fact that the characters are too "civilised"'.[8] Blanchot's essay has relevance in this respect, for it concerns Hölderlin's interrogation of modern man as a figure divided from both nature and the gods. The essay begins:

> The young Hölderlin, the author of *Hyperion*, yearns to take leave of his form, escape his limits, and be united with nature: "to be one with all that lives, and to return in blessed self-forgetfulness into the All of Nature – that is man's heaven."[9]

The 'All' will become synonymous with a divine presence, but one that fluctuates through time. Hölderlin's meditation upon ancient Greece and modern European civilisation led him to conceive of an alternation between times when the gods are present and times when they are absent: periods of light, periods of darkness. Our own separation from the gods is contrasted with the divine unity of the ancient Greeks, a unity manifest in their art. It is in this context that Blanchot discusses Hölderlin's change of the final line of *The Poet's Vocation*. Blanchot writes: 'This is a strange revision. What does it mean?' His conclusion is similar to Lang's: God's absence is seen by Hölderlin as ultimately more comforting. But Blanchot takes the question further, asking why this should be. He describes Hölderlin, on the point of madness (having returned from his own, dazzling Mediterranean odyssey to the South of France) feeling too close to the dangerously foreign realm of the divine. In these times one can only possess the divine safely through maintaining *separation*, decides the poet. The role of art becomes in part a defence against our being overwhelmed ('simplicity protects him . . .'). The ancient Greek poets meanwhile, living amongst very present gods, had to acquire 'to an exceptional degree the power of sober moderation; Homer remains its finest example.'[10]

Homer's sober art makes demands on Godard's cinema. Like the novel on which it is based, *Le Mépris* asks how modern man can respond to *The Odyssey*. For Godard, his own medium is an inevitable part of that response. Collet goes on to question Godard with regards to Lang's assertion of 'la réalité d'Homère': 'Homer does not let itself be sub-divided, it is either to be taken as it is or left alone.' Godard replies: 'This is the opposite of the modern world, which somehow wants to accommodate itself to everything.' Then, in a stream of associations, he continues:

> I see everything done in *Le Mépris* as if it were no longer possible to keep anyone on solid ground. We have five survivors of a shipwreck. This is what they are. The cinema replaces the point of view of the gods.[11]

The final sentence, thrown out as if in passing, highlights ambitions tied to the act of film making in *Le Mépris*. Fritz Lang himself, epitome of the film director, symbolises 'the poet, artist, creator' as we have seen, but in a 1963 interview in *Le Monde*, Godard also presents him as 'the voice of the gods, the man who looks at men'.[12] He is the conscience of cinema itself, and cold observer of mankind:

> The point of *Le Mépris* is that these are people who look at each other and judge each other, and then are in turn looked at and judged by the cinema – represented by Fritz Lang, who plays himself, or in effect the conscience of the film, its honesty.[13]

If cinema is in a position to judge then it must evade the compromise and solipsistic neuroses that mark modern civilisation. Its power of judgement is in fact its transparency.

Can cinema replicate the point of view of the gods? The question reflects Godard's ambitions at this moment in his career. To what degree can cinema treat an emotional drama *objectively*, without succumbing to sentimental (human) interiority? *Le Mépris* is intended to be 'a simple film without mystery, an Aristotelian film, stripped of appearances' Godard asserts, with a further gesture to classical ideals.[14] But what is it about *cinema* that might enable this?

For the hope that cinema might cast off the bad habits of previous forms we need to turn to its high priest, André Bazin, whose writings in *Cahiers du cinéma* celebrate a photographic medium that provides a direct index of reality. His essay, 'The Ontology of the Photographic Image', remains an unapologetic herald of progress:

> No matter how skilful the painter, his work was always in fee to an inescapable subjectivity. The fact that a human hand intervened cast a shadow of doubt over the image ... Originality in photography as distinct from originality in painting lies in the essentially objective character of photography ...... For the first time an image of the world is created automatically, without the creative intervention of man.[15]

Bazin plays on the French for 'photographic lens': 'objectif'. Though conceding that the personality of the photographer will be traced in his or her acts of selection, there remains a fundamental human absence to the artefact that Bazin identifies as unique to photography:

> All the arts are based on the presence of man, only photography derives an advantage from his absence. Photography affects us like a phenomenon in nature, like a flower or a snowflake whose vegetable or earthly origins are an inseparable part of their beauty.[16]

Again, photographic art is associated not simply with modernity or technology but with an unpremeditated 'nature'. Bazin's language comes close to Blanchot's own when Blanchot discusses the role of absence and impossibility in the creative process throughout *L'Espace littéraire*. Only Blanchot is concerned with universal phenomena. Whatever the psychological appeal of artworks free of human stain, it is clearly this ontological promise that must keep cinema distinct from other mediums. This leads to an inevitable tension with its narrative element.

When Godard describes *Il Disprezzo* as 'a nice, vulgar [novel] for a train journey, full of *classical*, old-fashioned sentiments in spite of the modernity of the situations', an implicit contrast with his own objective Bazinian cinema is established.[17] Slightly more favourably, Godard describes the script he was shooting as 'rather faithful to [Alberto Moravia's] novel ... [It] allowed me tell a *classic* film story, as if movies were really like that.'[18] Nicholas Paige notes that in *Cahiers du cinéma* during the 1950s and early 1960s, the terms 'classic' and 'modern' were 'continually if unsystematically invoked in order to map out the relation between present cinematic production and everything from Greek tragedy and Hollywood to Pierre Boulez and abstract expressionism.'[19] But the opposition is placed in the foreground in *Le Mépris*. Marc Cerisuelo describes *Le Mépris* as 'the only truly modern film in the sense that it *stages* the difference between classic and modern.'[20] Crucial to the staging is Godard's disruption of sentimentality and narrative itself by drawing attention back to the image, the cuts, the medium; to the cold gaze of the camera that faces us at the film's opening.

Yet the ideal of objectivity predates cinema, and can bring in very different associations with 'the classical'. Alberto Moravia himself identifies the *Odyssey* with an art that is godlike and, at the same time, almost part of *nature*. It can be found in a theory of epic outlined by Hegel in his *Philosophy of Fine Art*.[21] For Hegel, epic action acquires 'objective form . . . [it] becomes an *event*, in which the facts in question disclose themselves in free independence, and the poet retires into the background.'[22] The subjectivity of the poet takes second place to the deeds. The ancient world again promises objectivity.

'In Capri pictures are ready made, so to speak . . . All you have to do is put yourself in front of the landscape and copy it'.[23] The curious line from Moravia's novel is one of the few preserved almost exactly in the film, in the mouth of Jeremy Prokosch, of all people. In the film, Bazinian 'objectivity' is bound to a distinct, Mediterranean landscape, with its own epic which is not to be subjected to psychological readings:

> Everything was here, and there was nothing else. And now Rheingold wanted to make this bright and luminous world . . . into a kind of dark, visceral recess, bereft of colour and form, sunless and airless: the subconscious mind of Ulysses.[24]

Godard's complex relationship with his source text can be seen in the swapping of symbolic roles. In *Le Mépris* it is Lang, symbol of cinema, who pursues objectivity. In the novel Molteni, the novelist, stands in opposition to the film director, Rheingold, who expounds a *psychoanalytical* reading of the *Odyssey* (Rheingold's German nationality has very different associations from Lang's, identifying him with psychoanalysis). For Moravia, unsurprisingly, it is Molteni who is haunted by a sense of lost clarity, objectivity and *authenticity*, in his life as much as his screenwriting project:

> In order to have the Emilia I loved and to cause her to judge me for what I was, I should have to carry her off into a world as simple as herself, as genuine as herself, a world in which money did not count and in which language had retained its integrity.[25]

The muddied, modern world in which they find themselves precludes clear judgement. Language itself is corrupt. And it is Homer's *Odyssey* which preserves an ideal alternative:

> The beauty of the *Odyssey* consists precisely in the belief in reality as it is and as it presents itself objectively . . . in this same form, in fact, which allows of no

> analysis or dissection and which is exactly what it is ... Homer belonged to a civilisation which had developed in accordance with, not in antagonism to, nature.[26]

Homer's art is seen, again, as belonging to a pre-lapsarian age. Molteni longs nostalgically for a lost linguistic integrity. But it is not a simple aspiration, in so far as it is now impossible, inhuman even, while still haunting contemporary artists as a dream. If *Le Mépris* concerns a crisis in the history of cinema, it is also concerned with a crisis fundamental to artistic creativity. Art must steer between an impossible, original purity and the 'prostitution' that *Le Mépris* repeatedly associates with narrative. This tension is explored in the next section, through the symbolism of Homer's Sirens.

## Pure Wilderness

Having noted that 'Rome is the modern world ... Capri, the ancient world,' Godard goes on:

> *Le Mépris*, in other words, might have been called In Search of Homer [*A la recherche d'Homère*], but it means lost time trying to discover the language of Proust beneath that of Moravia, and anyway that isn't the point.[27]

Why this odd conjunction of Proust and Homer in Godard's thoughts, aside from the opportunity it presents for another swipe at Moravia? The influence of Blanchot may provide an explanation and lead further into the concerns of Godard's film. In his collection, *Le Livre à venir* (1959), Blanchot presents adjacent essays on Homer and Proust while discussing the Sirens' song in the *Odyssey*. Proust is introduced as 'this new Ulysses', one whose 'long, tedious wanderings were revealed as those vital moments which make the past present.'[28] An echo of these essays is heard in Godard's comments on *Le Mépris* when he describes how his 'castaways ... reach a mysterious deserted island, whose mystery is the inexorable lack of mystery, of truth that is to say.'[29] In Blanchot's 1959 essay this seductive emptiness is the deceptive lure of the Sirens themselves, who awoke

> hope and desire for a sublime elsewhere which, in fact, was only a wilderness – as though the birthplace of music were the one place that was totally devoid of music, a dry and arid place where silence and sound alike prevented all those who were drawn to song from acceding to it.[30]

It is Blanchot who makes a 'birthplace' of this wilderness, but the Sirens' conjoining of beauty and deathly stasis goes back to the *Odyssey* itself: 'They sit in their meadow, but the beach before it is piled with boneheaps/Of men now rotted away, and the skins shrivel upon them.'[31] When sailors approach, the wind dies away, the sea itself freezes. But those entranced do not notice. Blanchot asks:

> What was the nature of the Sirens' song? . . . Some have said that it was an inhuman song – a natural sound (is there such a thing as an unnatural sound?) but on the borderline of nature, at any rate foreign to man; almost inaudible.[32]

Again, 'natural' expression is not a straightforward ideal but a threatening impossibility. Even as Blanchot hesitates over the dichotomy he projects a fragile borderline. By taking a step further and connecting this resistance to the *source* of music, its birthplace, Blanchot renders each creative act a paradoxical quest.

Renata Salecl places Blanchot's Sirens within a wider tradition that reads the episode for the tensions it reveals within art.[33] The philosopher Tzvetan Todorov, for example, draws upon the Sirens in *The Poetics of Prose* (1971) when he seeks to distinguish 'speech as beauty' and 'speech as narrative':

> It is a song about itself. The Sirens say only one thing: that they are singing . . .. The loveliest speech is the one which speaks itself.[34]

This miraculous, contentless art is contrasted with the surrounding story. For the classicist Pietro Pucci, the Sirens' song becomes 'the negative, absent song that enables its replacement – the *Odyssey* – to become what it is.'[35] The repeated, frustrated, attempt to return to this ideal is the creative act itself. Blanchot sees it in Ulysses, 'the great teller of tales', whom the Sirens forced 'to undertake the successful, unsuccessful journey which is that of narration – that song no longer directly perceived but repeated and thus apparently harmless: an ode made episode.'[36] Hence the Sirens' song, in Salecl's account, becomes 'an empty point of self-referentiality that a story has to omit in order to attain the status of a story.'[37]

*Le Mépris* is built around one obvious point of self-referentiality: the film-within-a-film, Lang's own *Odyssey*. We have just received our first glimpses of this putative film when Lang quotes Hölderlin. The rushes depict what, in the English subtitles is described as a mermaid but, in the French, by the conventional term 'une sirène'.[38] As an anti-cinematic point of self-reference it is both haunting and hilarious, caught between the hollowness of trash erotica and the eerie silence of the plaster gods. It is an impossible project and Godard's film describes the activity around this empty centre.

But Homer's Sirens are more than just a tantalising absence. They promise that whoever will listen to their 'honey-sweet voice'

> then goes on, well pleased, knowing more than ever
> He did; for we know everything that the Argives and Trojans
> Did and suffered in wide Troy through the gods' despite.
> Over all the generous earth we know everything that happens.[39]

The Sirens represent an absolute, objective record. They promise knowledge: history as fact.[40] As Salecl observes, this is not in the sense of knowledge found in the counter-tradition of the muses, daughters of Zeus and Mnemosyne (memory). Where the muses preserve history in the form of narrative the Sirens serve it cold. It is this that renders their knowledge as deadly as it is desirable. Jean-Pierre Vernant writes:

> In the mirror of the Sirens' song Odysseus sees himself not as he is, struggling on the surface of the sea, but as he will be when he is dead, as death will make him, forever magnified in the memory of the living.[41]

'Mirror' is a curious metaphor for a song. Perhaps the Sirens' song is closer to cinema, or at least the inhuman, ontological aspect of cinema that is the reverse of its storytelling power.[42] The deathliness of the photographic image has become a major critical trope since Roland Barthes' *Camera Lucida* (1980). But it is there in Bazin's account also. The dramatic opening of his essay suggests that embalming the dead may be the source of all plastic arts. Only, where these superstitious practices provide 'a defence against the passage of time' cinema *reintroduces* time: it is 'objectivity *in time*'.[43] Cinema teeters between a deathly purity on one side and narrative time on the other, saving it and corrupting it. The conflict is central to *Le Mépris*, lending depth to its engagement with Homer and enriched by the influence of Blanchot.

## Coda

Godard cites Blanchot thirty-five years after *Le Mépris*, in his vast video essay *Histoire(s) du Cinéma* (1988–98). Amongst the intellectual figures that crowd the work, Blanchot is tangential, quoted only once towards the end of the final chapter, but he introduces these same concerns over time and the image. Four and a half minutes from the end, Blanchot's name appears on screen in an intertitle. There follows a quotation, read by Godard:

> Cinema thus had nothing to fear from others or from itself. It was not sheltered from time, but was a shelter for time. Yes, the image is joy, but alongside it nothingness lingers, and the entire power of the image can be expressed only by appealing to that nothingness.[44]

Blanchot allows Godard to articulate a familiar dialectic: representation and its failure, art and silence. But a closer look at the source of the citation is again revealing. The essay from which it is taken, 'The Museum, Art and Time', is one of three written by Blanchot in response to André Malraux's *Essais de psychologie de l'art* (and gathered in a collection published in memory of Blanchot's close friend, Bataille).[45] That Malraux underlies the encounter is significant: Hill identifies Malraux's theories behind Godard's contention that it is montage, the act of cutting and juxtaposing shots, that defines the medium of cinema. Malraux argues in *Esquisse d'un psychologie du cinema* that 'cinema's means of reproduction was the moving image, but its means of expression is the sequence of shots'. This alone is responsible 'for the birth of cinema as art.'[46]

Where, for Malraux, montage elevates cinema to the realm of art, for Godard it is one more tool for asserting its *separation*: 'montage is what made cinema unique and different as compared to painting and the novel.'[47] In a literal act of montage, a still from Malraux's 1939 Spanish civil war film *L'espoir*, can be seen amongst the photographs tacked to Bruno Forestier's bedroom wall in *Le Petit Soldat* (1963) – alongside photographs of Brigitte Bardot herself.[48] If montage makes cinema unique it also promises a way of saving the photographic fragment on which it is built, of steering between its polarities of image and narrative, ontology and language. Godard emphasises *Le Mépris*'s existence as an edited montage when he argues for its lack of old-fashioned 'interiority': '*Le Mépris* proves in 149 shots that in the cinema as in life there is no secret, nothing to elucidate, merely the need to live – and to make films.'[49]

Yet is this tension unique to cinema after all? Godard's citation of Blanchot in the *Histoire(s)* is itself a work of artful montage. He splices sentences that appear over two and a half pages apart in Blanchot's essay and, more significantly still, substitutes '*cinéma*' where Blanchot has written '*œuvre*'.[50] In fact it is not cinema to which Blanchot is referring but painting and sculpture. The immediate reference is to artworks of the 'classical age' and their compromised status in modern museums.[51] What do these fragments convey, Blanchot is asking, when the classical gods have fled and the subject of art is predominantly art itself? This paper has argued that conceptual tensions which may seem unique to cinema overlay old concerns general to art; it is these to which Blanchot returns in his work and for which Godard turns to Blanchot at critical moments in his own career. Blanchot's intricate probing of the creative process, along with his own use of fragmentation and his pointed engagement with the classical past all feed into *Le Mépris*'s reflections on cinema. Godard set out to make movies like books by Blanchot, and succeeded.

## Notes

1 Jean Collet, interview of September 12, 1963, in ibid. 95–111; extract quoted in English translation by Sam Rohdie, *Promised Lands* (London: BFI, 2001). Hereafter cited as 'Collet/Rohdie'.

2 Ibid., 109–10.

3 Maurice Blanchot, *L'Espace littéraire* (Paris: Editions Gallimard, 1955), 283–92. I have used Ann Smock, ed. and trans. *The Space of Literature* (London: Nebraska UP, 1982) (Hereafter cited as 'Smock'); the only commentators I have found who mention this are Kaja Silverman and Harun Farocki, *Speaking about Godard* (New York: NYU Press, 1998), 231.n.12

4 Original statement from press conference, Feb 1995, quoted in *Jean-Luc Godard par Jean-Luc Godard*, Alain Bergala ed. (Paris: Cahiers du cinéma, 1998) II, 301; cited in Leslie Hill, '"A Form that Thinks": Godard, Blanchot, Citation' in *For Ever Godard*, eds. Michael Temple, James S Williams, Michael Witt (London: Black Dog, 2004), 396.
5 Leslie Hill, 'A Form that Thinks', in Temple, Williams, Witt (2004).
6 See Bergala, 379.
7 *Cahiers du Cinéma* 146, August 1963, extract in *Godard on Godard* eds. Jean Narboni, Tom Milne (New York: Viking Press, 1968), 201. Hereafter cited as 'Narboni/Milne'.
8 Interview in *Télérama*, 761 (Aug 16, 1964); in Royal Brown, *Focus on Godard* (New Jersey: Prentice-Hall, 1972), 44.
9 Smock, 269.
10 Ibid., 271.
11 Collet/Rohdie, 110.
12 'Shipwrecked People from the Modern World' interview by Yvonne Baby, from *Le Monde*, December 20, 1963; reproduced in Brown (1972), 39.
13 Narboni/Milne, 201.
14 Ibid.
15 André Bazin, 'The Ontology of the Photographic Image', trans. Hugh Gray, *Film Quarterly*, vol.13, no.4, (Summer 1960), 4–9, originally in Bazin, *Problèmes de la peinture* (1945).
16 Ibid., 7.
17 Narboni/Milne, 200–1; my italics.
18 JLG, *Introduction à une veritable histoire du cinema* (Paris, 1980), 1:85.
19 Nicholas Paige, 'Bardot and Godard in 1963 (Historicizing the Postmodern Image), *Representations*, No.88 (Autumn, 2004), 1–25.
20 Marc Cerisuelo, "L'Instauration du cinéma', *Jean-Luc Godard (2): Au-delà de l'image*, ed. Marc Cerisuelo (Paris, 1993), 59. My italics.
21 Leo Bersani, Ulysse Detoit, *Forming Couples: Godard's Contempt* (Oxford: Legenda, 2003), 5; the theory is developed by Hegel in the section of the *Aesthetics* devoted to poetry.
22 G.W.F. Hegel, *Philosophy of Fine Art*, trans. F.P.B. Osmaston, (London: G.Bell and Sons, Ltd, 1920), 4:100/102.
23 Alberto Moravia, *Contempt*, trans. Angus Davidson (New York: New York Review Books, 1999), 81.
24 Ibid., 141.
25 Ibid., 232–3.
26 Ibid., 146.
27 Collet/Rohdie, 210.
28 Maurice Blanchot, 'Proust' in *The Sirens' Song: Selected Essays by Maurice Blanchot*, ed. Gabriel Josipovici, trans. Sacha Rabinovitch (Bloomington: Indiana UP, 1982), p.66 (hereafter 'Josipovici/Rabinovitch'); first published in *Le Livre à venir* (Paris: 1959).
29 Collet/Rohdie, 210.
30 Josipovici/Rabinovitch, 60.
31 Richmond Lattimore trans. *The Odyssey of Homer*, XII, 45–7; 167–9 (New York: HarperCollins, 1967).
32 Josipovici/Rabinovitch, 59.

33 Renata Salecl, 'The Silence of the Feminine Jouissance' in *Cogito and the Unconscious*, ed. Slavoj Žižek (London: Duke UP, 1998).
34 Tzvetan Todorov, *The Poetics of* Prose, trans. Jonathan Culler (Oxford: Basil Blackwell, 1977), 58.
35 Pietro Pucci, *Odysseus Polutropos: Intertextual Readings in the Odyssey and the Iliad* (Ithaca, London: Cornell, 1987), 212; cited by Salecl.
36 Josipovici/Rabinovitch, 60–61.
37 Salecl, 177.
38 Paul: C'est dans l'Odyssée, ca?/Francesca: oui, c'est une sirène.
39 Lattimore, XII,184–191.
40 See Gabriel Germain, 'The Sirens and the Temptation of Knowledge', from *Genèse de l'Odyssée* (1954), trans. George Steiner in *Homer: A Collection of Critical Essays*, eds. George Steiner and Robert Fagles (New Jersey: Prentice Hall, 1962), 91–7.
41 Jean-Pierre Vernant, *Mortals and Immortals: Collected Essays*, ed. Froma I. Zeitlin (Princeton: Princeton UP, 1991), 105.
42 For an extended discussion of this issue see Laura Mulvey, *Death 24x a Second* (Chicago: Reaktion, 2005), 71.
43 Bazin, 1/8; my italics.
44 *Histoire(s) du Cinéma VI: Les signes parmi nous* (1998).
45 Maurice Blanchot, *Friendship*, trans. Elizabeth Rottenberg, Stanford UP, 1997 (hereafter 'Rottenberg'); first published as *L'Amitié* (Gallimard, 1971). The essay itself first appeared in two parts in *Critique*, issues 43 (December 1950) and 44 (January 1951).
46 Malraux, in *Esquisse d'une psychologie du cinema* (Paris: Gallimard, 1946). The passage recurs in Malraux, *Le Musée imaginaire* (Paris: Galimard-Folio 1965), 86.
47 Jean-Luc Godard, 'Le Montage, Le Solitude, et la Liberté', *Confrontations: les mardis de la FEMIS*, Paris: FEMIS, 1990. See *For Ever Godard*, 380.
48 Paige, 12.
49 Narboni/Milne, 201.
50 'L'oeuvre ne craignait donc rien ni des autres, ni d'elle-même . . .': *L'Amitié*, 49/ Rottenberg, 37.
51 Rottenberg, 37.

JONATHAN LAW

# Stasis and statuary in Bazinian cinema

This essay takes as its starting point André Bazin's 1945 text on photography and cinema, 'The Ontology of the Photographic Image'. Drawing on Bazin's metaphors of statuary and the mummified body, which he uses to articulate the temporal and representational properties of photography and cinema, I explore the static images of the human form that feature in films by Chris Marker, Alain Resnais, Roberto Rossellini and Jean-Luc Godard. These sculptural images open up correspondences between the films in which they appear and coalesce to develop theories of the cinematic mode; they provide interpretations of the function of statues, the static and the still image, whilst mobilising the ambiguous sense of movement that is part of the cinematic form in which they appear. In his essay, Bazin uses a number of different, yet related metaphors in his description of photography and cinema, primarily statuary, death masks and the embalming practices of mummification. Though connected, these forms and processes vary, and I explore how they differ when considering them as representations and preservations of bodily form.

## Part one: Stasis

In his essay Bazin reflects on the essential condition of photography, articulating how still photographic images function by preserving the objects that they reproduce. Referencing the funerary practices of the Ancient Egyptians, who 'saw survival as depending on the continued existence of the corporeal body', he believes that this is linked with 'the primordial function of statuary, namely, the preservation of life by a representation of life'.[1] He later draws a comparison between the practice of photography and 'the moulding of death masks' (*OPI* 12). In comparing the static, yet persistent, nature of the photographic image to statuary, the death mask and the mummy, Bazin contends that photography is largely concerned with practices of memorial and mourning.

Again focusing on death in his discussion of the temporal properties of photography, Bazin writes that 'photography does not create eternity [. . .] it embalms time, rescuing it simply from its proper corruption' (*OPI* 14), thus underlining how representational art forms are chiefly concerned with the effects of time. Embalming is not a process that simply replaces movement and change with stasis; rather, the process of embalming and mummification is a corrupting effect in itself, a preservation of the body that disrupts its natural vicissitudes. It is a stifling stasis that necessitates the relocation of the body to a hidden site, to the catacomb in which it subsists, maintaining its memorial appearance only behind closed doors. This is an invisible procedure, and its concealment relates it back to that which it seeks to avoid: the standard putrefaction of entombment in which an obscured decay runs rampant.

Emphasising a developmental arc within the history of figurative representation, and recalling Bazin's opening remark 'that at the origin of painting and sculpture there lies a mummy complex' (*OPI* 9), Annette Michelson observes that:

> The icon [. . .] derives not all that distantly from the Egyptian portraits of the dead, placed in mummy cases, so as to be visible from within the mummy bands. The likeness, double, or *Ka* took the place in the grave of a mystic and vivifying image; it articulated the link between departed soul and deserted body preserved in the form of the mummy.[2]

Highlighting the indexical nature of the photographic image as both representation and trace, Michelson argues that 'the photograph once again reopens the question of the icon, of the image as both image and emanation',[3] stating further that 'the notion of the icon as in some way participating in the sacred presence of the figured personage is grounded in the doctrine of the Incarnation, as expressed in Paul's view: Christ is an image as well as an emanation of God'.[4] These reflections underline the magical properties of image-making whilst aligning photography with theological value systems. This notion of the index is key to Bazin's perception of photography, and supports his contention that in considering the medium's 'transference of reality from the thing to its reproduction' we can observe that 'the Holy Shroud of Turin combines the features alike of relic and photograph' (*OPI* 14).

Bazin's explicit reference to the corpus of Christ (a subject often considered to be 'unique, unrepresentable, and unnameable'[5]) invokes the incorruptibility and infinite temporality associated with the divine presence. As Robin Cormack notes of the Turin Shroud:

> If it was the true shroud of Christ, the imprint of the body must have been etched by a miracle; it would show the divinity of Christ [. . .] the true face of Christ in the tomb, when his body was not subject to the corruption of rotting flesh.[6]

This sense of the divine death-shroud as a miraculous exposure suggests a concealment that is also a revelation: the tomb as a camera in which this alchemical transformation from body to image takes place; a screening of the body that conjures both objective image and indexical emanation.[7]

Examining this relationship between an object and its photographic reproduction, Bazin contends that:

> The photographic image is the object itself, the object freed from the conditions of time and space that govern it. No matter how fuzzy, distorted, or discolored, no matter how lacking in documentary value the image may be, it shares, by virtue of the very process of its becoming, the being of the model of which it is the reproduction; it *is* the model. (*OPI* 14)

Bazin finds the key discrepancy between the object and its image to be a perversion of time and space. As with the reproductive function of statuary, the photographic image of the body is endowed with a curious persistence. Its reconstituted format promotes a revised longevity that positions the body outside of its regular timeframe, inhabiting an alternative dimension of extratemporal stasis that evokes the idealistic temporality of heavenly bodies.

Developing his argument to incorporate reflections on the nature of the cinematic image, Bazin discusses how this medium extends the still image into temporal duration, so introducing the further complexity of change and transformation. He states that:

> The cinema is objectivity in time. The film is no longer content to preserve the object, enshrouded as it were in an instant, as the bodies of insects are preserved intact, out of the distant past, in amber. [. . .] Now, for the first time, the image of things is likewise the image of their duration, change mummified as it were. (*OPI* 14–15)

Bazin thus articulates how cinema complicates our understanding of stasis, promoting not simply our morbid scrutiny of the instant but also of duration and change, with process itself now subject to preservation and memorial. Reflecting this argument, Karen Parna has written that:

> A still image is often looked at as a paralysed fragment of an otherwise dynamic reality [. . .] What makes the strict separation between the fixed and the moving images even more complex is a consideration of images that are neither one or the other, yet have characteristics of both.[8]

Similarly, Catherine Russell observes that 'the freeze-frame *replaces* the corpse, preserving the living body in the ontology of the photographic image', while also noting that in 'the protraction of the dying process that occurs with slow motion [. . .] death and stasis are virtually effaced and disavowed'.[9] This collision between stillness, movement and time is key to the grammar of cinematic representation; the filmic use of freeze-frames and slow-motion engages with stillness to provide complex renderings of time – animations, reanimations and de-animations of the moment – that cannot be oversimplified into an opposition between motion and stasis.

Describing one of the functions of fixed images within cinematic presentations, Michelson attests that:

> The still photograph cuts into time, causing a kind of gap, bringing it to an instant of arrest [...] cinema, grounded in the persistence of vision, hypostasizes our inability to think that gap in time. [...] the still photograph [...] inserts, within our experience of lived time, the extratemporality of death. And it is this that gives to the freeze-frame and to other cinematic forms of temporal digression their particular effect of power. Within the flow of cinematic representation, that semblance of temporality itself, we can insert this arrest that figures the perpetual freezing of the image as a kind of posthumous life within the flow of the film. The image, thus released from that flow, and from that of the narrative syntagm, attains extratemporality.[10]

This articulation of the status of still images within a moving-image sequence suggests a revised function of stillness while reasserting Bazin's belief that photography engages with 'the disturbing presence of lives halted at a set moment in their duration, freed from their destiny' (*OPI* 14), a view that again underlines the liberation of the body from its advance through finitude.

## Part two: Statuary

Like the cinematic freeze-frame, ancient statuary stands apart from the supple flow that surrounds and supports it, pregnant with the conditions of a past age. Yet while a sense of decay lingers, frozen, in the death mask, statues are neither index nor relic. While these sculpted forms of permanence represent an ideal of the infinite, encapsulating an impression of a distant moment, they have themselves endured the gulf of duration that has passed in between, a duration that has similarly ravaged their surfaces and corrupted their forms. Like all persisting textual matter, statues from classical antiquity are cultural markers, immobile indications of illusory permanence. Standing in substitution for the body in space as well as time, they are transmissions from time past that will continue into time future, and are indelible, if not incorruptible.

Chris Marker's 1962 film *La Jetée* demonstrates, in both its narrative – concerning memory, time-travel and apocalypse – and its still images of statuary, archaeological remains and taxidermy, a preoccupation with stasis and preservation. As Bruce Kawin observes, the film features 'an overwhelming imagery of stasis'.[11] *La Jetée*'s post-apocalyptic world is populated by figures who subsist beneath the earth, away from the light of the sun, deep within the Chaillot catacombs – the Paris tombs beneath the site of Henri Langlois's La Cinémathèque Française (Figure 1). Entombed in this darkness, away from the eroding pollution of the elements and amongst arrangements of broken statuary, the characters have lost both their temporal bearings and any sense of fixed identity.

**Figure 1** *La Jetée*, dir. Chris Marker, 1962

The tombstones that we see above ground, appearing at the culmination of a particularly vivid remembrance experienced by the protagonist, are markers of time, functioning as both symbols and icons of disappeared lives and a lost culture. The narration describes them as 'real graves', thus conferring an authenticity upon them that belies their status as mere memorials (Figure 2). As Sarah Cooper writes:

> The ontological connection between the photographic and the cinematic image, as discussed by Bazin, is implicated in Marker's manipulation of the static image, and is also reassessed. [. . .] Haunted by death, and doubled by eternity [. . .] *La Jetée* is concerned with the endurance of the photograph rather than its loss.[12]

In *La Jetée*, corridors are lined with fragmented sculptural remains: the subsisting shadows of permanence and perfection, their distressed materiality indicative of the chaotic and amorphous nature of spatiotemporal interrelations. Marker's dissection of the moving image in *La Jetée*, with its explicit illusion of movement (at one point the rate of edits accelerates towards, and immediately recedes from, 24 frames per second), further complicates the relationships between time and space, movement and stasis, memory and premonition.

Marker punctuates a montage showing the static bodies of subjects of failed time-travel experiments with images of broken statuary (Figures 3, 4) in a sequence that recalls his 1953 collaboration with Alain Resnais, *Les Statues meurent aussi*. This documentary features strikingly photographed statues and icons that have been removed from their cultural sites of origin.

**Figure 2** *La Jetée*, dir. Chris Marker, 1962

Some are shown in conditions of disrepair, underlining how monuments are subject to decrepitude and decay in the same way as the bodies they serve to recompose (Figure 5, 6). As Cooper suggests, in these films Marker 'situates the artwork on the side of reality and temporality rather than in the realm of the shadows of eternal stasis [...] If statues can die, then so can images.'[12]

The forms in *Les statues meurent aussi* represent a dislocation of culture that disrupts the permanence and infinity of their spatial stasis, and so perverts the correlating temporal dimension.

Resnais's fictional work from this period likewise utilises images of statuary in order to explore time, memory and trauma. His *Hiroshima mon amour* (1959) shows embracing bodies taking on the appearance of petrifaction (Figure 7), while *L'Année dernière à Marienbad* (1961) features not only statuary but the static forms of the living frozen unnaturally in time as part of a nightmarish reconstruction of reality (Figures 8, 9). The latter film emphasises the uncanny stasis of these bodies, both flesh and stone, by virtue of the camera's swooping movements around and between their forms, the probing lens gliding and circulating in an unstoppable trajectory of repetition that collapses notions of past, present and future.

Roberto Rossellini's 1954 film *Viaggio in Italia* is furnished with similar imagery. Throughout the film the protagonists Katherine and Alex Joyce (whose dissolving marriage prompts an investigation of the landscape and artefacts of Naples) are surrounded by different kinds of sculptural forms. As Laura Mulvey writes, in this film:

> The space is dominated by the ruins and traces of an ancient civilization. Rossellini used this terrain to extend into cinema the blurred boundaries

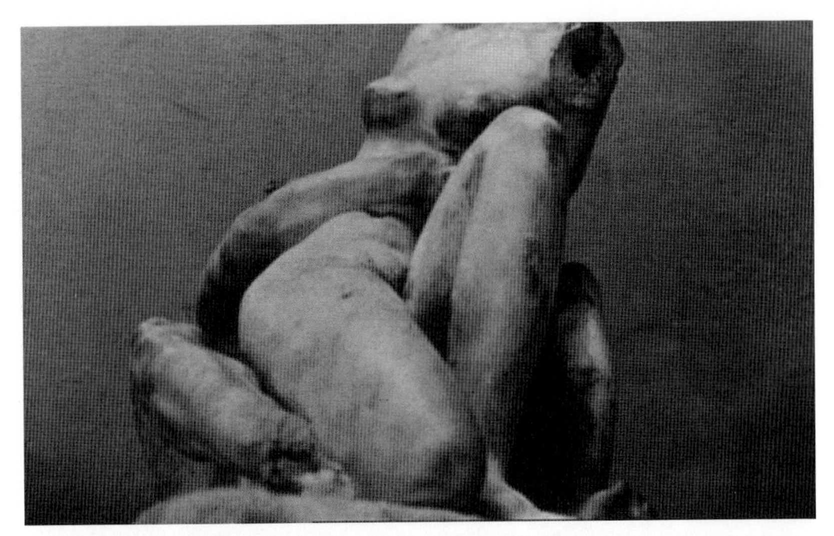

**Figure 3** *La Jetée*, dir. Chris Marker, 1962

**Figure 4** *La Jetée*, dir. Chris Marker, 1962

> between the material and the spiritual, reality and magic, and between life and death that Bazin and Barthes associated with photography.[14]

Stating that 'death forms a central thematic element', Mulvey argues that *Viaggio in Italia* enables 'the cinema's paradoxical relation between movement and stillness to achieve a degree of visibility'.[15] This tendency is exemplified in extended sequences in which Katherine explores the National Archaeological Museum (Figure 10), before being taken on a tour

**Figure 5** *Les Statues meurent aussi*, dir. Chris Marker and Alain Resnais, 1953

**Figure 6** *Les statues meurent aussi*, dir. Chris Marker and Alain Resnais, 1953

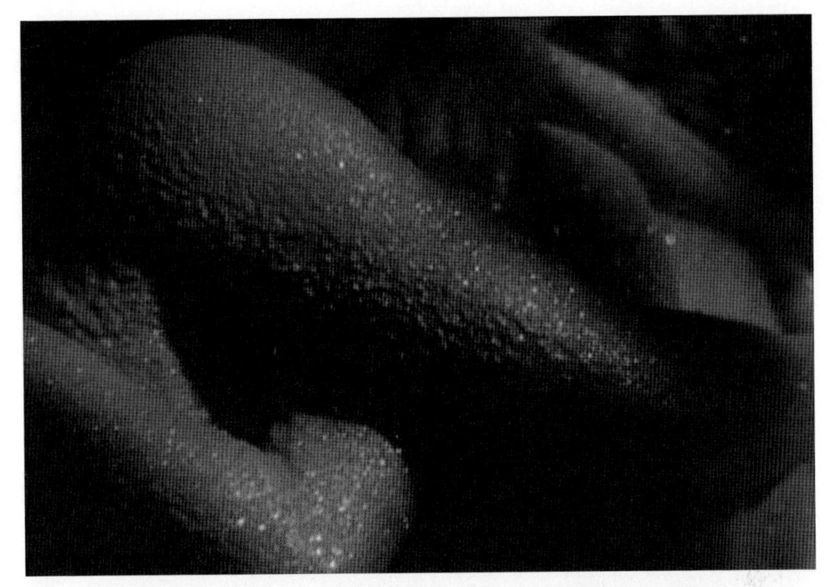

**Figure 7** *Hiroshima mon amour*, dir. Alain Resnais, 1959

**Figure 8** *L'année dernière à Marienbad*, dir. Alain Resnais, 1961

of ancient catacombs (Figures 11, 12). At the museum Katherine uneasily surveys statues depicting arrested bodies. As she encircles these forms, the passage of the camera imbues them with a sense of borrowed motion, later leading her to remark excitedly on their capacity to evoke the past.

While visiting an excavation site in the ruins of Pompeii, Katherine witnesses the transformation of bodies into images, as plaster is poured into the subterranean cavities left by two long-since decomposed corpses. These figures have survived as empty shells, defined in space only by the ravaging and consuming decomposition of the millennia; time rendering them vacant whilst denying them of their materiality, insisting upon a void of concealed formlessness. Upon the discovery of these hollows they are

**Figure 9** *L'année dernière à Marienbad*, dir. Alain Resnais, 1961

**Figure 10** *Viaggio in Italia*, dir. Roberto Rossellini, 1954

redefined and given a new permanence. The analogy with photography is clear, as negative impressions of absence prefigure an indexical positive. As the reconstituted bodies are materialised, we see light come out of darkness, and form out of formlessness (Figure 13, 14).

Time and putrefaction have rendered these bodies absent; corporeality now incorporated into the subterranean vacuum around which the form and contours of the body were invisibly preserved. The plaster casts of these cavities are a horrifying emanation that has preserved not life but the process of painful suffocation and death, a revelation that disturbs

**Figure 11** *Viaggio in Italia*, dir. Roberto Rossellini, 1954

**Figure 12** *Viaggio in Italia*, dir. Roberto Rossellini, 1954

**Figure 13** *Viaggio in Italia*, dir. Roberto Rossellini, 1954

Katherine enormously. *Viaggio in Italia* thus distinguishes between a range of reconstituted bodies in which the value of time, stasis and preservation varies according to the precise nature of the forms' construction.

Signalling his debt to Bazin at the beginning of his 1963 film *Le Mépris*, Jean-Luc Godard begins the spoken credits sequence by paraphrasing the critic. Writing on 'The Ontology of the Photographic Image', Colin MacCabe has suggested that 'this short essay, which places cinema in a cultural perspective that takes in the 4,000 years from Egyptian funeral art [. . .] is absolutely crucial to understanding Godard's œuvre. It is [. . .] the "axiom" from which all of Godard's theorems derive.'[16] *Le Mépris* features recurrent imagery of statuary, presented mainly as fragmented images from the film-within-a-film, Fritz Lang's version of Homer's *The Odyssey*. The statues function as totems that suggest a coalesced sedimentation of text and culture, whilst also indicating a movement towards finitude. The camera rotates around these figures, identifying and locating them as central pillars or axes, and insisting on their immobile fixity (Figure 15). At the end of *Le Mépris* this rotational aspect is replicated, but this time it moves around the lifeless bodies of Prokosch and Camille, as in a tableau in which the corpse replaces the statue (Figure 16). Russell notes that 'Bardot and Palance were not required to act but simply to "be in" the narrative of *Le Mépris*. As corpses, their status as mere signs of characters is made explicit.'[17]

*Le Mépris* is often compared with Rossellini's film, MacCabe stating that it might accurately be read 'as a remake of *Viaggio in Italia*'.[18] Noting

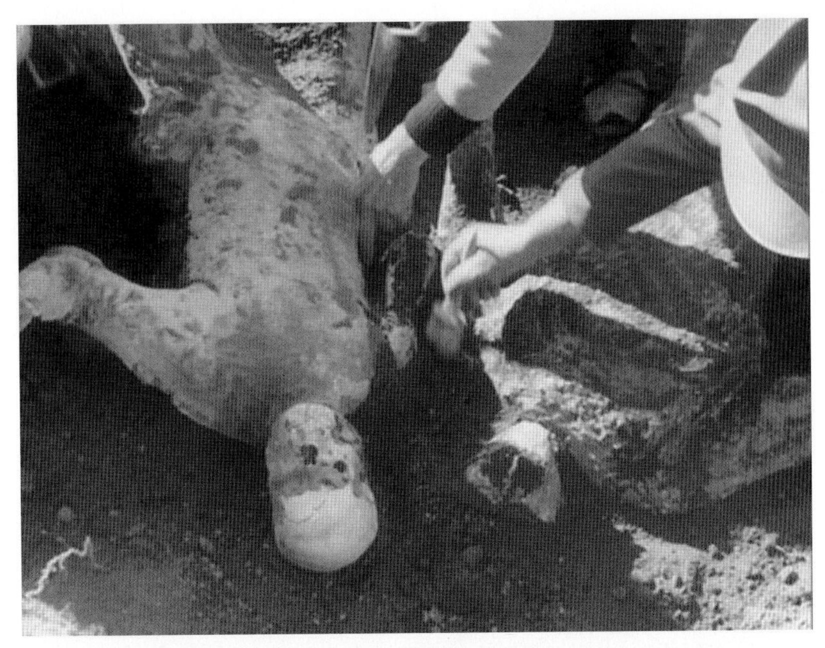

**Figure 14** *Viaggio in Italia*, dir. Roberto Rossellini, 1954

**Figure 15** *Le Mépris*, dir. Jean-Luc Godard, 1963

similarities between the two films' depictions of statuary, Jacques Aumont writes that:

> Both films give the same feeling of an almost physical presence of the gods, and not just because Godard films his plaster reproductions with the same majesty as Rossellini does the statues in the Naples Archaeological Museum.[19]

While Godard supplements these images with photographs of ancient fragments, including an artefact that had also featured prominently in

**Figure 16** *Le Mépris*, dir. Jean-Luc Godard, 1963

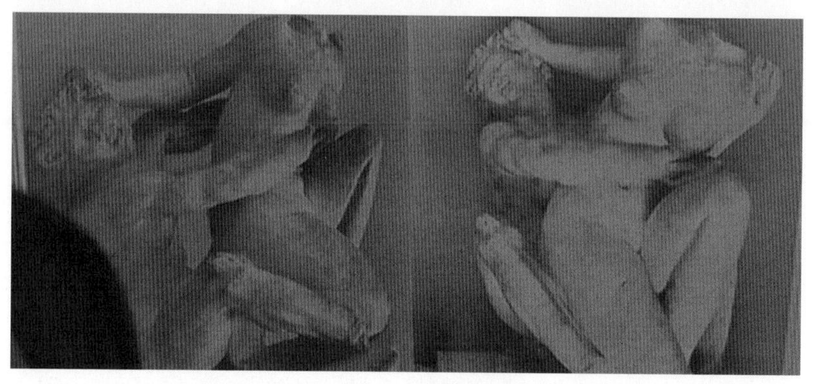

**Figure 17** *Le Mépris*, dir. Jean-Luc Godard, 1963

*La Jetée* (Figures 3, 17), his plaster casts are untainted by time: vividly polychromed, fresh and complete. These reproductions appear on screen, abruptly interrupting the narrative flow in their depiction of Homer, Ulysses and gods such as Neptune and Minerva. The statues of gods are here outside of time, their subjects immaterial, disembodied and apart from our spatiotemporal scheme.

## Conclusion

Writing in 1949 on the relationship between representation and reality, Bazin comments that 'the reality that cinema reproduces at will and organizes is the same worldly reality of which we are a part, the sensible continuum out of which the celluloid makes a mold both spatial and temporal', arguing that 'before cinema there was only the profanation of corpses and the desecration of tombs'.[19] Bazin's persistent use of competing metaphors, in which the natural attributes of the body become central to the question of its reproduction in time and space, find expression in the intermingling of alternative art forms: cinematic sequences in which statues figure prominently as totems of time and space, challenging the objective lens to restore their mobility and distort their duration.

Bazin's writing and the films discussed engage with enduring traditions of Western representation, enquiring about the relationship between time and the image, between statuary and the body, between preservation and reproduction. More than simply illuminating Bazin's text, Marker, Resnais, Rossellini and Godard weave his discourse into the narratives and visual schemes of their work, embedding static bodies within moving-image sequences in a way that emphasises the ambiguity of the cinematic mode's sense of time and motion. They acknowledge the origins of representation as intimately involved with the desire to make visible the invisible, to make material the immaterial, and as a means of engaging with the incomprehensible.

## Notes

1 André Bazin, 'The Ontology of the Photographic Image', *What is Cinema?*, trans. by Hugh Gray, 2 vols (Los Angeles: University of California Press, 1967–71), vol. 1 (1967), 9–10. Hereafter referred to in the main text as *OPI*.
2 Annette Michelson, 'The Kinetic Icon in the Work of Mourning: Prolegomena to the Analysis of a Textual System', *October*, 52 (Spring 1990), 24–5.
3 Ibid., 30.
4 Ibid., 29.
5 Robin Margaret Jensen, *Face to Face: Portraits of the Divine in Early Christianity* (Minneapolis: Fortress Press, 2005), 70.
6 Robin Cormack, *Painting the Soul: Icons, Death Masks, and Shrouds* (London: Reaktion Books, 1997), 120.
7 The power and significance of the Shroud of Turin as a unique and peculiar feat of magical image-making gained further momentum in 1898, when photographic negatives revealed the 'face' of Christ imprinted on the shroud – transforming what had been a relic into a objective image of the divine body; reverting the nature of this holy image – itself a negative – one step closer to that of its model. Ibid., 119–20.
8 Karen Parna, 'Narrative, Time and the Fixed Image', in *Time, Narrative and the Fixed Image*, ed. by Mireille Ribière and Jan Baetens (Amsterdam: Rodopi, 2001), 34.
9 Catherine Russell, *Narrative Mortality: Death, Closure, and New Wave Cinemas* (Minneapolis: University of Minnesota Press, 1995), 187.
10 Michelson, 'The Kinetic Icon in the Work of Mourning', 31–2.
11 Bruce Kawin, 'Time and Stasis in "La Jetée"', *Film Quarterly*, 1:36 (Autumn 1982), 17–18.
12 Sarah Cooper, *Chris Marker* (Manchester: Manchester University Press, 2008), 46.
13 Ibid., 52/53.
14 Laura Mulvey, *Death 24x a Second* (London: Reaktion Books, 2006), 104.
15 Ibid.

16 Colin MacCabe, *Godard: A Portrait of the Artist at 70* (London: Bloomsbury, 2003), 62.
17 Russell, *Narrative Mortality*, 156.
18 MacCabe, *Godard*, 162.
19 Jacques Aumont, 'The Fall of the Gods: Jean-Luc Godard's *Le Mépris* (1963)', in *French Film: Texts and Contexts*, ed. by Susan Hayward and Ginette Vincendeau (London: Routledge, 2000), 177.
20 André Bazin, 'Death Every Afternoon', trans. by Mark A. Cohen, in *Rites of Realism: Essays on Corporeal Cinema*, ed. by Ivone Margulies (Durham: Duke University Press, 2003), 30/31.

ROB GALLAGHER

# 'FAUX RACCORD': Mismatch, Noise and Transformation in the Work of Jean-Luc Godard

This essay will argue for the importance of the mismatch, of conjunction, collision and dissonance, in Jean-Luc Godard's filmmaking. Mismatch will also characterise my method: I will be focussing chiefly on *Le Mépris* (*Contempt*) (1963) and *Histoire(s) du Cinéma* (1988–1998), texts poles apart in terms of their respective media, moments, methodologies and genres. In doing so I aim to demonstrate the continuity of certain Godardian preoccupations, not least his belief in the productive potential of *dis*continuity. I also want to stress the role of technology in Godard's filmmaking. In *Alphaville* (1965) he leaves it to a computer to observe that 'once we know the number one we think we know the number two, because one plus one equals two. We forget that first we must know the meaning of plus.' As computers continue to transform our modes of composing and consuming filmic images, it seems all the more important to understand the part played by technologically-effected mediations, juxtapositions and interruptions in Godard's work. For, if Godard in some respects anticipates the modern, multimedia order of things, he also looks beyond it, levying technology in the attempt to forge a fundamentally cinematic mode of expression. As we shall see, this centrally involves probing 'the meaning of plus', rethinking relations between words and images, language and identity, bodies and machines.

The proliferation, in recent decades, of new modes of viewing, disseminating, archiving, remediating and restoring visual media has enabled film to take on all manner of new bodies and, consequently, to enter into new relations with the bodies of viewers, actors and directors. Film is, as Vivian Sobchack stresses, a cyborg medium, 'emerging from the symbiotic cooperation of humans and technology . . . partially mechanical and inhuman – and as well, partially intentional and human'.[1] Godard's appreciation of cinematic materiality (a beneficiary of the Cinémathèque Française collection Henri Langlois had both helped to amass and to save from Nazi destruction, he understood the fallacy of 'believing that a strip of celluloid is less perishable than a block of stone or even memory') often manifests itself in the representation of techno-organic circuits or assemblages akin to those Sobchack describes.[2] The viewer is (literally) confronted by one at the start of *Le Mépris* as Coutard and his team track toward and focus on the auditorium itself. In *Histoire(s)* 1b, meanwhile, Godard anthropomorphises the cinematic apparatus by associating the two Lumière brothers with the film camera's twin reels (Figure 1).

Godard's own ageing body also functions, throughout the *Histoire(s)*, both as an index of the passage of time and as an example of humans' ability to appropriate and employ objects and machines. Of course, these technologies also alter their users in return; if, as Godard notes in 1b, the left video reel is the 'slave' and the right the 'master' then human/machine relations are harder to hierarchise. Indeed, mediated and prosthetised by an array of books, cameras, pens, screens, typewriters and angle poise lamps, the Godard of *Histoire(s)* seems as dependent as he does masterful. When, in 2b, he appears shirtless, suddenly even the most naturalised and quotidian prostheses – spectacles, sun visor, watch – are newly apparent. By electronically manipulating his voice and the tempo of his movements, Godard is able to appear both uncannily mechanical and humanly vulnerable, foregrounding cinema's capacity not so much to immortalise as to *materialise mortality*. This capacity has fascinated the director from the first: as he stated in 1962, 'whoever one films is growing older and will die... cinema is interesting because it seizes life and the mortal side of life'.[3] But while the filmed may die, as may film itself (indeed, it only records in the first place via despoliation), *cinema* is alive. More than the sum of its components and material supports, a film's 'body' is, as Sobchack argues, no more reducible to 'camera, projector, screen, film, stock, chemicals' than a human being is to 'organs, bone, skin, tissue, blood'.[4]

**Figure 1** *Histoire(s) du Cinéma* 1b, dir. Jean-Luc Godard, 1989

The form the camera's seizure of life takes, whether celluloid, video or digital, is not immortal or immutable. However, this very mutability creates the potential for adaptation and transformation. Video, a medium 'controlled *by the finger and the eye*', enabled Godard to 'see at the same time as I do', facilitating an intimate, dynamic and embodied relation between film and filmmaker.[5] Among other things, it became a means for Godard to revisit and transform his past work. Thus, in *Histoire(s)* 1b he returns to *Le Mépris*, layering Fritz Lang's praise of Homer's representation of objective reality 'in a form that is not going to break down' over images of Brigitte Bardot, Lang and Godard himself. Elegiac in its evocation of the passage of time, the sequence also demonstrates film's ability to re-present the past while investing it with new meanings. Lang's praise of immutable forms begins to sound both idealistic and wrongheaded in this light; Bresson's dictum, cited elsewhere in the *Histoire(s)*, that images which 'clearly express' a meaning that 'won't change when put in contact with other images' are 'unusable in the cinematographer's system' seems far more in keeping with Godard's practice. For him, an *Odyssey* as immutable as Lang's would be inert, unusable. Godard acknowledges the cinematic utility of Homer's epic *and* Moravia's 'vulgar' novel, of Beethoven, *bandes desinées* and his own *œuvre*.[6] What counts is what emerges from these texts' redeployment and juxtaposition, the noise they can generate in concert.

Godard's manipulation of *Le Mépris*, facilitated by video, affirms Laura Mulvey's contention that 'delaying' and fragmenting films can produce 'otherwise hidden, deferred meanings'.[7] Certainly, seeing fragments of *Le Mépris* layered over other images is revelatory insofar as it emphasises the presence and significance of similar layerings both within the original film and throughout Godard's work. Perhaps especially evocative of Godard's later, video-era superimpositions is the early scene in *Le Mépris* that takes place outside the screening room. The posters in its background relate their own particular *histoire du cinéma*, delimit a canon and, in their torn and degraded condition, suggest both the film industry's state of crisis circa 1963 and celluloid's fragility as a medium. But they also perform another function, generating visual rhymes with the actors in the foreground in a manner not dissimilar to Godard's video compositions in the *Histoire(s)*: John Wayne is cropped in the *Hatari* (1962) poster just as the shot and the Alfa Romeo's frame crop Palance; Bardot's blue ensemble and her posture link her to *Vivre sa vie*'s (1962) Nana; Hitchcock looks somewhat Lang-esque in the *Psycho* (1960) poster (Figures 2, 3). The fixed plane of postures and precedents invites comparisons, suggesting ways of classifying the characters (and the actors playing them) in relation to pre-existing 'types': the domineering American, the sagacious European director, the tragic beauty and so on.

It is crucial, though, to recognise that the posters do not operate like a Rosetta stone, enabling a fixed, permanent relation between signs to be recovered. They cannot confirm identity; they only invite comparison.

**Figure 2** *Le Mépris*, dir. Jean-Luc Godard, 1963

**Figure 3** *Le Mépris*, dir. Jean-Luc Godard, 1963

The same might be said of cinema in general, characterised by Roland Barthes as a 'metonymic art'.[8] Barthes was also to argue, this time with reference to literary representation, that beauty 'cannot assert itself save in the form of a citation ... or simile'.[9] Godard's repeated juxtapositions of bodies and their images suggest Barthes' observation holds true for film, demonstrating how both beauty and identity circulate between rather than radiating from or embedding themselves within bodies. Patricia's superimpositions of her 'live' body in front of first a Renoir print and then a picture of herself in *À bout de souffle* (1960), for example (Figures 4, 5), exemplify both beauty's basis in comparison and the difficulty of coinciding even with one's own beauty, one's own image, whether we take that word to mean pictorial representation or 'star' persona. The latter, as Laura Mulvey has shown, is often a matter of cultivating characteristic attitudes or gestures that match with prior images, Bardot's lying on her front with one or both of her feet in the air being one such 'pose' (Figures 6–10).[10] The play

**Figure 4** *À bout de souffle*, dir. Jean-Luc Godard, 1960

**Figure 5** *À bout de souffle*, dir. Jean-Luc Godard, 1960

of synecdoche, resemblance and allusion often proves hard to close in Godard's films; we need only think of the multiplicity of associations generated when, in *Vivre sa vie*, Anna Karina's Nana wears a Louise Brooks-like wig (later worn by Bardot/Camille in *Le Mépris)* to watch Falconetti play Jeanne d'Arc – a role in which Preminger had cast Seberg prior to her portraying Godard's Patricia.

Camille is denying this transcorporeal semiotic traffic when, at the beginning of *Le Mépris*, she reasons that because Paul loves each part of her body he loves her 'totally'. While Camille supposes that bodies produce

**Figure 6** Brigitte Bardot[32]

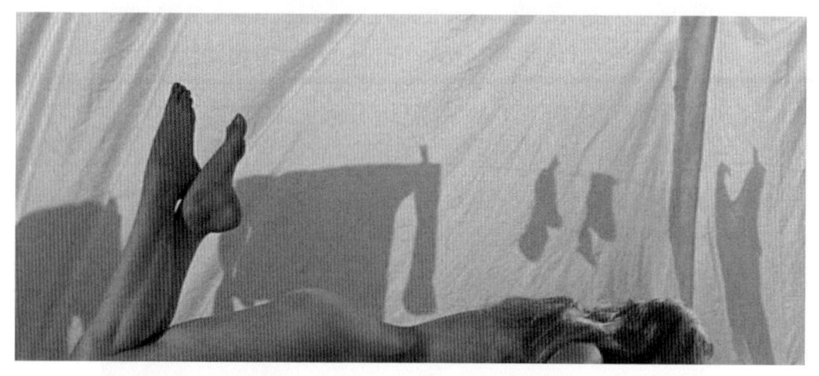

**Figure 7** *Et Dieu... créa la femme*, dir. Roger Vadim, 1956

desire, Godard repeatedly shows that desire emerges and migrates *between* signs and bodies. The film's famous bedroom scene foregrounds the role of cinematic artifice in this process. Its use of obtrusive coloured filters foregrounds the images' mediation, undercutting the actors' performance of secluded intimacy (and, consequently, the viewer's sense of voyeuristic privilege). The use of a technique largely neglected since the silent era also underscores the extent to which film's claims to verisimilitude have always entailed the disavowal of the artificial, the conventional, and the symbolic. Indeed, Bardot's own status as 'the symbol of France' is also evoked by the overlay of red, white and blue onto a body that had already, by 1963, been thoroughly coded and commodified (as Colin MacCabe contends, 'Bardot *was* nudity').[11]

Godard was well aware that that the cinematic apparatus has traditionally operated to ground desire in the mediated, mechanised bodies it constructs for its female stars. Functioning as sexualised commodities, these bodies permit viewers to fetishistically forestall the acknowledgement

**Figure 8** *Le Mépris*, dir. Jean-Luc Godard, 1963

**Figure 9** *Le Mépris*, dir. Jean-Luc Godard, 1963

**Figure 10** *Histoire(s) du Cinéma* 1b, dir. Jean-Luc Godard, 1989

of their desires' fundamental incoherence (as Juliette puts it in *2 ou 3 choses que je sais d'elle* (1967), 'my feelings haven't always a specific object. Desire, for example ... Does any expression not refer to a specific object?'). *Le Mépris* offers an especially eloquent portrayal of the attempt to incarnate or coincide with a desirable 'image'/body in the shape of Nausicca's karaoke performance. Michael Moon has read karaoke in David Lynch's *Blue Velvet* (1986) as serving to suggest the mimetic, derivative character of both identity and desire, which, he argues, emerge via citation and technological prosthesis, by way of the sort of 'lip-synching' Nausicca attempts.[12] Nausicca, however, has difficulties staying 'in sync': performing to a pre-recorded pop song, she is not only audibly out of tune and out of time but also struggles to stay in the tracking camera's field of view. Similarly jarring is Godard's unconventional use of audio in this scene. Rather than ducking the sound of the performance to allow viewers to hear the characters speak, he simply cuts the music altogether for the duration of their exchanges, rendering awkwardly apparent the contrivances (ordinarily camouflaged) whereby audiences are afforded access to certain scenes and sounds. Songs, which occur with surprising frequency in Godard's work, serve to exemplify, via their highly formalised language and performative mode of address, the status of personality and communication as forms of *recital*, perennially vulnerable to noise and incoherence, to the threat (as the intertitle that interrupts Valerie Lagrange's dying guerrilla's song in *Week-end* (1967) has it) of '*faux raccord*'.

That term generally refers to the style of discontinuous 'jump-cutting' that made Godard's name, but, in its literal sense of a mismatch, clumsy transition or visible stitch, *faux raccord* also suggests the Godardian love of unexpected conjunctions and transitions. While mismatches can produce bathetic travesties such as Nausicca's inept performance or Paul's failure to evoke Dean Martin in his hat (more 'like the ass Martin' is Camille's verdict), they can also prove surprisingly fecund. As Michel Serres writes, 'if the relation succeeds, if it is perfect, optimum, and immediate; it disappears as a relation'; without noise 'there would be no spaces for transformation anywhere'.[13] With noise included, however, Godard's attempt at translating *Scarface* (1932) to 1950s Paris produces a glorious mutation like *À bout de souffle*. Not for nothing does he add Francesca, a translator whose paraphrases often seem less faithful than they might be, to Moravia's scenario in *Le Mépris*.

Indeed, the quadrilingual *Le Mépris*, in which the unspoken and the misunderstood prove so crucial, is also a demonstration of Godard's attitude to the relation between words and images. If language can operate either to reduce images' affective intensity or to 'amplify' their 'noise', 'resonat[ing]' with rather than contextualising or explaining them, then Godard unquestionably prefers resonation to explication.[14] Consequently, his work often proves resistant to commentary, rationalisation or paraphrase. As an example, we might return to *Vivre sa vie*'s Nana watching *La Passion de Jeanne d'Arc* (1928). The scene both represents and produces a form of affective contagion: it is hard, as we watch a crying Karina watching Falconetti cry, not to begin crying ourselves. Devoid of any clear narrative motivation, our tears are, however, senseless, gratuitous. We are responding to nothing more than juxtapositions of bodies and images. Most narrative cinema recuperates affect by giving audiences tools to convert it into emotion, expediting the process of 'sociolinguistic fixing' whereby it becomes 'semantically and semiotically' identifiable (and, thus, narrativisable). In the *Jean d'Arc* sequence, however, Godard hampers this process by refusing to offer a rationale or narrative frame, troubling human/machine distinctions by demonstrating how easily (how mechanically) film can elicit irrational, embodied responses.[15]

The sequence also pays tribute to silent film, which Godard believed might hold 'part of the answer' to creating a uniquely cinematic mode of expression, one less dependent on subordinating images to words.[16] It can hardly be coincidence that the extract from *Jeanne d'Arc* prominently features Antonin Artaud, who praised Balinese theatre's capacity to 'render useless any translation into logical or discursive language' and who rejected the cinema when it fell prey, like Western theatre before it, to the 'dictatorship of speech'.[17] As we have seen, *Le Mépris'* Nausicca sequence highlights the undue precedence given to dialogue by violently 'cutting out' all other sound, despite the fact that the dialogue in question is entirely inconsequential. In doing so it suggests both the limitations of language, and the limitations verbocentrism imposes on cinema.

In *Une Femme est Une Femme* (1961), *Pierrot le Fou* (1965) and *Le Mépris* language's limitations are demonstrated via breakdowns in communication between heterosexual couples. Just as words fail to 'close' the cinematic images, so they fail to fix relations between people. But it would be a mistake to suggest that Godard is merely stating that words cannot convey the 'true depth' of love, emotion or identity. Rather, as the comical use of book titles to trade slurs and slights in *Une Femme est Une Femme* or Camille's habitual use of the most banal colloquialisms in *Le Mépris* show, the issue is not so much that language might be incommensurable with or insufficient to express human subjectivity as that human subjectivity itself might be derivative and relational. Paul claims bad language doesn't suit Camille; Camille's litany of coarse slang (which she utters without inflection or interest) proves it can be as chic 'on' a woman as Coco Chanel had proven masculine suits could be, that words are not proprietary or permanent aspects of ourselves anymore than Godard's glasses or typewriter are bodily organs.

Godard's belief that words should amplify rather than reduce 'noise' also informs his interpolations of other's writings (usually unattributed, often misquoted), his re-dubbing and de-synchronisation of voices and his use of intertitles, signs and typed messages, which frequently decompose or rearrange before the viewer's eyes. These devices also suggest his suspicion of traditional notions of originality and ownership. Precociously intertextual even before *Tel Quel* had proposed the term, *Histoire(s)* affirms that Godard also 'understands copyright as a crucial artistic and political issue' in the multimedia age.[18] Ownership over one's creative output is, of course, already a key issue in *Le Mépris*. The scene in the screening room offers an especially dense portrayal of the mechanics of selling out and cashing in, demonstrating how the circulation of money and writing echoes and regulates the circulation of meanings and identities. Lang and Prokosch's row over whether what is 'on that screen' corresponds to what is 'in the script' sets in motion a connotatively rich series of relays and displacements, a play of gestures and objects across bodies, contexts and spaces: the sexualized conjunction of Vanini's and Prokosch's bodies as she forms a desk for him is displaced from the bedroom to the screening room; Hanns Johst's gun becomes Prokosch's chequebook ('when I hear the word culture I bring out my chequebook'); Francesca's handing of the cheque to Paul and his pocketing of it mark him as feminised and exploited by the transaction. Ultimately, the scene suggests the complexity and ubiquity of both semiotic and economic ties, implicating all the characters in networks as hard to opt out of as they are to control.

As such, while it is tempting to see Paul as exploiting himself (or his muse, or Homer, or Camille), we must first ask what such exploitation would mean for Godard, suspicious as he is of the notions of self-identity, originality and ownership ordinarily mobilised in tales of artists signing Faustian pacts. After all, in *Vivre sa vie*, which pursues questions of property, identity and inspiration within a *milieu* of thievery and prostitution, Godard appears to identify, at least to some extent, with Nana. Charged with robbery, she cites Rimbaud's famous declaration '*Je est une autre*', from the same text in which the poet proposes a rethinking of grammar and attribution, suggesting one should say 'I am thought' rather than 'I think'.[19] The construction perfectly describes Godard's own willingness to admit 'I don't know', to submit himself to 'completely spontaneous' inspirations and allow things to *occur to* him.[20] Often (as with his deciding to incorporate Poe's 'Oval Portrait' into *Vivre sa vie*) what occurs to him is to appropriate what he finds lying around.[21] This is one reason why video, a medium in which 'the operator discovers the effect live' as he handles the equipment, had such an appeal for him.[22] If, then, Godard sees nothing as essentially one's own, and, to this extent, identifies with Nana the poet/thief/prostitute, then what is there to despoil or give away, to 'prostitute'? Why should this term have a negative connotation?

In a 1967 interview, Godard defines a prostitute as 'anyone who does something he doesn't want to. If I worked for Simca and all day long I said nice things about Simcas, even though I really preferred Ferraris, then I would be prostituting myself to Simca'.[23] What is at stake, then, is not so much truth, ownership or money as the right to spontaneity, contradiction and 'live' discovery. A car-lover, Godard thinks this relation in terms of automobiles; he does so again in *Pierrot le Fou*, when Belmondo spins the wheel '*a droit . . . a gauche. . . a droit. . .. a gauche*' before careering right off of the road and into the sea (typically for Godard, this 'spontaneous' act is also a quotation of a scene in King Vidor's *Ruby Gentry* (1952)). Later it is not the car on the strip of road but the figure on the strip of video tape which allows him to develop the idea; having begun to experiment with using video to slow, fragment or syncopate footage of figures in motion, Godard remarked that 'as soon as you freeze an image in a movement . . . you notice in a shot you have filmed, according to how you stop it, that suddenly there are billions of possibilities' – the vast majority of which will, of course, never be realised.[24] It is the right to veer or digress, to acknowledge the plenitude of possibility and the 'otherness' at the core of the self, that the prostitute, as Godard understands the term, sacrifices in order to embody and give (apparent) consistency to the desires of their employer. The body, in such instances, becomes *mechanised*, and Paul is culpable only to the extent to which he is complicit with this mechanisation.

This desire to mechanically fix, 'flesh out' or 'bring to life' a fantastic form underwrites both Nausicca's performance and (in a more exalted register) the tableaux vivants in *Passion* (1982): a live body moving in time to a record, a fleshly, navigable, zoomable-into Velasquez. Indeed, the wish to enter into new and more intimate relations with images, to remediate them in forms more amenable to our spectatorial desires, to close the gap between viewed body and viewing body, continues to drive the development of audiovisual technologies. Just as Godard's setup in the *Histoire(s)* anticipates the modes of interacting with films now available to any cinephile with a modern computer (as YouTube's wealth of mash-ups, re-dubs, fan-made trailers and tributes testify) so *Passion*'s tableaux anticipate contemporary attempts by 'the entertainment industry to enhance the classic 2D video into an immersive and interactive 3D medium'.[25] Such software would 'enabl[e] the viewer to choose an arbitrary viewpoint onto the scene in real-time and without loss of visual quality', pandering to the desire for 'mastery' over represented spaces and bodies that drives Laura Mulvey's 'possessive spectator'.[26]

Godard undoubtedly understands the appeal of this attitude, admitting, for example, the pleasure he took in directing Seberg, 'an actress who I wanted to see doing little things which amused me'.[27] He is, however, also aware that attempts to technologically smooth over or fetishistically obfuscate *faux raccord* are pernicious. Ultimately more of a 'pensive spectator', the Godard of the *Histoire(s)* lets the stitches show, using technology to *emphasise* gaps, losses and contradictions.[28] If technology facilitates what he dubs, in *Histoire(s)* 4b, the 'totalitarianism of the present', the 'abolition of time' in favour of the 'unified time of the moment', the *right now* of the consumer's whim, then Godard shows that it can also be used 'to show an ear that listens to time and try to make it heard'. The project represents his attempt to 'metabolise the former means of survival into new ones' (*Histoire(s)* 4b) and 'to tell the story of all the films that were never made' (*Histoire(s)* 1a). Using video to explore lost or latent possibilities at a micro-level (by looping, altering the tempo of and juxtaposing recorded motions to suggest other ways that they might have played out) *Histoire(s)* simultaneously, at a macro-level, asks what other *histoires* could or should have been, which glimpsed possibilities were truly and tragically *'sans avenir'*. Thus, in *Histoire(s)* 1b, Godard weaves together images of projectors, trains and the Nazi mechanisation of genocide so that a still of a woman poised to switch a railway signal becomes an indictment of culture's failure to avert Auschwitz, acquiring new meaning and moral force from the interplay of images (Figure 11).

Godard can in many ways be seen as a forerunner of those contemporary artists whose work, informed by Derrida's concept of 'hauntology', uses technology to effect juxtapositions and hybridisations as a means of political critique or a form of elegy.[29] Film's registration and re-presentation of already-vanished moments is, of course, fundamentally ghostly, and never more so than in the *Histoire(s)*, a séance at which the ghosts who haunt the cinema are made to speak, both to one another and to new audiences. Its method anticipates that of video collagist Michael Robinson, or the practice of The Otolith Group, whose *Otolith III* (2009), a 'premake' of an unrealised Satyajit Ray sci-fi film, imagines an alternate 1967 by splicing archive material with new footage. Godard's attempt to draw images into dialogue also anticipates Richard Wright's Mimeticon search engine, which, questioning our practice of thinking the visual in terms of the verbal, retrieves images not on the basis of text accompanying or appended to them (as with traditional search engines) but by way of pictures that the user constructs from alphabetical characters.[30] The relation between language

**Figure 11** *Histoire(s) du Cinéma* 1b, dir. Jean-Luc Godard, 1989

and the image, the attempt to find a language *of* the image, remains, for Godard, the crux of the cinematic problem: 'just as painting succeeded in reproducing perspective, cinema should have succeeded in something, too, but was unable to, due to the application of the invention of sound'.[31] Cinema could perhaps, have 'succeeded' in answering Juliette's call for a mode of expression that 'does not refer to a specific object' but seeks, instead to move beyond portrayals of subjects operating on objects.

Godard's mutually transformative conjunctions of texts, images, objects and bodies may not solve the problem. They continue nevertheless to pose a challenge not merely to practitioners and theorists of film but to anyone concerned with representation and communication in the age of 'New Media'. In its use of technology to evoke im/possible pasts, presents and futures Godard's is a truly 'virtual' cinema, alive to the structures (aesthetic, syntactical, sociopolitical) that new technologies endorse, encode or camouflage, but also receptive to their artistic potential. As the range and sophistication of software used to deny or palliate *faux raccord* increases, the question of how to develop Godard's strategies for exposing or generating noise remains pressing, not least because so many of his methods have been routinised and recuperated. It is all the more crucial, in this context, that we learn to attend not merely to the nature of the media and the technologies used to compose images, but also to 'the meaning of plus', to the dissonant tones, latent meanings and accesses of affect that conjunction and juxtaposition can release.

## Notes

1 Vivian Sobchack, *The Address of the Eye: A Phenomenology of Film Experience* (Princeton, New Jersey, Oxford: Princeton University Press, 1992), 219.
2 Tom Milne and Jean Narboni (eds), *Godard on Godard* (New York: Viking, 1972), 166.
3 Milne and Narboni, *Godard on Godard*, 181.
4 Sobchack, *The Address of the Eye, 220.*
5 Philippe Dubois, 'Video Thinks What Cinema Creates: Notes on Jean-Luc Godard's Work in Video and Television', in *Jean-Luc Godard – Son+Image, 1974–1991*, eds. Mary Lea Bandy and Raymond Bellour (New York: The Museum of Modern Art, 1992), 177, 178, emphasis original.
6 Milne and Narboni, *Godard on Godard*, 200.
7 Laura Mulvey, *Death 24x a Second: Stillness and the Moving Image* (London: Reaktion, 2006), 148.
8 Roland Barthes, 'Towards a Semiotics of Cinema: Barthes in Interview with Michel Delahaye, Jacques Rivette (September 1963)' in *Cahiers du Cinéma 1960–1968: New Wave, New Cinema, Reevaluating Hollywood*, ed. Jim Hillier (Cambridge: Harvard University Press, 1992), 276–285, 279.
9 Roland Barthes, *S/Z*, trans. Richard Miller (Oxford: Blackwell, 1990), 33.
10 Mulvey, *Death 24x a Second*, 172.

11 Peter Haining, *The Legend of Brigitte Bardot* (London: W.H. Allen, 1983), 175; Colin MacCabe, *Godard: A Portrait of the Artist at 70* (London: Bloomsbury, 2004), 153, emphasis original.
12 Michael Moon, *A Small Boy and Others: Imitation and Initiation in American Culture from Henry James to Andy Warhol* (Durham; London: Duke University Press, 198), 21.
13 Michel Serres, *The Parasite*, trans. Lawrence R. Scher (Minneapolis: University of Minneapolis Press, 2007), 79.
14 Brian Massumi, *Parables for the Virtual: Movement, Affect, Sensation* (Durham; London: Duke University Press, 2002), 26.
15 Ibid., 27–8.
16 David Steritt (ed.), *Jean-Luc Godard: interviews* (Jackson: University Press of Mississippi, 1998), 24.
17 Antonin Artaud, *Selected Writings*, trans. Helen Weaver, ed. Susan Sontag, (Berkley and Los Angeles: University of California Press, 1988), 216, 233.
18 MacCabe, *Godard*, 301.
19 Arthur Rimbaud, *Rimbaud Complete*, trans. Wyatt Mason (New York: Modern Library, 2002), 365.
20 Milne and Narboni, *Godard on Godard*, 218.
21 Ibid., 180.
22 Dubois, 'Video Thinks What Cinema Creates', 177.
23 Richard Roud, *Jean-Luc Godard* (London: Secker & Warburg, 1967), 32.
24 Dubois, 'Video Thinks What Cinema Creates', 178–9.
25 Jose Carranza, Marus A. Magnor, Hans-Peter Seidel, and Christian Theobalt, 'Combining 3D Flow Fields with Silhouette-based Human Motion Capture for Immersive Video', *Graphical Models*, 66 (2004), 334.
26 Ibid., 334; Mulvey, *Death 24x a Second*, 171.
27 Milne and Narboni, *Godard on Godard*, 177.
28 Mulvey, *Death 24x a Second*, 186.
29 Jacques Derrida, *Spectres of Marx: The State of the Debt, the Work of Mourning, and the New International*, trans. Peggy Kamuf (New York: Routledge, 1994), 10.
30 Richard Wright, *Mimeticon* (2006), accessed 3 January 2010, http://www.mimeticon.net/.
31 Daney, 'Godard makes [Hi]stories', 167.
32 Simone De Beauvoir, *Brigitte Bardot and the Lolita Syndrome* (London: The New English Library, 1962), 54.

ELENA CRIPPA

# Anti-theatricality and gesture as antidotes to the commodification of cinema: Godard's *Le Mépris* and Pasolini's *La Ricotta*

By the late 1960s, the relationship between filmmakers Jean-Luc Godard and Pier Paolo Pasolini was marked by open conflicts on both aesthetic and political grounds. Godard had accused Pasolini of being 'a bureaucrat' and Pasolini had responded labelling Godard 'a moralist'.[1] Yet, their filmmaking had, at least for a period, been guided by similar preoccupations. In particular, in 1963, they directed two films which bore striking similarities, not just on a formal level but in their ethical and political stance. Those films are Godard's relatively high budget feature film *Le Mépris* and Pasolini's short *La Ricotta*.[2] These films have many similarities but this essay aims to highlight their relationship with theatre and analyse their shared anti-theatrical stance. In doing so, reference will be made to the theories and techniques developed by Bertolt Brecht and Samuel Beckett, who shaped their work against the legacy of Wagner's gestural theatre. Moreover, anti-theatricality will be analysed as an act of resistance against an art that overwhelms its audience by drowning it in an all-encompassing experience that collapses critical distance and prevents analytic response.

By 1963, Godard and Pasolini had already caught the attention of both critics and public with their feature films. Their work was shaped by a love for cinema and writing, social engagement and a passion for all forms of visual arts. It is in this year that both filmmakers released movies that acted as an 'embittered discourse on the film *industry*'.[3] Godard's *Le Mépris* and Pasolini's *La Ricotta* are both films in which a human drama is intertwined with the story of the making of a film and the portrayal of the world of cinema. *Le Mépris*, an adaptation of Alberto Moravia's novel *A Ghost at Noon*, narrates the disintegration of the marriage between Paul (Michel Piccoli), and Camille Javal (Brigitte Bardot), amid jealousy, misunderstandings, silences and betrayed expectations. While Camille's love drifts into contempt, Paul is working on a script for an adaptation of the Homeric *Ulysses* commissioned by the crass producer Jeremy Prokosch (Jack Palance). The director of the film is Fritz Lang, playing himself. Ulysses' attempts to return home are repeatedly compared with Paul's personal drama, his desperate need to act and incapacity to do so. Pasolini's *La Ricotta* also stars a famous filmmaker playing himself. In this case, the director is Orson Welles and the subject of the film within the film is another story of epic proportions: the Passion of Jesus Christ. In *La Ricotta*, as in *Le Mépris*, the drama of the protagonist resonates with the one at the core of the film within the film. *La Ricotta* tells the story of a day shooting the scenes of Christ's crucifixion. The camera records the actors strolling around in costume while the extras occupy their spare time playing music, dancing and organising a striptease. The frenetic atmosphere is counterbalanced by the inexpressive features of the main actress and by the motionless stance of the filmmaker, who unenthusiastically goes through different takes without ever getting up from his chair. The protagonist is Stracci, a poor and simple man, generous and yet greedy, whose role in the film within the film is that of the 'Good Thief' dying on the cross next to Christ. After having given his lunch pack to his wife to feed his family, Stracci spends most of his time between takes trying to obtain food by theft or trickery; and his perennial hunger is the cause of continuous mocking and bullying. At the end of *Le Mépris*, Camille and Prokosch die in a car accident. At the end of *La Ricotta*, Stracci dies while playing his part attached to the cross, a victim of indigestion caused by eating too much while already ill.

Another similarity between the two films is that they both feature numerous quotations, appropriations and repetitions.[4] Like collages, they feature incongruous elements that only precariously coexist, resisting any attempt to fit them into univocal narratives. If Nicholas Paige has written that *Le Mépris* is 'constructed as a nearly endless chain of allusions' and that 'pastiching' is its signature tropes,[5] Pasolini stylistically defined himself as a *pasticheur* by passion, always coalescing different styles.[6] In both films, quotations and references are often taken from the cinema. In *Le Mépris*, conversations between the characters often refer to other films and famous actors. Posters of other films are visible at Cinecittà and in a film theatre, where an audition takes place; while the framing of the camera marks the beginning and end of the film. In *La Ricotta*, a journalist asks Orson Welles about his views on Federico Fellini. The filmmaker answers by reading a poem from Pasolini's screen play of *Mamma Roma* – a detail that can hardly escape the spectator, as Welles holds up the book making its cover clearly visible.[7] The film is punctuated by the voiceover of the assistant director giving orders through his megaphone, and Pasolini makes fun of the redundant role of large crews when the orders of the director are repeated at ridiculous length. Both Godard and Pasolini chose their actors in relation to the history of the cinema, obviously in the case of the directors but also each actor brings with them aspects of previous roles. Both directors make an appearance in the films playing minor roles: Godard as Lang's assistant and Pasolini as an extra playing a shepherd in the staging of the deposition. Thematically, both films deal with the anguish of physical and professional prostitution. If Godard is obliged to include Bardot's nudity, her readiness to strip for the camera is a warning sign of the fact that the female body is becoming a capitalist commodity. The stripping bare of Bardot is echoed in *La Ricotta* by the striptease of Natalina (Maria Bernardini), an extra who is persuaded to undress in front of a large group of men in exchange for payment. In this respect, both films announce their break with the status quo of the film industry by exposing the economic logic governing the commodification of pleasure in which they participate. Finally, if *Le Mépris* plays homage to Rossellini's *Viaggio in Italia* (1954),[8] Pasolini's *La Ricotta* is still attached to the narration of tragic stories of underpriveleged individuals. As in *Roma città aperta* (1945), from the very start of the film, it is clear that the seeds of disaster have been sown and that death is inevitable. Yet, despite their attachment to Neo-Realism, and particularly to the cinema of Rossellini, both films reject naturalism, at least as expressed in Bazinian terms.[9] In fact, in both films the action, style of acting, use of décor, insertion of quotations and use of colour is not firmly subordinated to the production of the illusion of reality. On the contrary, their particular style functions with the suspension of such an illusion.

The two films under discussion, filmed at an important stage in the career of both directors, seem to embody a struggle between two drives. On one side, the desire to reach a wide audience, respecting the need to generate coherent and continuous narratives that guarantee a degree of suspension of disbelief. On the other side, the desire to offer a non-engrossing experience that creates a space of critical distance and a sense of detached presence. Although a clear narrative persists, it is generated working against one of the major bastions of cinema: a personal identification with the story and, in particular, with the vicissitudes of the protagonists. The two films overtly distance themselves from what we could define as a mimetic or realistic rendering of filmic narratives. Instead, they attain a collage-like structure in which the viewer is constantly pulled back from the risk of being engulfed in the cinematic flow of images. Such formal choices could simply be interpreted as part of a stylistic programme wanting to break with the tradition of integral realism. At the same time, Godard and Pasolini's aesthetic programme transcends the confined territories of cinema and can be analysed as an expression of broader cultural tendencies. One such cultural trope is 'anti-theatricality', which characterised the work of the most influential dramatists of the twentieth century while also permeating the visual arts.[10]

Both Godard and Pasolini had an interest in theatre and Godard's work has been read in relation to Brechtian techniques, to the point that Colin MacCabe argues that 'Brecht is the most important thinker through which Godard tries to theorise his relationship to the audience'.[11] Godard was passionate about theatre and, in the 1960s, became a close friend of actor and theatre director Antoine Bourseiller, for whom he bought a theatre.[12] Pasolini had also been engaged with theatre since a young age, acting and writing plays. In 1959, he was asked to translate Aeschylus's *Oresteia* for the

Greek Theatre of Syracuse; in the mid to late 1960s, Pasolini wrote six tragedies, constantly returning to the codes of dramatic genre; and most of the films from this period are either filmic translations of plays for theatre (*Teorema* and *Pigsty*) or cinematic versions of classical tragedies (*Edipo re* and *Medea*).[13] In both films analysed, the framed images can often be compared to stages in which characters walk in and out of a scene. The space of the stage is often clearly set and framed by the architecture. In *Le Mépris*, the producer's living room in his Roman villa and the couple's flat have all the characteristics of theatrical interior settings, dominated by props, sculptures and mirrors. Other settings appear like monumental sites for the staging of epic actions. This is the case of the empty roads and the raised entrance to Teatro n. 6 in Cinecittà, as well as the nearly empty open space of Prokosch's villa in Capri and its spectacular roof-terrace. There seems to be a great deal of pleasure and playfulness in the setting up of stages for dramatic exploits. Nevertheless, the awaited action never takes place, or only in gratuitous and yet highly staged manifestations of violence – such as when Prokosch hits the film canisters – or in the final, non-redemptive death. In *La Ricotta*, particular sites are demarcated as being stage-like settings, existing in a direct physical relation with the presence of an audience. When Stracci is liberated from his cross and can go back to the cave where he had hidden his lunch, a growing public materialises to enjoy the spectacle of Stacci's gluttony, laughing out loudly and initiating a processional offering of lavish dishes. When journalists and politicians arrive on the set, they create a large audience facing the scene of the crucifixion and, at the same time, the viewers in the film theatre.

If both films reference the spaces of the stage and the stalls, the predominant relationship they establish with theatre is antagonistic rather than flirtatious. In fact, the two films embrace the spirit of anti-theatricality that dominated the twentieth century and affected the fine arts, music and cinema as well as theatre itself. Martin Puchner has dissected the concept of 'anti-theatricality' in his book *Stage Fright* (2002). He describes the way in which the sentiments of anti-theatricality were shaped through the criticism of philosophers such as Friedrich Nietzsche, Walter Benjamin and Theodor W. Adorno as a response against the totalising theatre of Wagner. Those thinkers rejected the power of theatre to turn live characters into absolute values and disdained the mimetic aspect of acting, which calls for a passive receiver, an a-critical identification with the actors and an engrossing experience of the totality of theatre. These anti-theatrical conceptions were shaped through the closet drama of Stéphane Mallarmé, the writing of James Joyce and the dramaturgy of Brecht and Beckett. As part of the anti-theatrical tradition developed by those authors, stage directions and diegetic speech are crucial devises through which representation is estranged, controlled, framed, fragmented and fundamentally questioned in its material integrity. Through textual or diegetic mediation the liveliness and presence of the human actor, and with it the aura of the theatre, is under attack.[14] The story is not just lived out – through the mimetic impersonation of actors – but narrated, in the third person, by the equivalent of a modern chorus of narrators.

The two films analysed are powerful examples of cinematic rendering of the anti-theatrical tradition. In both films, diegetic narrative is constructed through a number of expedients. It is embodied in the profuse use of literary and visual quotations. It is manifested in the pleasure for storytelling, as in the case of the two stories told in *Le Mépris*, of Râma Krishna and his disciple and of the adventures of the ass Martin. Finally, it materialises in the appropriations of extra-narrative references, such as the film posters in *Le Mépris* and the staging of Rosso Fiorentino and Pontormo's paintings in *La Ricotta*. All these different sorts of diegetic strategies act as framing, controlling and interrupting devises, shattering the wholeness of the mimetic space. Moreover, different authors have addressed the debt of *Le Mépris* to the theatre of Bertolt Brecht. 'B.B.' is overtly introduced in the scene staged in the film theatre, which clearly adopts the German director's techniques by separating speech, music, acting and set design from one another, in order to prevent the numbing effect of theatre.[15] It is in such a scene that the space of the stage is set against the space of the public; the music is interrupted when the characters speak; and Lang quotes Brecht's poem on Hollywood's merchants of lies. Apart from the debt to Brecht, *Le Mépris* creates a sense of estrangement and critical distance in a number of ways: fostering an acting style defined by a nearly mechanical precision of gestures and a sense of cold distance; giving away little of the history of the characters, for whom we can only very partially feel; inserting diegetic elements that either break with the narrative or comment upon it; or using quotations and appropriations that bring alien elements into the main story. Some of these estrangement techniques do not rely on the theatrical tradition but are purely cinematic. Among them is the insertion of small fragments of moving images that break the narrative. Those fragments suggest a past in the characters' life that would be impossible to deduce from the main events; strike because of their visual qualities but seem to lack any narrative role; anticipate a future event or location; or contradict events previously seen in the film, telling the same story in a different way. *La Ricotta* pushes even further the disintegration of the wholeness of the film and highlights the discontinuity of isolated fragments. Two different paintings of the deposition of Christ are staged as tableaux vivants, attempting to reproduce the celebrated representations of such scene by two famous Mannerist painters. The overall sense of continuity is denied by the use of both black and white and colour film. While the real-life passion of Stracci is filmed in black and white, the story of the Passion, as well as other highly mannerist visual digressions, are shot in Technicolor. With *La Ricotta*, Pasolini truly engages in the attempt to realise his 'cinema of poetry' before the letter, inserting fragments of moving images that are not necessary to the understanding and unrolling of the main narrative and giving way to moments of pure form and rhythm.[16]

Furthermore, in both films, the aspect that seems the most indebted to the anti-theatrical tradition of Brecht and Beckett is the representation of gestures, which often appear as isolated moments of punctuation and hold an extraordinary plasticity or comic appeal. It is again Martin Puchner who has outlined the historical development of theories on the representation of human gestures, from Wagner's gestural theatre to the gesticulative language of Beckett's plays.[17] Undoubtedly, as Giorgio Agamben has pointed out, the modern interest for gestures is not relegated to theatre, but is characteristic of many other disciplines. Gesture can be considered the subject of Muybridge's photography, it was at the heart of Aby Warburg's art historical project *Mnemosyne Atlas*, 1925–29, is central to the study of motor and phonic tics in Neuropsychiatry; and encountered a moment of extraordinary celebration in silent cinema.[18] All those disciplines shared an interest in breaking down the integrity of the human body into single movements. Similarly, in both films analysed, habitual gestures are isolated, taken out of their context and played off against the integrity of both the character and the actor. Highly staged movements and gestures punctuate *Le Mépris*. Fritz Lang's habit of quotation is often reinforced by a pointing finger while, on more than one occasion, emphatic expressions completely substitute for words. Prokosch often stands like a public orator, quoting from his little red book, and he often enforces his power with theatrical gestures. He pulls Paul's tie while telling him that he wants him to write new scenes for the script, and he uses his assistant's back as a desk to write a cheque. Like Beckett's characters in *Waiting for Godot*, Paul Javal always wears a hat and is characterised by inaction while being devoted to much activity, which is carried out in a vaudeville-type style. Paul's incapacity to detect his wife's emotions and shape his own life is echoed by the awkward way in which he touches or strikes objects, such as the sculpture in his apartment or the harp in Prokosch's villa. His inadequacy is echoed by the clumsiness and ridicule of many of his gestures. He takes down his trousers while walking into the bedroom, nearly tripping over, while Camille hides behind the door. On more than one occasion he pulls up his trousers in an exaggerated and farcical manner. He bathes wearing his hat, trying to look like the character played by Dean Martin in the American film *Some Came Running* (1958), but his wife tells him that he resembles more Martin's ass than Dean Martin. Many of those gestures are reminiscent of the theatre of Beckett and of slapstick comedy. Props are used and manipulated interrupting or punctuating dialogues. There are moments of abrupt violence or sudden activity, as when Camille kicks Paul or Paul catches a taxi on the run. Conversely, as pointed out by Paul Coates, Camille's halcyon demure, her 'absent presence', is reminiscent of the inertia of gods, of the stars who exist outside and overshadow narratives, as in the fragmented world of the idealised and unmovable statues seen in Lang's *Odyssey*.[19]

In a similar way, *La Ricotta* is populated by a large number of exaggerated expressions and movements. When the filmmaker stages the first tableau vivant, he has to keep correcting the actors because they have unsuitable expressions or are not static, as in the case of an old man picking his nose. When staging the second scene, the young men supporting Jesus let him fall on the floor, causing the uncontrollable laugh of all actors. Apart from quoting his most admired mannerist painters, Pasolini pays homage to his favourite actor and filmmaker: Charlie Chaplin. His slapstick techniques are clearly evoked in the sketches in which Stracci frantically runs after his lunch. Many of these scenes are played at an increased speed and are dominated by repetitions. Stracci dresses as a woman in order to get hold of a second lunch pack, after having given his first one to his family. After the diva's dog eats his second meal, he runs to a stall where a man is selling ricotta, at which point both men are taken by the unstoppable urgency to energetically scratch their backsides. On his way back to the set, Stracci runs past a group of men doing mechanical exercises while standing in a line along the main road and crosses a group of policemen picking flowers in a field. The group of journalists and politicians joining the set are characterised by affected smiles, while the paparazzi jump around to take their precious pictures. Although many of the gestures that can be isolated in the two films find their *raison d'être* in the diegesis, the fact that they are rendered in an overemphatic manner does not contribute to an illusion of reality. On the contrary: they are resources that create interruptions and moments of estrangement. In his essay on Brecht's theatre, Benjamin argues that the theory on *gestus* points at the dismantling of actors into isolated fragments and the disruption of the continuum of material mimesis.[20] In this respect, gestures act as deixis, pointing towards themselves. They contribute to the weaving of a multilayered work that fosters a complex experience of seeing and an enhanced critical viewpoint.[21]

It seems at this point useful to expand on the concept of the resistance to theatricality as a resistance to mimesis. In the context of the post-war philosophical and cultural tradition, the aversion to the absolute value of acting as a sort of aping activity coincides with a fear of a passive and a-critical identification with another being.[22] The complete identification accomplished first by the actor and then by the audience does not allow the development of individual subjectivity. For that the viewer must be confronted with an external object which is distant and incomplete. This is why, for Adorno, the state of incompleteness is critical in the definition of artworks. Tom Huhn has attempted to construe Adorno's reading of artworks as incomplete entities from at least two perspectives.[23] Artworks address subjects whose experience and interpretation they presuppose; and they are specimens of the world that they imply, standing as evidence of their incompletely realised status. For Huhn, artworks project new worlds or ways of thinking as a result of their incompleteness, because they foster an exploration while signalling the inability of a subjectivity to fully consume it. Following this reading, artworks are the occasions for subjective dissolution and reconstitution. It is the unfinished status of the object that holds the greatest promises: it is an occasion for the subject to liken him/herself to a state of unfinishedness and understand the development of subjectivity as a historical and dialectical process. As in Beckett's theatre, in *Le Mépris* and *La Ricotta* objects and isolated gestures compose an ensemble of primary signifiers on which the diegesis relies and upon which it invests much of its signifying energy. Objects and gestures seem to be given a similar weight to speech, as happens in symbolist theatre. Nevertheless, neither Beckett nor Godard nor Pasolini's work can be read in such a light. The three authors inherited this symbolist project in as much as their work is invested in the staging of objects and isolated gestures, an investment that leads them to develop very meticulous stage or filmic directions. At the same time, the act of isolating objects and gestures is carried out in the absence of any faith for their symbolic interpretation. The fact that individual actions do not have a specific symbolic meaning is reinforced by the fact that the same gestures are repeated throughout the movie in different situations and contexts, denying their power to reveal unspeakable and circumstantial meanings. The content of objects and the meaning of gestures are not self-sufficient standings to be deciphered by a subject. Instead, they act as occasions for viewers to become actively aware of their role as implied by the work, and to liken themselves to a status of unfinishedness, a sense of potentiality and projection towards an active, critical stance.

In both films, the different techniques of estrangement used and the way characters are depicted, in a fragmented and often contradictory manner, generate a sense of ambiguity. This ambiguity, as in Beckett's theatre, can appear as a drawback of certain dramatic expectations, but it also represents an intriguing and powerful resource, capable of engaging the imagination of active spectators. It is compelling to analyse *Le Mépris* and *La Ricotta* as self-aware in their condition of being 'incomplete artefacts', as they constantly refer to or imply to the viewers that they presuppose, and stand as examples of possible alternative worlds. While both directors articulate their refusal of reality and its social norms, they also express their love for a possible reality that needs to be cherished or, at least, longed for. If we read *Le Mépris* and *La Ricotta* as 'incomplete objects', we can also argue that these films embody a rejection of commercial films not just in their overt criticism of the mechanisms underpinning the film industry but, foremost, in their form. In fact, if for Marx the appearance of a commodity depends on the disappearance of the social relations that allowed it coming into being, for Adorno an artwork does not efface a world for the sake of coming into being. Instead, it makes apparent the instruments, choices and relationships that shaped its genesis and project a possible world that bears the traits of a promising potentiality.[24] At a time when cinema seemed to be condemned to the status of an industry turning films into commercial enterprises, Godard and Pasolini struggled for a different cinema both with the stories that they told and, more importantly, with aesthetics which fundamentally refused such commodification.

## Notes

1 Godard qualified Pasolini as a 'bureaucrat' in an interview published in *Vie Nuove*, a weekly publication of the Italian Communist Party, which was re-published in the preface of the Italian edition of *Jean-Luc Godard. Il cinema è il cinema*, ed. by Aldo Garzanti (Milano: Garzanti, 1971). Pasolini's response, in a short essay titled 'Godard', is re-published (without bibliographical references) in *Pasolini Cinéaste*, ed. by Alain Bergala and Jean Narboni (Paris: Éditions de l'Étoile, Cahiers du Cinéma, 1984), 27–28. In the same book (7–10), Bergala retraces the aesthetical and political disagreements that finally led to the complete silence of the editorial board of *Cahiers du Cinéma* on Pasolini's work, after his open criticism of the Italian students who, in 1968, engaged in violent confrontations with the police.

2 *La Ricotta* was produced for the compilation Ro.Go.Pa.G., a 1963 film in four episodes directed by Roberto Rossellini, Jean-Luc Godard, Pier Paolo Pasolini and Ugo Gregoretti. As per Pasolini's account, the directors engaged in the four short films did not have any contact with each other. In fact the producer, Alfredo Bini, had conceived Ro.Go.Pa.G. as the anthology of four independent films. On this subject, see the comments of Pasolini in Osward Stack, *Pasolini on Pasolini: Interviews with Osward Stack* (London: Thames & Hudson, 1969), 59.

3 With this sentence Jacques Aumont describes *Le Mépris* in his essay 'The Fall of the Gods: Jean-Luc Godard's Le Mépris (1963)', in *French Film: Texts and Contexts*, 2nd ed, ed. by Susan Hayward and Ginette Vincendeau (London; New York: Routledge, 2000), 174–188, (176).

4 Although Godard's *Le Mépris* certainly does not, as others of his lower budget films, feel messy and improvised (as Nicholas Paige has described his style), it maintains the impression that a sense of playfulness and caprice guides particular aesthetic and formal choices or insertions. Godard's passion for quotation is the subject of many essays and Godard said that 'Criticism taught us to admire both Rouch and Eisenstein. From it we learned not to deny one aspect of the cinema in favour of another' See 'Jean Luc Godard: "From Critic to Film-Maker": Godard in interview (extracts)', in Jim Hillier, *Cahiers du Cinéma vol. 2, the 1960s* (London: Routledge and Kegan Paul, 1986), 59–67, (59). As pointed out by Jacques Aumont, by the time *Le Mépris* was released, there was already a clear sense not just that Godard's style was characterised by quotations, but that quotations were introduced in a casual way. In Jacques Aumont, 'The Fall of the Gods', 176.

5 Nicholas Paige, 'Bardot and Godard in 1963 (Historicizing the Postmodern Image)', *Representations*, 88 (2004), 1–25 (10).

6 Stack, *Pasolini on Pasolini*, 28.

7 The screenplay of Pasolini's *Mamma Roma* was published by Rizzoli in 1962, the same year in which the film was released.

8 Jacques Aumont, 'The Fall of the Gods', 176–177.

9 For a critical review of Bazin's criticism of stylistic choices when not subordinated to the interests of realism see: Christopher Williams, 'Bazin on Neo-Realism', *Screen*, 14:4 (1973–74), 61–69.

10 Famously, contemporary art has been dominated by Michael Fried's powerful criticism of the aspects of theatricality that he perceived as dominating in minimal art. See Michael Fried's essay 'Art and Objecthood', first published in *Artforum* in 1967, re-published in *Art in Theory, 1900–2000*, new edition, ed. by Charles Harrison and Paul Wood (Oxford: Blackwell, 2003), 835–846.

11 Colin MacCabe, *Godard: A Portrait of the Artist at Seventy* (London: Bloomsbury, 2003), 160.

12 Ibid., 143.

13 On Pasolini's relationship to theatre see Edi Liccioli, *La scena della parola. Teatro e poesia in Pier Paolo Pasolini* (Firenze: Le Lettere, 1997).

14 In *Stage Fright* Puchner gives specific examples of Mallarmé's closet drama, Brecht and Beckett's plays as well as Joyce's stage directions, in particular analysing 'Circe', the fifteenth dramatic chapter of *Ulysses*.

15 For Brecht the only way to control total theatricality of the opera is to turn the arts against one another so that, in an estranging effort, they interrupt and dissolve the totality of the work of art.

16 These techniques have been theorised by Pasolini in *Empirismo Eretico*, a collection of essays of cinematographic theory and practice that were written in 1968 and first published in 1972. For a detailed recount of *La Ricotta* as a manifestation of Pasolini's poetic theories see Silvia Carlorosi, 'Pier Paolo Pasolini's La ricotta: the power of cinepoiesis', *Italica* 86:2 (2009), 254–271.

17 Martin Puchner, *Stage Fright: Modernism, Anti-Theatricality, and Drama* (Baltimore: Johns Hopkins University Press, 2002), 91–97 and 142–171.

18 Giorgio Agamben, *Notes on Gesture*, in Giorgio Agamben, *Means Without End: Notes on Politics*, trans. by Vincenzo Binetti and Cesare Casarino (Minneapolis: University of Minnesota Press, 2000), 48–59. The representation of gestures has since been recuperated and has become a popular subject in contemporary fine arts, especially in the work of artists using video and photography and referencing cinema and theatre, such as Nan Goldin, Catherine Sullivan and Keren Cytter.

19 Paul Coates, 'Le Mépris: Women, Statues, Gods', *Film Criticism*, 22:3 (1998), 38–50.

20 Benjamin's essay on Brecht's theatre begins stating that 'Epic theatre is gestural', and all the features of epic theatre (such as interruption, montage, episodic nature and quotation) are defined as gestural. For Benjamin, the more an action is interrupted, the more gestures become prominent and, in this sense, the interruption of actions is the central concern of epic theatre. See Walter Benjamin, 'What is Epic Theatre?', in Walter Benjamin, *Understanding Brecht*, trans. by Anna Bostock (London: NLB, 1977), 1–14; and Puchner, *Stage Fright*, 151.

21 As Puchner has noted: 'If we feel that the deixis of gestus resembles the raised finger of a didactic gesture, we may remember that the complexity of Brecht's work depends on what he calls "art of watching a play" and on the insistence that "complex seeing must be practiced"'. Ibid., 153.

22 This apprehension had been nourished by a long sociological and political tradition, including Jürgen Habermas' critique of the public sphere and the interpretation of the theatres as training grounds for the formation of a political

arena. The analysis of the use (or instrumentalisation) of the theatre for politics was aggravated by the horrors of Nazism and Fascism and also stands behind Walter Benjamin's diagnosis of the fascist aestheticisation of politics.

23 Tom Huhn, *The Cambridge Companion to Adorno* (Cambridge: Cambridge University Press, 2004), 8–21.

24 Huhn, *The Cambridge Companion to Adorno*, 6–12 and 79–100.

WILLIAM VINEY

# 'Not necessarily in that order': *Contempt*, Adaptation and the Metacinematic

## Introduction

If the text is 'a tissue of quotations drawn from the innumerable centres of culture',[1] then Godard's *Le Mépris* provides a tissue of indeterminate depth or density; it is a fabric of fraying and uncertain limits. With its churning system of citation, allusion, and adaptation, *Le Mépris* does not simply quote but relentlessly questions the very act of quotation. The referential schemes that give Godard's film its texture frequently draw attention to its manipulation and management of texts, to the hazy parameters that assure our engagement with the film. By problematising the provenance and boundaries of his work, Godard interrogates the place of the cinema and its role as narrative technique and technology. Of particular interest is how this effort to problematise the limits and boundaries of the film affects our experience of narrative closure, resolution, and sense of ending. The shifting coordinates of *Le Mépris*, the textual relays and circuits upon which the film's narrative structure depends, requires us to rethink traditional notions interpretation. *Le Mépris* scrutinises the very act of interpretation. Through its open reliance on an adapted work relentlessly staging and displaying the technology that achieves this work of adaptation, the film seems to question the reliability of cinematic narrative and the authority of cinema's attempts to interpret and be interpreted. Since one of the central objects of *Le Mépris* is the technology of its own utterance, the narratorial potential of the camera puts under tension what we see and the manner in which we see it. The following analysis seeks to elaborate how the work of adaptation and the metacinematic display of cinema's material apparatus affects the certainties of interpretation, the trajectory of narrative, and the possibility of closure.

## Interpreting the Adaptation

'One does not find film-makers asserting a bold approach to their source material'[2], writes Brian McFarlane, yet Jean-Luc Godard asserts a bold and explicit approach to his source material and allows this approach to form part of the narrative content of his films. The work of adaptation is often seen to trap two works on a spectrum bound by two extremes; the adaptation either takes from or adds to its source material. Adaptation Studies, the sub-discipline that attempts to schematise and theorise the relationship between literature and film, tends to think in these somewhat mathematical terms, implicitly judging the adapted work according to the 'amount' of the source text it contains. The whole question of 'fidelity' to the source text, so routinely maligned by adaptation theorists,[3] is a symptom rather than the cause of this quantitative view of adaptation. So, even the theories which attempt to stand in opposition to ideas of 'faithfulness' or 'authenticity', depend upon this quantitative bias; works are evaluated according to whether adaptations 'keep, drop, or add'[4] material from their source texts. Geoffrey Wagner suggests three categories by which to assess a film's relation to a work of literature. Firstly, the adaptation might be called a 'transposition' where the literary text is transferred as accurately as possible. Secondly, an adaptation might provide a 'commentary' in which the original is altered whilst retaining some of its salient characteristics. Lastly, 'analogy' describes how the source text provides a point of departure for an entirely different narrative.[5] These categories tally with Dudley Andrew's 'transforming', where the film is judged to reproduce the essential text, 'intersecting', which recreates the distinctiveness of the original, and 'borrowing', which makes no claims to fidelity to the original.[6] Whilst Deborah Cartmell is right to question whether these categories are appropriate to every adaptation, she surely misses the point when she concludes, 'the more we study adaptations, the more it becomes apparent that the categories [by which we distinguish one adaptation from another] are limitless.'[7] This leaves the basic premise of each category untouched. The quantitative basis by which Desmond, Hawkes, Wagner and Andrew mean their evaluations are predicated upon the idea that the source text has stable, determined, or reliable content. It is not the 'fidelity' issue that plagues many theories of adaptation so much as how an analysis of adaptation depends upon the semantic inertia of the source. So, for all Brian McFarlane's sophisticated engagement with structuralist and poststructuralist theory, he argues for a method of analysing adaptations by 'isolat[ing] the chief character functions of the original and observ[ing] how far these are retained in the film version.'[8] McFarlane not only assumes that the 'chief' characters and/or their functions can be isolated but also argues that their 'original' meanings can be agreed upon. Godard's use of Alberto Moravia's novel exemplifies the problems with this conception of the source text since the instability of Molteni's narrative means that interpretative certainty is by no means assured.

The peculiar constitution of written texts cannot permit a singular view or interpretation of the source. Following Bakhtin's theory of the dialogical, Julia Kristeva's conception of intertextuality details how meaning becomes dispersed in and through the texts that it mediates. The author does not create meaning in their text but compiles it from pre-existent texts. The author's work is 'a permutation of texts, an intertextuality in the space of a given text' where 'several utterances, taken from other texts, intersect and neutralise one another.'[9] Kristeva stresses the plural and dialogical nature of language, a nature that 'between the different units of a sentence or narrative structure, indicat[es] a *becoming* [...] a logic of analogy and nonexclusive opposition, opposed to monological levels of causality and identifying determination.'[10] All words have been used before and carry with them the traces of this former use into works of adaptation; texts are palimpsests that continually reuse and rewrite. Words take the position of '*mediator*, linking structural models to cultural (historical) environment, as well as *regulator*, controlling mutations from diachrony to synchrony.'[11] Kristeva's theory of the text complicates the notion of adaptation that seeks to stage a simple comparison between a source and an adapted work. Whilst an analysis of adaptation might try to demonstrate a correspondence between one text and another, it offers an impoverished view of a much more plural, overarching transtextual process, emphasising that, with varying degrees of reflexivity, meaning does not simply stand *outside* the work but shuttles *between innumerable texts and contexts*. In fact, one might argue that Adaptation Studies, with its quantitative emphasis on what is kept, dropped, or added, might fabricate a continual series of Kristevian *ideologemes*, establishing an illusory 'outside' or pre-existent meaning in the hope of bringing unity to the adaptation.

The effect that this inter- or transtextuality has on how unity is perceived in the work is well summarised by André Bazin, 'we are moving toward a reign of the adaptation in which the notion of the unity of the work of art, if not the notion of the author itself, will be destroyed.'[12] Godard's *Le Mépris*, with its multiple literary and filmic influences, allusions and citations, certainly complicates our sense of narrative coherence and places the concept of the singular, all-powerful author under tension. It might be argued that the act of adaptation therefore increases the 'writerly' content of Godard's film, its co-creative potential. For Roland Barthes, the writerly text is a work that requires the reader to co-produce, to be active in the composition of the work's meaning. The 'goal' of the literary work is 'to make the reader no longer a consumer, but a producer of the text.'[13] The 'readerly' text, on the other hand, renders the reader's interaction with the text a passive transfer of a fixed, pre-determined reading; the text's meaning is the author's alone. On the other hand, the perfectly writerly text is 'a galaxy of signifiers, not a structure of signifieds; it has no beginning; it is reversible; we gain access to it by several entrances, none of which can be authoritatively declared to be the main one'.[14] The writerly text is open, plural, and radically unstable, without limit or determination. With its blend of traditional forms and incongruously manipulated allusions to exterior texts, *Le Mépris* is what Barthes might call an 'incompletely plural' work; popular narrative forms still seep through, traditional narrative trajectories are projected and realised, meaning knots and bunches around particular stereotypes: a familiar story is told. It is precisely this sense of assumed familiarity that makes the adapted work enter an interesting exchange with Barthes' distinction between the readerly and the writerly. Since the readerly is a text of repetition, a programmatic repetition of expectations, the work of adaptation oscillates between the expected and the unexpected, the readerly and the writerly.

The presence of extrinsic and intrinsic texts, which mix, blend and displace one another, means that the viewer must constantly manage their expectations and surprise, their sense of repetition and difference. In this sense, adaptation merely intensifies interpretative tensions already in operation when we watch a film. For David Bordwell, 'the spectator comes to a film with a schemata, and these are derived in part from experience with intrinsic norms. The viewer applies these schemata to the film, matching the expectations appropriate to the norms with their fulfilment within the film. Greater or lesser deviations from these norms stand out as prominent.'[15] Bordwell's model of understanding film is predicated upon the correspondence between pre-established expectations and those built up and modified whilst viewing the film. Although the film may generate its own sets of norms these only generate meaning insofar as they replicate or differentiate themselves from the viewers evaluative position. Whilst *Le Mépris* does replicate a surprising amount of material from Moravia's novel,[16] it does so inconsistently and elliptically. A brief example from Godard's film proves how any clear distinction between 'intrinsic' and 'extrinsic' cannot be maintained. The appearance of Paul's Communist card during the long scene in the apartment suggests the arbitrary and diffuse relationship Godard establishes between his source and his adaptation. Moravia's Ricardo is cajoled into joining the Communist Party by a friend, at a time when he 'felt more desperate than usual.'[17] Ricardo agonises that by joining the Party he had betrayed his 'genius' and taken another step closer to becoming the 'starving journalist or the scraggy employee' (*C*, 23). He is clearly not interested in or aligned to the traditional attitudes of the political left. He treats Emilia's former employment as a typist with derision and patronisingly imagines 'the people of the working class' as being 'closer to nature than others, and whose consciousness is not obscured by any convention or prejudice' (*C*, 112). One might speculate that this is all done to undermine Ricardo as a reliable or coherent narrator, yet this remains at the level of speculation. On the other hand, the appearance of the Communist card in the film creates an empty reference to the novel without causal explanation. It remains uncertain as to exactly what has been kept, dropped, or added. Paul's membership of the Communist Party defies the quantitative models of adaptation explored earlier and increases the writerly rather than the readerly content of Godard's film. Whilst the expectation that parts of Moravia's work will appear in the film might constitute an extrinsic norm for Bordwell, the inexplicable meaning attached to the Communist card disrupts any coherent norm being developed. Bordwell's 'normalisation' of cinema's effects attempts to overcome this, leading him to develop the idea that whenever the viewer senses something ambiguous in a film this ambiguity simply fulfils an extrinsic norm particular to what he calls the 'art-cinema mode of narration'. But even he concedes there are moments when, 'there is no way to resolve these disparities; we can only note them as ambivalent effects, working to jar expectations and to make the film an object of interpretation [...] the uncertainty is never dispelled.'[18] Clearly there are techniques that can dissolve any norm, and Godard subtly subverts the expectations of his audience. The appearance of the card replicates the noisy surplus of meaning found elsewhere in the film, doing so through an incongruent non-identical repetition of its source. A simple, quantitative analysis of Paul's political affiliations would miss how Godard empties his narrative of coherent content under the playful guise of being 'faithful' to his sources. And although we might speculate as to the relationship between the card as a sign of political commitment and Godard's own increasing interest in the politics of the left, the ambiguous citational framework in which the card appears serves to erode the completeness of a biographical explanation. Godard thus renders aspects of his film unstable, creating a writerly, indeterminate surplus that frustrates independent interpretative mastery.

## Staring the Narrator in the Lens

We noted earlier how the unreliability of Ricardo's narrative complicates traditional views of adaptation, as they rely on the semantic transparency of the source. Moravia's narrator is entirely self-conscious, opening his narrative, 'The story sets out to relate how ...' (*C*, 3). Even Ricardo seems aware of the fabula he spins; he sets out to tell a 'story' and not simply the 'facts' of what happened. Indeed, Ricardo's story is riddled with self-doubt. From very early on, long before the 'hallucination' sequences that cloud and confuse the novel's conclusion, Ricardo qualifies Battista's introduction to Emilia with, 'Looking back, I am aware of having preserved a confused memory of an incident' (*C*, 4). He observes how 'love has a great capacity not only for illusion but also for forgetfulness,' noting how Emilia had become 'a semblance in a mirage, with a haze of impossibility of nostalgia [...] outside reality' (*C*, 37, 35). So, from an early stage, the reader is reminded of their limited and contingent access to the story. This raises the issue of how cinema generates narrative perspective, how cinematic narrative establishes and maintains a mode of telling. In his discussion of *Le Mépris*, Robert Stam argues that 'the film itself seems to tell the story without mediation, without any characterised narrator. The first-person point of view of the novel becomes the 'no-person' point of view of the film. Since the film has no marked narrator, the question of narrational 'reliability,' so essential to the novel, does not even come up.'[19] Whilst Stam is right to point out how cinema struggles to find an equivalent to Moravia's first-person narrative, the issues of mediated points of view and narrational reliability prove relentless themes in Godard's film. It seems that Godard, in the spirit of Brechtian theatre, wilfully displays the contingent, even arbitrary terms by which narrative information is presented. By doing so, *Le Mépris* contradicts the stable, unobtrusive, omniscient narratives of classical Hollywood cinema.[20] It also frustrates the more traditional view of film narrative that argues that, 'with plays and films, it is generally easier to assess how we should feel about what is narrated, where the emphasis should fall, what is important and what is not, and how we should judge the characters involved.'[21] In particular, by filming the camera Godard generates deep ambiguities surrounding who, what, or how *Le Mépris* narrates. As if to say 'This story sets out to relate *with* . . .' Although Bordwell might argue that 'all filmic techniques, even those involving the 'profilmic event,' function narrationally, constructing the story world for specific effects,'[22] we might question what 'specific effects' accrue by displaying the technology of these techniques.

There are three occasions when the camera becomes directly represented in *Le Mépris*, offering a complex and ambiguous commentary on the nature of cinema. These appearances of cinema's integral piece of technology seem to mark the beginning, middle, and end of the film's narrative. The first of these appearances gives an analogue for the self-referentiality repeated in the other two, a telescopic view of the camera and the making of the moving image. The object of their shot is Prokosch's translator, Francesca Vanini, set against the drab and empty backdrop of the Cinecittà Studios. The focus of *our* shot is their filming; viewing the medium of our viewing. We witness the filming of the filming of cinema, placing us both inside and outside what is being represented. It is precisely this liminal position that the shot documents, where cinema becomes both the object and medium by which we comprehend the action. The shot serves as a kind of metacinematic preface to the rest of the film, forever reminding the audience of their instantiated, mediated position in relation to the cinema's recording process. The shot is a fixed view of a small crew, making a slow tracking shot along rails, smoothly moving towards us. We see the assistants pushing the camera, the sound engineers and their microphones, the complex assemblage of technique and technology. We see what is so frequently forbidden in conventional cinema; the means of cinematic production. The shot ends with us looking up at Godard's director of photography, Raoul Coutard, who is checking his light meter and scrutinising the controls of the camera. Godard foregrounds the labour and technique of his and Coutard's production at the instant when we are quoted Bazin's maxim, 'The cinema substitutes for our gaze a world more in harmony with our desires.' Perhaps in accordance with Godard's desires, Coutard turns his camera towards the camera that is filming him.

For Nicholas Paige, Bazin's quote clarifies the film's objective, to be 'a film about the world-making power of cinematic art.'[23] This is all very well, but the world being represented to us here involves a reflexivity that does not so much amount to a 'world' as an interpretative frame, a frame by which to observe the construction of a world. It is this rich and complex metacinematic gesture that begins Godard's film, one that allows the narration of a story to absorb and distort the means by which that story is told. After the quote from Bazin, the camera lingers. We are asked to stare the production of artifice in the lens, as if to say that we desire to observe ourselves being observed, or rather, observe technology observing yet more technology. A series of unanswerable questions are posed: are we being shown what we desire? Is this confrontation with labour and technology any more or less in harmony with what we demand from cinema? What is the narrative status of this 'look,' how does it relate to the rest of the film? What happens to the face-to-face of human interaction when mediated by technology; is the camera an instrument of prosthesis or does it offer a radically different means of seeing? These problems, posed in the first scene of the film are never resolved. The disclosure of cinema's apparatus is at the cost of any narrative closure we might hope for.

The second instance where the camera appears on the screen is just before everyone sets off for Capri. Camille sits at the bow of the boat, quizzically looking into the shot. Suddenly, we take on her perspective and see what she was looking at. She's looking up, of course, at a camera, flanked by two identically dressed technicians. We are suddenly shown the mechanism for our viewing, the rationale for our (or her) perspective. The camera's lens hood and the two blue lights mounted above display the 'true' face of cinema, as the lens meets the iconic face of contemporary stardom. That the crew are preparing to film 'the Cyclops scene' offers an obvious, ironic reading of this exchange. Nevertheless, the scene continues with Paul entering from the left, sitting beside Camille and asking, 'what are you doing?' to which Camille replies, 'looking.' It is hard to tell who is answering Paul's question, the character of Camille, idling away a few minutes before leaving for Capri, or Bardot herself, repeating her instructions for the scene. In this way, the metacinematic tension of the film seems to want to erode any clear distinction between the various productions represented. This is compounded when the scene ends, Godard himself enters the picture as Lang's assistant to say, 'Please, you're in the frame.' He implicitly refers to two frames, Lang's and Godard's – that of the film, and that of the film within the film. Yet both frames are Coutard's. One of the oddest and rarely observed overlaps between the fabula and syuzhet *of both films represented* is that they share Coutard's cinematography. Indeed, when we view the rushes and the clapperboard appears on our screens, we can clearly see that Lang's cinematographer is one 'R. Kutard'. The Germanic variation of Coutard's name serves as an analogue for the intimate connections drawn between the various levels of artifice on show, both proximate and diverging.

The final appearance of the camera marks the film's final sequence. Again, just as in the first scene, the crew are busy establishing a tracking shot. Lang and Paul are saying goodbye to one another when, rather inexplicably, the camera in the background wheels round in our direction. It is as if we do not have permission to see a camera without it being first directed at us. The climax of *Le Mépris* is a panning shot of the filming of the panning shot; we follow in parallel what Lang's film is recording. And yet, being slightly behind and to the left of the other camera, we notice Odysseus, arms aloft, side-stepping to counter balance the panning camera that follows him, perhaps to simulate the rocking of his ship. We are allowed to see what the other camera does not reveal, the secrets that otherwise go undetected. Our camera then out pans the other and we are left with the same perspective as Odysseus but without his presence. For Paige this is a shot 'that returns us to the simple (but always technically evolving) recording power of the camera–the building block of any cinema to come.'[24] Our awareness of the camera's place in the production of this spectacle does something to remove the subject from and the naturalism of film. We are not left with an empty image, as Paige suggests, but an image intensely aware of what may or may not be happening behind the camera.

## Conclusion

Godard's *Le Mépris* is a film that stages the transmission of meaning, as it passes from text to text, from text to image, from that which is quoted and that which quotes. This transmission is by no means perfect; noise is a constant presence within the system, a writerly presence that affirms its status as an object of interpretation. This noise works at the level of translation, though the figure of Francesca, and it works through the Hollywood system, in the conflicts of interpretation we witness throughout the film. More importantly, *Le Mépris* frustrates any coherent theory of adaptation, the quantitative bias of adaptation theory crumbles under the piecemeal and, at times, arbitrary, correspondence between the film and the 'original' text. Godard once famously replied to the question as to whether he thought a film should have a beginning, middle and end, with, 'yes, but not necessarily in that order.'[25] *Le Mépris*'s relentless citations – filmic, literary, and so on – and its frequent display of the cinematic means of production shows how beginnings, middles and ends can be absorbed within a wider cultural and technological continuum. By both blurring the status of the camera's narratorial position and confusing the provenance of the work, Godard examines how beginnings, middles and ends can become infinitely rearranged.

## Notes

1 Roland Barthes, *Image-Music-Text*, trans. Stephen Heath (London: Fontana, 1977), 146.

2 Brian McFarlane, *Novel to Film: An Introduction to the Theory of Adaptation* (Oxford: Oxford University Press, 1996), 11.
3 See, Thomas Leitch, 'Adaptation Studies at a Crossroads', *Adaptation* 1:1 (2008), 63–77, for an overview of recent developments in adaptation studies.
4 See, John M. Desmond and Peter Hawkes, *Adaptation: Studying Film and Literature* (New York: McGraw-Hill, 2005), 51.
5 Geoffrey Wagner, *The Novel and the Cinema* (Cranbury: Associated University Presses, 1975), 222–6.
6 Dudley Andrew, *Concepts in Film Theory* (Oxford: Oxford University Press, 1984), 98–104.
7 Deborah Cartmell, 'From Text to Screen: Introduction', in *Adaptations: From Text to Screen, Screen to Text* eds. Deborah Cartmell and Imelda Whelehan (London: Routledge, 1999), 24.
8 Brian McFarlane, *Novel to Film*, 25.
9 Julia Kristeva, 'The Bounded Text', in *Desire in Language: A Semiotic Approach to Literature and Art*, trans. Thomas Gora, Alice Jardine, and Leon S. Roudiez, ed. Leon S. Roudiez (Columbia: Columbia University Press, 1980), 36.
10 Julia Kristeva, 'Word, Dialogue, and Novel', 71, 72.
11 Julia Kristeva, 'Word, Dialogue, and Novel', 66.
12 André Bazin, 'Adaptation, or the Cinema as Digest', in *Bazin at Work: Major Essays and Reviews From the Forties and Fifties*, trans. Alain Piette and Bert Cardullo, ed. Bert Cardullo (London: Routledge, 1997), 46.
13 Roland Barthes, *S/Z*, trans. Richard Howard (London: Jonathan Cape, 1975), 4.
14 Roland Barthes, *S/Z*, 5.
15 David Bordwell, *Narration in Fiction Film* (London: Routledge, 1997), 153.
16 Displaying all the problems witnessed in Adaptation Studies, Jacques Aumont argues that *Le Mépris* adapts so much of Moravia's novel that it is Godard's only adaptation in the Hollywood style, see, Jacques Aumont, 'The Fall of the Gods: Jean-Luc Godard's *Le Mépris* (1963)', in *French Film: Texts and Contexts*, eds Susan Hayward and Ginette Vincendeau (London: Routledge, 2000), 185.
17 Alberto Moravia, *Contempt*, Angus Davidson (New York: New York Review Books, 1999), 23. Hereafter cited in the text as *C*.
18 See Bordwell, *Narration in Fiction Film*, (London: Routledge, 1997), 226.
19 Robert Stam, *Literature Through Film: Realism, Magic, and the Art of Adaptation* (Oxford: Blackwell, 2005), 282.
20 See, David Bordwell, *Narration in Fiction Film* (London: Routledge, 1997), 160.
21 H. Porter Abbott, *The Cambridge Introduction to Narrative* (Cambridge: Cambridge University Press, 2008), 80.
22 David Bordwell, *Narration in Fiction Film* (London: Routledge, 1997), 12.
23 Nicholas Paige, 'Bardot and Godard in 1963 (Historicizing the Postmodern Image)', *Representations* 88 (2004), 6.
24 Paige, 'Bardot and Godard in 1963 (Historicizing the Postmodern Image)', 18.
25 Quoted in Kenneth Tynan, 'Verdict on Cannes' *The Observer*, 22 May 1966, 24.

RICHARD MARTIN

# 'So What Am I Supposed To Do?' Thoughts of Action and Actions of Thought in Godard's *Contempt*

Action, *n.*
1. The process or condition of acting or doing. [. . .]
4. The thing represented as done in a drama; the event or series of events, real or imaginary, forming the subject of a fable, poem, or other composition. [. . .]
6. d. Used as a film director's word of command.

*Oxford English Dictionary*

The time for action is over; the time for reflection has just begun.

Jean-Luc Godard, *Le Petit Soldat*

From its opening moments to the elegiac final scene, Jean-Luc Godard's *Contempt* (1963) continuously wrestles with the meaning of action in both life and cinema. Its initial sequence culminates in Godard's cinematographer Raoul Coutard rotating his camera to face the audience – a sinister, uncanny movement that immediately creates suspicion over where the film's true action is taking place. The film finishes with Godard himself barking orders at the crew of Fritz Lang's adaptation of *The Odyssey*. His last commands are the banal, everyday terms of the film-set, but are deeply suggestive in the context of both *Contempt* and Godard's career as a whole: 'Action! [. . .] Silence!'

In two distinct sections, this essay will investigate the tensions between action and thought in *Contempt*. Firstly, a close reading of the film will establish how the constant negotiation between intellectual reasoning and physical decisiveness, most prominently displayed in the character of Paul Javal, becomes its central theme. The second half of the essay will place this analysis in the context of Godard's other work in this period, principally *Le Petit Soldat* (1960), *Pierrot Le Fou* (1965) and *La Chinoise* (1967), to demonstrate that the notion of effective action – whether in politics or personal relations – was a persistent concern for the director. Assessing these films alongside *Contempt*, it becomes clear that a tension between action and thought is inherent within Godard's own conception of cinema and the film-making process. *Contempt* itself is a bold attempt to represent those essential struggles on-screen.

## 'Do you mind if your wife comes along with me?'

Doubt and indecision are the key features of *Contempt*'s primary source, Alberto Moravia's 1954 novel *Il Disprezzo* (published in English as *A Ghost at Noon* and later as *Contempt*). Here, Riccardo Molteni's relentless questioning of his wife is combined with severe anxiety over his script-writing career. 'I was all nerves and imagination, morbidly sensitive and complex', the narrator confesses.[1] Crucially, he concludes: 'I was, in effect, the civilised man who, in a primitive situation – a crime in which honour is concerned – refuses to resort to the knife'.[2]

While Godard rejects the first-person subjectivity of *Il Disprezzo*, Riccardo's strained notion of civilisation, a battle between intellectual reasoning and primal passion, remains at the forefront of his cinematic adaptation. It is Paul Javal who most epitomises Godard's representation of a world in which instinct and spontaneity clash with reason and contemplation. Analysed in turn, Paul's relationships with three figures – his wife Camille, the American producer Jerry Prokosch and the mythical Ulysses (as portrayed in Lang's film within *Contempt*) – offer a complex interrogation of the notion of action.

The first manifestation of this theme comes in the marital disharmony at the heart of the film, a conflict which centres upon an unresolved ambiguity concerning active and passive behaviour. In short, does Paul actively push his wife towards Jerry, or is he passive while she is seduced by the American? This question is never formally settled and its inherent contradictions are immediately established when the three characters first meet, early in *Contempt*. As Camille rushes to greet Paul within the studio complex, they are momentarily divided, anticipating their later separation, by Jerry's speeding red sports car, an emblem of crude masculine vitality. It is Paul who eagerly introduces Camille to Jerry and, significantly, it is *he* who ushers her into the producer's car, despite her palpable discomfort. In a parallel scene in Capri, Jerry brazenly asks, 'Do you mind if your wife comes along with me?' Paul's reply – 'No, go ahead, Camille. Go ahead' – is again dangerously accommodating. As they race off in a red speedboat, another symbol of impulsive motion, the camera closes in on Paul, but the image offers us nothing. The action resonates, yet Godard refuses to provide any simple psychological explanation.

Three years earlier, in *Le Petit Soldat*, Godard filmed a female Front de Libération Nationale (FLN) activist reading a Mao Tse-Tung pamphlet emblazoned with the famous expression, 'A Single Spark Can Start a Prairie Fire'. In *Contempt*, the scene involving Jerry's car creates an irreversible rupture in Paul and Camille's relationship: this spark sets fire to an entire marriage. Godard underscores the significance of the incident by replaying it three times during *Contempt* within a series of flashback montage sequences.

This brief event, which barely seems to register as a conscious action on Paul's behalf, confirms Godard's belief that 'there are moments in life when you can't turn back, when something breaks definitively'.[3] It is useful here to relate Godard's admiration for Ingmar Bergman, which focuses on the Swedish director as a film-maker of the *moment*, who can produce 'a twenty-fourth of a second which is metamorphosed and prolonged for an hour and a half'.[4] Godard takes a similar approach in *Contempt*: the reverberations from a single mistake, a momentary hesitation that transformed an entire relationship, are extended throughout the next eighty minutes. 'I don't know whether or not you can 'see' contempt or scorn', explained Godard. 'Perhaps one can only capture the instant during which it exercises its force – after a certain gesture, after a misunderstanding'.[5] Paul's action, or inaction, surrounding Camille's trip in Jerry's car is the moment when certain contemptuous forces – Paul's carelessness for his marriage and his wife's disappointed response – begin to make their presence felt. Godard thus mimics Moravia's novel in investing this sequence with a 'decisive importance'.[6]

The metamorphosis and prolongation of this episode manifests itself in an aftermath of exhausting and painful conversations which further highlight Paul's failure to take decisive action. During the lengthy scene in the couple's apartment – thirty minutes of screen-time which features almost no conventional cinematic action, composed as it is of looping arguments within a banal domestic environment – Paul's persistent questioning of Camille, and uncertainty over his career, unveils a chronic inability to make firm, lasting choices. What is more, he again seems determined to drive his wife towards Jerry. Even when she repeatedly refuses, he continues to ask her to accompany him to Capri, where the producer will be prowling. When Paul finally concludes, 'you don't love me anymore', it is as if he is willing the words to be true. Such a self-defeating action is akin to picking a scab until the wound becomes permanent.

Towards the end of the apartment scene, we hear revealing statements from Paul and Camille during the longest and most important of *Contempt*'s three flashback sequences. The voiceovers in this montage are the only examples of Godard allowing us direct access to the thoughts of his characters and therefore provide a rare insight into the psychology of their relationship. Moreover, the following extracts are spoken at both the beginning and the end of the montage, heightening their resonance:

> Paul: 'I'd thought Camille might leave me and how terrible it would be. Now it's happening'.
>
> Camille: 'Everything used to happen instinctively in a shared ecstasy. Things happened with impetuous, enchanted, mad spontaneity'.

Paul's account demonstrates how his thoughts anticipated reality and suggests an unconscious will to destroy the relationship; Camille's lament reveals how thought itself was absent during the relationship's happiest moments, when actions were simple and uninhibited. Paul, as Toby Mussman points out, is always 'a second or so behind the life-pulse [...] because he has to stop and think about it'.[7] Notably, the argument in the living room is followed by Paul retreating to his study to write. The passage he subsequently reads aloud – 'Paula had to make a decision, which was contrary to her nature' – is full of dramatic irony and intimates that, at some level, he is aware of his own crippling weakness.

*Contempt*'s domestic dilemmas are illustrative of wider social concerns, as Godard suggested in 1963: 'I feel that misunderstandings represent a modern phenomenon'.[8] Violence is posited as one potentially decisive solution to contemporary confusions; a tool of mediation between the fear of inaction and more satisfactory deeds. As *Le Petit Soldat* and *Pierrot Le Fou* confirm, the use of violence has continually fascinated Godard. In *Contempt*, Paul's efforts to wrestle back control of his life increasingly lead him to consider acts of brutality. The film's guiding moral force, Fritz Lang – a classical god watching over the characters and a cinematic god in the eyes of Godard, his self-appointed assistant – is quoted by Camille: 'one must rebel when one is trapped by circumstances or convention'. Murder, however, is directly ruled out as a solution, with the explanation that 'the crime of passion is pointless'. Yet, impotent elsewhere, Paul begins to physically abuse Camille and to carry a gun. It is an essentially 'pointless' act, nonetheless, a gesture that his wavering courage cannot sustain. Indeed, Paul's emasculation is completed in Capri through verbal taunts ('I kissed Prokosch, yet you still dither over doing the script [...] You're not a man') and symbolic castration (Camille removes the bullets from his weapon). Paradoxically, while Camille earlier complained of Paul's roughness ('you frighten me') and also criticised Jerry's abuse of Francesca, it is with the more aggressive man that she eventually leaves the island. Godard, it seems, is fully aware of the ambivalent desires that surround physical strength. Paul, we should note, is asleep when Camille leaves – further exhibition, if it was needed, of his passivity at the most critical moments in their relationship.

As Elena del Rio has noted, 'passivity does not mean absence of action. On the contrary, the passive synthesis implies a heightening of the power one has of being acted upon, no less a power than acting itself'.[9] It is in this light that we can best assess Paul's relationship with Jerry. In direct contrast to Paul, Jerry is strident and dynamic – a man of fast action, not delaying thought. Their encounters are distinguished by the producer's physical and verbal dominance: he grabs Paul's tie, places his arms upon his shoulders and directs his movements ('you stay right there'). Whilst Paul is consistently forced into concessions, Jerry takes the initiative. The American constantly *makes things happen* – asking Camille to visit Capri contributes to the Javals' marital disharmony, while his phone call to their apartment (even after he has expressly asked Paul to contact him) interrupts the couple's conciliatory kiss – and yet his dominance is also dependent on Paul's complicity and natural subservience. By asking 'So what am I supposed to do?', Paul *chooses* to place himself under the control of his opponent.

Instinctive as he is, Jerry is also another example of a character whose actions are guided by text – in this case, a small red book of trite quotations. Furthermore, his relationship with Paul is not entirely one-sided. For example, Jerry feels intellectually humiliated by his rival's lecture on cinematic history, a demonstration of Paul's learning brought into action. *Contempt*'s exploration of modern tensions between thought and action specifically question whether such intellectual prowess can be combined with vigorous, influential decision-making. By 1967 and *La Chinoise*, Godard demonstrates how a very different little red book unites effective political action with intellectual integrity.

Perhaps, Godard implies, the solution is to be found in self-knowledge. Jerry is highly aware of his limitations and alters the terms of battle to suit his own strengths. Indeed, the first quotation he reads out begins, 'To know what one does not know is the gift of a superior spirit'. It is revealing that when Jerry explains why he is so sure Paul will rewrite the script – 'someone told me you have a *very* beautiful wife' – this explicit link between financial and sexual reward is not questioned by Paul. Jerry assumes the world functions according to his own primal values – money, physical prowess and sheer willpower – and is angered when others (such as Lang) present an alternative mode of being. Paul, by contrast, acquiesces and damages both his career and his marriage in the process. He never openly confronts his sexual rival over the issue of infidelity – indeed, possibly Paul never admits it to himself – preferring to use false alibis (an intellectual disgust with script-writing, the demands of modern capitalism) to justify his actions.

In a film in which questions of language, translation and nationality are omnipresent, it seems inevitable that we view Jerry's actions as representative of a dynamic, uncomplicated, yet intellectually inferior American society. Paul, by this reading, is symbolic of a post-war France paralysed by fear and indecision. Eric Rohmer's comments, as part of a 1957 discussion in *Cahiers du Cinéma*, certainly support this perspective:

> In twenty years the face of France has changed very little, while America and even Italy have evolved a lot. Nothing new has altered the French way of life since, let's say, 1930, except what reaches us from America.[10]

Of course, what had reached Rohmer, and the rest of the critics and film-makers surrounding *Cahiers du Cinéma* (including Godard), was Hollywood cinema. Their attraction centred upon the vitality and immediacy of vision demonstrated by American films. Equally, as André Bazin noted, American cinema showed American society as it wanted to be seen: spontaneous and dynamic.[11] Significantly, and in direct contrast to the era's prevailing critical viewpoint, this dynamism was praised by Godard and his colleagues, rather than frowned upon as a lesser version of European cinema. Raymond Durgnat claims that Hollywood, in the shape of Howard Hawks (a key early influence on Godard), appealed to French thinkers as a corrective to European culture and its 'contempt for decision, action, efficacy, simplicity.'[12] Here, again, it is easy to draw parallels with Godard's representation of Jerry and Paul. Thomas Elsaesser neatly summarises the broader appeal that the United States held:

> What French intellectuals expected from things American were works of fiction that could serve as creative models, representative of their own situation and embodying specifically modern tensions – between intellect and emotion, action and reflection, consciousness and instinct, choice and spontaneity.[13]

As we have seen, Elsaesser's list of modern tensions constitute the central themes of *Contempt*, yet it must be stated that by 1963 Godard was complaining about Hollywood's current direction: 'what was good about American cinema was that it was spontaneous, at whatever level; now it's become calculated. The American character is not that well-suited to calculation'.[14] Such comments explain why, despite his assertiveness, Jerry is portrayed as such an unpleasant, dangerous and ridiculous individual. In Godard's eyes, he represents a breed of American who is undermining the great art form that Hollywood once helped to define.

It is also evident that *Contempt* places the opposition between action and thought beyond national boundaries and into more classical terms. In particular, Godard emphasises the stark contrast between Paul's uncertainty and the decisiveness of Ulysses. In Lang's adaptation, Homer's hero is shown clambering over rocks with sword in hand and firing arrows at suitors while Penelope looks on in admiration. As the German director confirms, Ulysses is 'a simple, cunning and daring man', rather than a 'modern neurotic' – the latter description surely belonging to Paul instead. Paul, nevertheless, clings to a different interpretation of *The Odyssey*, one initially forced upon him by Jerry and later modified to justify his own actions concerning Camille – that is, a story of 'a simple woman' who misinterprets her husband's trust.

In the closing stages of *Contempt*, Godard brings Ulysses (or, at least, his cinematic representative) and Paul face-to-face. It is, in many ways, the quintessential image of the film: a final confrontation between the classical and the modern, framed specifically in terms of action and contemplation. The robed warrior meets the suited intellectual, with a classical setting of rocks and the sea behind them and the modern paraphernalia of the film-set in the foreground. The pair are separated by the peeling wall of a modernist architectural icon, the Casa Malaparte, famed for its relationship with the timeless landscape surrounding it. And yet, as the sword is raised and their eyes meet, what is the result of this encounter? Nothing, it appears, but blank incomprehension, without a note of recognition, before they continue on their separate journeys. Action and thought are irreconcilable.

## 'I'll finish the film. Always finish what you've begun'

In *The Radical Faces of Godard and Bertolucci* (1995), Yosefa Loshitzky claims that the French film-maker's career contains a distinct shift from its early focus on tough action heroes, influenced by American cinema, to the contemplative students and intellectuals of his work in the latter stages of the 1960s.[15] This is a rather misleading argument. For, from the outset of his career, Godard has frequently portrayed characters, especially men, who are divided, uncertain and conflicted by thoughts of action, as an analysis of *Le Petit Soldat* reveals.

*Le Petit Soldat* belongs in a tradition of texts, perhaps best epitomised by John Osborne's *Look Back In Anger* (1956), that present protagonists striving for the political certainties of the past, most notably those of the Spanish Civil War, within a corrupt and festering post-war world. As Godard confirms, 'I wanted to show a confused mind in a confused situation'.[16] That confused mind belongs to Bruno Forestier, a man who is tortured both literally and metaphorically in the film. In a perfect illustration of his torn nature, and of the conflict between mind and body that haunts *Contempt* too, Bruno stares at his reflection in a mirror, before asking: 'What do you think is more important, the inside or the outside?' He then opens up the mirror (it is merely the façade of a bathroom cabinet) to remove a gun from the shelf inside, emphasising how a killer's cool exterior can mask internal violence. Later, when wavering over his assassination assignment, Bruno's narration is instructive:

> My friend Raoul Coutard called it 'the pain in the backside law'. Every time I was ready to fire, something happened to stop me. Every time the coast was clear, I hesitated. And once again, it was too late.

By attributing this quotation to his own camera operator, the man who literally 'shoots' the action for him, Godard links the instinctive requirements of assassination with his own concept of a spontaneous approach to film-making.

What complicates matters is that Godard by no means privileges the consequences of decisive action in the rest of the film. If the brutish Jerry is the face of forceful deeds in *Contempt*, *Le Petit Soldat* shows us in graphic detail the 'monotonous and sad' reality of politically-motivated torture. Bruno may equivocate over murder, a delay that results in his own suffering, as well as the eventual death of his lover Véronica, but would it be better, Godard asks, if he was more vigorous in his actions, like the FLN terrorists who carry out brutal violence in domestic settings? Notably, and in typically playful style, it is Godard himself who brings in the apparatus used in Bruno's torture; of course, as director, he is already ultimately 'responsible' for these scenes of terror. We are left to ponder whether Bruno, unsuccessful even in his attempts at suicide, is correct in his assertion that 'strength is superior to intelligence'. After all, as with Paul in *Contempt*, it is this most indecisive of characters who has survived at the end of the film. The ambiguities of the situation are better captured by the protagonist's mournful conclusion: 'It's terrible these days. If you remain calm and do nothing, you get into trouble for doing nothing. So, you end up doing things you don't believe in'.

*Pierrot Le Fou* presents an even more convincing case for the impossibility of both lasting personal relationships and effective political change. Indeed, the film's pessimism persuaded Godard's sister that her brother was contemplating suicide.[17] Ferdinand's increasing introspection, highlighted by a retreat into his personal journal, is combined with Marianne's more restless uncertainty: 'What shall we do? I don't know what to do', she repeatedly tells him. Violence is again a mediating force: the film is flooded with images of warfare and torture. The couple's tragic situation supports Peter Harcourt's claim that Godard's characters 'long for the reality of meaningful action outside themselves and yet long to retreat into a world away from action, a world given up to the celebration of personal love'.[18] It is this predicament, with Ferdinand and Marianne trapped eternally between thought and action, that adds particular resonance to the American director Samuel Fuller's assertion in *Pierrot Le Fou* that 'films are like battlegrounds'. For Godard, the battle is being fought continuously, but the usual rules of engagement have changed: it is the very terms of the conflict that are in permanent dispute and neither action nor thought can produce a decisive breakthrough. Resolution is impossible and this stalemate is so all-encompassing, so self-defeating, that Ferdinand's last available avenue is suicide. Ironically, his only dynamic act is wrapping dynamite around his head; even then, he regrets his actions immediately. The scene is almost Beckettian in its representation of active paralysis.

As the 1960s progressed, however, Godard's films more explicitly promoted a form of collective political action that denigrated individual thought. Those who remain conflicted, such as Henri in *La Chinoise*, are now definitively the outsiders. As Godard himself became more closely aligned with radical leftist groups, his activities within revolutionary circles were reflected in the slogans littering his films. *La Chinoise*, in particular, features explicit conversations about the effectiveness and justice of political violence, most notably in the scene with Francis Jeanson. The philosopher tells a Maoist revolutionary (and, we might surmise, Godard himself) that with terrorism, 'you're heading towards a dead-end'.

Such contradictions and complexities are fought out in a much more implicit manner in Godard's earlier films, yet they remain inherent within his very conception of cinema. It is evident that tensions between thought and action are built into the fabric of Godard's film-making and that *Contempt* self-consciously endeavours to represent these conflicts. Godard's approach to film-making is based around spontaneity, born out by the speed at which he has worked – *Une Femme Mariée* (1964), for instance, was made in just one month.[19] His early films, with their immense self-confidence and dazzling technical displays, not only reflect such spontaneity, but are also directly contingent on coincidences, surprises and accidents. Paradoxically, this reliance on the impulsive moment had been carefully thought-out in advance. For Godard, the camera does not simply passively absorb reality; it actively creates it. In 1962, he stated: 'the cinema is interesting because *it seizes life* and the mortal aspect of it' and thus a director's role is to orchestrate the specific action needed to 'capture the definitive by chance'.[20] Richard Roud has astutely noted Godard's methods for achieving this, most notably his 'perpetual contrast between movement and stasis: an ever-changing balance between his use of brief takes and long ones, and the building up of these takes into sequences of varying length'.[21] This 'perpetual contrast' is simultaneously a playful conception of cinema's possibilities, a fierce intellectual argument about cinematic representation and, most of all, a stark manifestation of Godard's notion of reality.

From its uncanny opening onwards, *Contempt* openly discusses the choices available to a director in his creation of reality; how thoughts of action can become actions of thought. Consider, for example, the scene in which Paul and Camille sit facing each other in their apartment, divided by a large lamp. As the conversation develops and their marriage unravels, the camera tracks slowly back and forth between their faces. However, its movements refuse to match the timing of the words spoken by the characters. This denial of the conventional, unbreakable link between sound and image not only accurately reflects the discordance at the heart of the Javals' relationship; it also foregrounds a consideration of the very terms of representation. Furthermore, potentially the most spectacular piece of action in *Contempt*, the climactic car crash involving Camille and Jerry, is not even shown by Godard: it occurs as sound only, as the text of Camille's letter slides across the screen, before the bloody aftermath appears. Again, this decision, which apparently amazed Fritz Lang, resists normal cinematic expectations.[22] In constantly making us aware of the camera and the action he has taken, Godard ensures it is impossible to be passive while watching *Contempt*: actions of thought are required from a spectator. Indeed, as Mussman points out, 'Godard's demands upon his audience are so wide-ranging and thorough-going that they result in nothing less than what amounts to a collaboration in what is being projected onto the screen'.[23] Given this combination of spontaneous decision-making with a rigorous theoretical stance, Mussman's labelling of Godard as 'an action-intellectual' seems wholly appropriate.[24]

*Contempt*, however, also highlights an alternative approach to film-making. Lang's version of *The Odyssey* demonstrates the suffocating slowness of epic productions. The script is constantly re-written beneath the overbearing shadow of its literary source, while a money-obsessed producer anxiously observes an unwieldy crew in an exotic location – all of which form the very antithesis to Godard's own methods. Conversely, though, this parody takes place within arguably Godard's most conventional film – a picture which necessitated a formal script, his largest budget, a world-famous actress and a disagreeable American producer (Joe Levine). *Contempt*, therefore, acts as the perfect illustration of what Jacques Rancière calls the 'thwarted fable' of film-making: the 'indecisiveness at the heart of its artistic nature', wherein cinema can only be faithful to its aesthetic potential by use of a technical nature that immediately constrains it.[25] Lang, the only character in *Contempt* who seems to have found a balance between intellectual pursuits and the prosaic demands of living, is rueful but accepting of this predicament: 'I'll finish the film. Always finish what you've begun'.

As Wheeler Winston Dixon notes, Paul finishes *Contempt* as 'a drifting husk, bereft of direction'.[26] If we doubt whether Paul will ever fulfil his creative ambitions in writing for the theatre, *Contempt* constituted Godard's sixth feature film in just four years. Thus, any tentative similarities between the director and his lead character, from their identical hats to their disintegrating marriages, remain negligible. The final shots of *Contempt* see Godard furiously organising Lang's shoot, a physical manifestation of his command 'Action!' His last demand – a call for 'Silence!' – is again doubled-edged: this is both the end of his film and a nod toward the death of the studio system; it also represents the beginning of a shot for *The Odyssey* (a film we can never see) and the initiation of a critical discourse surrounding *Contempt* (an argument we can never settle). In Godard's own words, *Contempt* 'proves in 149 shots that in the cinema as in life there is no secret, nothing to elucidate, merely the need to live – and to make films'.[27] Thought and action are therefore united in the only reality possible for Godard: that of the cinema.

## Notes

1 Alberto Moravia, *Contempt*, trans. Angus Davidson (New York: New York Review of Books, 1999), 49.
2 Ibid., 230.
3 Yvonne Baby, 'Shipwrecked People from the Modern World: Interview with Jean-Luc Godard on *Le Mépris*', in Royal S. Brown (ed.), *Focus on Godard* (Englewood Cliffs: Spectrum, 1972), 39.
4 Richard Roud, *Jean-Luc Godard* (London: Thames and Hudson, 1970), 75.
5 Baby, 'Shipwrecked People from the Modern World', 39.
6 Moravia, *Contempt*, 5.
7 Toby Mussman, 'Notes on *Contempt*', in Toby Mussman (ed.), *Jean-Luc Godard: A Critical Anthology* (New York: E. P. Dutton, 1968), 155.
8 Baby, 'Shipwrecked People from the Modern World', 39.

9 Elena del Rio, 'Alchemies of Thought in Godard's Cinema: Deleuze and Merleau-Ponty', *SubStance* 34.3 (2005), 71.
10 'Six Characters in Search of *Auteurs*: A Discussion about the French Cinema', trans. Liz Heron, in *Cahiers du Cinéma; The 1950s: Neo-Realism, Hollywood, New Wave*, ed. Jim Hillier (Cambridge: Harvard University Press, 1985), 44.
11 André Bazin, 'La Politique des Auteurs', *Cahiers du Cinéma*, 70 (April 1957). Reprinted in Peter Graham (ed.), *The New Wave* (London: Secker and Warburg, 1968), 143.
12 Raymond Durgnat, *Films and Feelings* (London: Faber, 1967), 82.
13 Thomas Elsaesser, *European Cinema: Face to Face With Hollywood* (Amsterdam: Amsterdam University Press, 2005), 243.
14 'Questions about American Cinema', in *Cahiers du Cinéma; 1960–1968: New Wave, New Cinema, Re-evaluating Hollywood*, ed. Jim Hillier (Cambridge: Harvard University Press, 1986), 177.
15 Yosefa Loshitzky, *The Radical Faces of Godard and Bertolucci* (Detroit: Wayne State University Press, 1995), 136.
16 Roud, *Jean-Luc Godard*, 39.
17 Colin MacCabe, *Godard: A Portrait of the Artist at 70* (London: Bloomsbury, 2004), 170.
18 Peter Harcourt, *Six European Directors: Essays on the Meaning of Film Style* (London: Penguin, 1974), 233.
19 MacCabe, *Godard*, 164.
20 Mussman, 'Notes on *Contempt*', 152; Harcourt, *Six European Directors*, 212.
21 Roud, *Jean-Luc Godard*, 13.
22 Wheeler Winston Dixon, *The Films of Jean-Luc Godard* (New York: State University of New York Press, 1997), 51.
23 Toby Mussman, 'Introductory Notes', in Mussman (ed.), *Jean-Luc Godard*, 21.
24 Ibid., 23.
25 Jacques Rancière, *Film Fables*, trans. Emiliano Battista (Oxford: Berg, 2006), 11.
26 Dixon, *The Films of Jean-Luc Godard*, 48.
27 *'Le Mépris'*, in *Godard on Godard*, eds. Tom Milne and Jean Narboni (London: Da Capo Press, 1986), 201.

JONATHAN GROSS

# In Translation: re-conceptualising "home" through *Le Mépris* and its source texts

Godard's *Le Mépris* (*Contempt*) is full of translations. At the centre of the narrative is the collaboration of a French scriptwriter, a German director and an American producer: working through an Italian translator to adapt *The Odyssey* from page to screen. Moreover, *Le Mépris* is itself an adaptation of another work, Alberto Moravia's novel *A Ghost At Noon*. To translate is 'to turn from one language into another.'[1] But an older meaning, 'to bear, convey, or remove from one person, place or condition to another, to transfer, transport',[2] indicates a further and important feature of the term: that the activity of translation is inextricably linked to notions of place. The need for translation arises from the condition of foreignness: from being abroad, out of place, away from home. This essay suggests that the prominence of acts of translation in *Le Mépris* is best understood by reading the film through the category of "home", particularly in relation to themes of subjectivity, artistic creation and – perhaps most importantly for Godard – the history of cinema itself. I begin by examining *The Odyssey* and *A Ghost at Noon*, showing that both texts are structured around their own particular conceptualisation of home. In the second half of the essay I then examine the ways in which Godard's film both exemplifies and subverts the notions of home identified in these two source texts. I thereby show how a reading of *Le Mépris* through this category provides an account of some of the most striking features of the film, and suggests, in turn, what implications *Le Mépris* may have for the notion of home as a category of thought.

## The Odyssey

The word "home" can indicate both a specific physical location and a more metaphorically located place of belonging. The *Oxford English Dictionary (OED)* offers the following definition:

> **home**: [. . .] **2. a.** A dwelling-place, house, abode; the fixed residence of a family or household; the seat of domestic life and interests; one's own house; the dwelling in which one habitually lives, or which one regards as one's proper abode. Sometimes including the members of a family collectively [. . .].[3]

Here we see some of the possible physical conditions of home: a particular building in which one dwells, and which may also be characterised by the physical presence of other members of one's family. And yet, the specification of home as that which 'one regards as one's proper abode' also indicates the more metaphorical modes of homeliness. This is elaborated by a further definition offered by the *OED*, in which the non-physical conditions of being-at-home emerge even more strongly:

> **home**: [. . .] **5.** A place, region, or state to which one properly belongs, in which one's affections centre, or where one finds refuge, rest, or satisfaction.[4]

Such places may often require specific physical conditions – such as the familiarity, fixity and comfort of a particular house. But, of course, refuge, rest, satisfaction and belonging are seldom straightforwardly physical states. Instead, they are conditioned by the full range of psychosocial conditions within which humans think and experience.

We may ask, then, what does it mean for Odysseus to return home? *The Odyssey* is perhaps the earliest and best known of all homecomings. But is the home that Odysseus returns to a straightforwardly physical place? He says to Alcinous, 'Once let me see my own estate, my servants, and the high roof of my great house, and I shall be content to breathe my last.'[5] And yet when arriving at Ithaca, by no means does Odysseus proceed directly to his house. He initially spends a considerable time in the hut of the swineherd Eumaeus, before traveling to town incognito, concealing his identity even when inside his own hall, and even from Penelope. An analysis of the delay between his arrival at Ithaca and his full 'homecoming' indicates the nature of home operating within *The Odyssey*.

Early in the epic, one of the suitors, Leocritus, explains that:

> Even if Odysseus of Ithaca himself came back and took it into his head to drive us nobles from the palace because he found us dining in his hall, his wife would have no joy of his return, much as she may have missed him. Then and there he'd come to an ignominious end, fighting alone against so many.[6]

Even though Odysseus may arrive at his estate, there are obstacles to re-establishing himself as its master. This is most obviously the case with the suitors who are occupying his house, but they are merely one amongst several potential dangers. A repeated presence in the poem is the story of Agamemnon's murder by his wife Clytemnestra upon his return from Troy.[7] Agamemnon's spirit tells Odysseus: 'I had certainly expected a joyful welcome from my children and my servants when I reached my home', and warns his friend, 'Never be too trustful even of your wife [. . .] Do not sail openly into port when you reach your home country.'[8] Once in Ithaca, Odysseus, dressed as a beggar, proceeds to test everyone he meets – including his son and wife – in order to establish their loyalty to him. Whether or not Odysseus would really, having seen his palace, be 'content to breathe his last', his homecoming is incomplete until he has ensured the loyalty of his family and servants.

But whilst Odysseus needs to confirm his family's loyalty in order to establish his house as a home, his homecoming is also very much the return to a particular physical place. When Penelope questions the disguised Odysseus about himself, she asks, 'who are you and where do you come from? What is your city and who are your parents?'[9] The four queries serve as a single question, each essentially asking who he is, with geographical origin and parentage the essential constituents of identity. Later, testing the stranger's claim that he is indeed Odysseus, the final confirmation that Penelope seeks is the secret of their marriage bed: that it is constructed around the trunk of a tree. It is by this intimate knowledge that Odysseus's identity is fully and finally established. It is only at this moment that Penelope is convinced of who he is, and that they are reunited. Homer describes Penelope's confirmation of Odysseus's identity as 'like the moment when the blissful land is seen by struggling sailors'.[10] It is only via the site of his marriage bed, where his identity can be fully established by his wife, that Odysseus finally completes his homecoming.

Identity and a physically located family abode are thereby inextricably linked. They are also the source of life's greatest pleasures, as Odysseus repeatedly says that to be a wanderer is 'a miserable existence',[11] and 'a man's fatherland and his parents are what he holds sweetest'.[12] Telemachus makes a "mini-Odyssey" in search of his father, and Nancy Sultan explains that he is the typical figure of a:

> *neos* [youth] who has little social power because he lacks military or travel experience. He gains respect and makes his first break into the realm of manhood by successfully completing his dangerous nautical foray.[13]

But whilst Telemachus enters manhood through his journey, it is only at the site of family residence that his identity is fully established, as 'he finally comes of age with his first battle against the suitors, and with his final disposal of [...] the traitorous household servants.'[14] Just as Odysseus's identity is only confirmed at the specific site of his marital bed, so Telemachus establishes himself by helping purge his father's house. In each case, whilst journeying may be a constitutive feature of Odysseus's and Telemachus's manhood, it is only at the site of family origin that full identity is secured.

## A Ghost at Noon

We find, then, that whilst Odysseus's homecoming is a return to a literal, physical place, it is also a process by which he reestablishes his identity. In Moravia's *A Ghost at Noon*, the text is also structured around the relationship between identity and home, but whereas in Homer this is a home regained, in Moravia this is a home irredeemably lost.

There are two dominant notions of home operating in *A Ghost At Noon*. Most conspicuously, there is the sense of bourgeois homeliness that Riccardo repeatedly attributes to his wife. 'With Emila, love of home had all the characteristics of a passion',[15] he says, and he illustrates this 'domestic spirit' from the earliest, happiest days of their marriage, right up until their relationship has collapsed. Even in spaces not her own, nor by any means permanent residences, Emilia "makes herself at home". Riccardo says that at the beginning of the marriage, when living in a rented room, Emilia:

> wanted to deceive herself into believing that she had a home of her own; and that, lacking her own household furniture, she wanted at least to infuse her own concentrated domestic spirit into the lodging-house-keeper's shabby utensils. There were always flowers in a vase on my desk; my papers were always arranged with loving, inviting orderliness, as though to encourage me to work and guarantee me the greatest possible privacy and quietness[16]

Emilia makes a home by establishing physical order and comfort within the space she occupies. Even at Battista's villa, Riccardo observes her home-making impulse at work, as 'I noticed signs of her domestic instinct – the dressing-gown carefully laid out on the armchair at the foot of the bed, the slippers placed neatly beside it'.[17] But whilst Emilia maintains her capacity to make herself at home through physical means regardless of the condition of her marriage, at the centre of the novel is Riccardo's struggle to respond to the loss of love and increasing contempt that his wife feels for him. This can be understood as a struggle with a kind of psychic homelessness.

Riccardo describes his response to signs that Emilia no longer loves him in terms of destabilisation, 'as if, all of a sudden, I had felt the ground give way beneath my feet.'[18] Later in the novel, when the relationship has completely collapsed, the undermining is even greater:

> I had, in truth, been suddenly uprooted, and my roots, like those of the tree, were up in the air, and the sweet earth, Emilia, who had nourished them with her love, was far away from my roots[19]

But the uprooting effect on Riccardo is not straightforwardly the effect of the break up of a marriage. Quite specifically, the novel succeeds in maintaining an uncertainty as to the causes of Emilia's loss of love and her growing feeling of contempt. Repeatedly Riccardo seeks to explain and understand the change in his relations with his wife. But his attempts fail, until he comes to the point at which he recognises that:

> She had no wish to explain herself, or perhaps, [. . .] she was unable to do so. Clearly some reason for her contempt existed; but it was not so clear that she was able to indicate it precisely.[20]

Given that he cannot understand the changes in Emilia, and she seemingly cannot explain them even to herself, for Riccardo, Emilia's feelings increasingly constitute an inscrutable judgment on his deepest nature. He is forced into a condition of intense self analysis as he attempts to find the explanation in himself: the effect of which is to destabilise his sense of identity. Consequently, the period before the change in Emilia's feelings acquires prelapsarian qualities in Riccardo's account of it:

> a complete, profound, harmony of the senses was accompanied by a kind of numbness – or should I say silence? – of the mind which, in such circumstances, causes an entire suspension of judgment and looks only to love for any estimate of the beloved person [. . .] we did not judge: we loved each other[21]

Riccardo's description manifests a nostalgia for a childlike condition in which not only is one unconditionally loved, but the mind is untroubled by demands of introspection. This harmonious state contrasts directly with the psychic dissonance that he suffers as a result of Emilia's contempt. Here we see most clearly the psychoanalytic parallels of his situation, as his account of the transition from love to its absence is analogous to psychoanalytic descriptions of the unavoidable developmental process through which children lose their seemingly symbiotic relationship with their mother, but cannot understand the loss.

And yet Riccardo's sense of uprootedness expresses itself not only in direct relation to Emilia. It also concerns his employment, and "modernity" at large. He repeatedly notes that his dissatisfaction with scriptwriting becomes intermingled with feelings about his marriage: that once Emilia's love is gone he feels no motivation for the work. Moreover, as the relationship disintegrates, Riccardo becomes almost absurdly and naïvely hostile to the cinema in contrast to his nostalgia for his 'beloved theatre'. He declares:

> my ideal is to write for the theatre!. . .Why am I unable to do so? Because the world today is so constructed that no one can do what he would like to do, and he is forced, instead, to do what others wish him to do. . .Because the question of money always intrudes – into what we do, into what we are, into what we wish to become, into our highest aspirations, even into our relations with the people we love![22]

His personal discontentment takes on the form of a generalised complaint against modern society. It can be seen particularly in his attitude to the project of adapting *The Odyssey*. He says of Joyce's *Ulysses* that it embraces 'everything modern, in other words debased, degraded, reduced to our own miserable stature'.[23] Revealingly, his complaint against the film director Rhinegold's psychoanalytic version of *The Odyssey* is that it was 'no longer that miraculous adventure, the discovery of the Mediterranean, in humanity's fantastic infancy, but had become the interior drama of a modern man entangled in the contradictions of a psychosis.' Riccardo's attitudes and hopes increasingly resemble childhood fantasies – or perhaps, rather, adult fantasies *of* childhood - as he indicates his desire to return to conditions in which actions and words are simple, not undermined by society's intrusions, nor by the mind's mysterious interiorities. His nostalgia can be characterised as utopian – in the ambiguous sense of the word's etymology – as he desires a 'good-place' that is also a 'no-place'.[24] This becomes most apparent in the final few pages of the novel. Here Riccardo admits that:

> in order to have the Emilia I loved and to bring it about that she judged me for what I was, I should have to carry her away from the world in which she lived and introduce her into a world as simple as herself, as genuine as herself, a world in which money did not count and in which language had retained its integrity, a world – as Rhinegold has pointed out to me – after which I could aspire, certainly, but which did not in fact exist.[25]

We see in Riccardo a desire for a place in which he 'properly belongs, in which one's affections centre, or where one finds refuge, rest, or satisfaction'. And this is not a physical place. It is a set of psychological conditions which have been removed, if they ever fully existed, by Emilia's changed feelings, and which Riccardo can never recover. By the end of the novel Riccardo has been left, in a profound sense, homeless.

## *Le Mépris*

*The Odyssey* presents a notion of home according to which identity is established by a return to origins, whilst *A Ghost at Noon* depicts the psychic homelessness of a psychologised "modern" man. By contrast, *Le Mépris* negotiates between the two: between the commitment to origins as the site of coherent selfhood, and, on the other hand, the abandonment of belief that these origins are still habitable.

In several respects *Le Mépris* is strikingly undermining of homeliness. The central domestic scene of the film culminates in Camille's declaration that she despises her husband, a pronouncement punctuated by her physical departure from the flat. During this scene, the breakdown of their home together is presented by several means. The couple's movements around the apartment indicate their mutual isolation. For example, at exactly the moment Paul enters the living room, Camille exits the shot by another route. Most shots are composed with sections of two or three rooms visible within the frame simultaneously: so when at one point Paul picks up the phone in the bedroom, there are two doors and the hallway between him and the camera, presenting a relationship in which domestic space is not a medium of intimacy, but of separation. The scene is also marked by conversations across these separating thresholds, with questions through doorways left unanswered, and threads of speech abandoned. At one point Camille begins to literally destroy the domestic infrastructure, dropping and smashing a set of plates; whilst Paul never takes off his hat, even in the bath, suggesting he is a traveler: not settled, not at home. Cumulatively, and culminating in Camille's departure from the flat, the homeliness of this inhabited space is thoroughly undercut.

But the sense of homelessness extends not only to the domestic sphere. Early in the film, Paul comments to Francesca on the emptiness of the Cinecittà Studios and she explains that 'Jerry has sent almost everyone home. Italian film is in a bad way.' The studio is presented as a place of activity and life which has now been abandoned. Such is the emptiness of the place that initially Francesca and Paul cannot locate the producer, Prokosch. When they do find him, he enters in a state of anguished nostalgia: not only lamenting the demise of the studio, but, in doing so, seeming to act out the films that might have been made there. He declaims, 'only yesterday there were kings here', in the style of the epic films of the 1950s and early 1960s. When he goes on to declare, 'this is my lost kingdom', Francesca translates his words as, 'It's the end of the film industry'. This mistranslation is indicative of a key feature of *Le Mépris*: that notions of home and homelessness operate not primarily in regards to the domestic, but in relation to cinema itself.

This can be observed through a comparison of nostalgia in the film and the novel. Whilst in *A Ghost at Noon* Riccardo is nostalgic for the theatre – this being the desired alternative to the unhappy world of cinema in which he has to work – in *Le Mépris,* if Paul displays any nostalgia at all it is a sadness for a lost world of film making. In reply to Jerry's question as to what interests him in making a film version of *The Odyssey,* Paul replies, 'Maybe this can be different from the modern films that I hate. We must get back to Griffith and Chaplin...To the great days of United Artists.' Even more revealingly, whilst in Moravia it is Riccardo who celebrates and defends Homer against psychoanalytic reinterpretation, in *Le Mépris* these attitudes are expressed by Fritz Lang. It is primarily Lang rather than Paul who becomes not only the mouthpiece, but also the object, of the film's nostalgia. In these two changes from the novel, we can see how the centre of the film's interest moves from the psychological questions explored by Moravia to questions about the nature and history of cinema itself. The home for which the film displays nostalgia is less the prelapsarian state of love than the history of cinema, of which Lang was a part, and which he represents.

The word "nostalgia" is often employed with a broad meaning, indicating '**2.** Regret or sorrowful longing for the conditions of a past age'.[26] But the term's Greek etymology, 'return home+pain', indicates a more specific usage: '**1.** A form of melancholia caused by prolonged absence from one's home or country; severe homesickness'.[27] We have identified a kind of nostalgia in *Le Mépris*. But exactly what kind of 'homesickness' is this? There are moments in which Godard thoroughly undermines the impulse to return to origins, as in Prokosch's ridiculous claim that, 'The Odyssey needs a German director: everyone knows that a German, Schlieman, discovered Troy.' Here the desire to return to origins is made absurd. But *Le Mépris* is by no means simply caught between nostalgic attachment and the rejection of any possible return. Instead, one of the most striking features of the film is the way it orientates itself to "source texts": playfully integrating and constructing itself through a plethora of references, quotations, and transformations of language.

Translations abound. And yet, whilst the difficulties of effective communication are readily suggestive of psychological exile, foreignness, and the pain of homelessness – as they are in *A Ghost at Noon* – in *Le Mépris* language problems operate rather differently. The fuller version of the first definition of *translation* given above is, 'To turn from one language into another; to change into another language retaining the sense'.[28] If the despairing, even tragic possibilities of the trope of (mis)translation lie in the inability to successfully 'retain the sense', *Le Mépris* not only finds humour in this inability, but perhaps even celebrates it for the opportunities it affords.

To understand this, we can observe that *Le Mépris* is full of references to other films. These include *Johnny Guitar*, which Paul tells Camille is showing at the Regina; *Viaggio in Italia*, advertised above the entrance to the cinema where the Naussica audition is being held; and 'the Dietrich western [that Paul and Camille] saw on Friday', but to which Lang prefers '*M*'. Moreover, the characters behave with an acute consciousness not only of other films, but also of themselves as performers. Camille "dresses-up" in a wig and temporarily conceals Brigitte Bardot's iconic blonde hair (whilst referencing Anna Karina's look in Godard's *Vivre sa vie* (1962) and the haircut made famous by Louise Brookes); Paul says he is 'Dean Martin in *Some Came Running*'; and Fritz Lang is Fritz Lang. The film's various modes and subtleties of reference and performance also extend from the visual to the verbal, as the characters freely quote to each other from such diverse sources of wisdom as Dante, Brecht, Prokosch's pocket book of epigrams, and Fritz Lang. *Le Mépris* overlays quotations and references in a way that does not straightforwardly lament the distance from the original. Enjoyment is taken in playing with and mingling these texts. The inevitable failure to reach the "original", to fully 'retain the sense', frees the film to invoke and transform.

Rather than seeking to establish a sense of definite origin or identity, or despairing at its homelessness, by taking a highly self-conscious, sometimes ironical, approach to language, to source texts, to various figures of western culture, to the history of cinema, and to cinematic form, *Le Mépris* utilises the inevitability of foreignness. If the film manifests both a degree of psychic homelessness that emanates from Camille and Paul's failing marriage and the depiction of their flat, and also a nostalgic sadness attached to Fritz Lang and the ailing film industry, yet *Le Mépris'* invocation of the texts it translates suggests a way of orienting oneself to the notion of home that is neither reactionary nor despairing. The film enacts a way of making oneself at home in psycho-historical conditions in which returning to a singular origin and establishing a fixed identity has become untenable. It suggests making oneself at home by first embracing the fact that homes have to be made anew repeatedly – from the resources available within the political, historical and artistic mélange we inhabit – and are never simply returned to.

## Conclusion

Between the epochs of Homer and Moravia, the conceptualisation of home as a stable, recoverable place suffered a metaphysical, psychological and political onslaught. Not only are the gods not in harmony with Riccardo, they no longer even exist to hear his appeal. Moreover, Freud indicated that humans can never be entirely at home with themselves, because the possibility of that frightening transformation of the homely (*das heimliche*) into the unhomely (*das unheimliche*) – the uncanny – is not an external threat. Psychic comfort is endangered by the return of the familiar, the return of the repressed, and Freud illustrates this by showing that the German word *heimlich* – what is familiar and agreeable – can also mean what is concealed and kept out of sight: *heimlich's* meaning morphing into its opposite, *unheimlich*.[29] After Freud the homely contains within itself the possibility of its transformation into the unhomely, as living with the unconscious we bear an internal 'foreign body that prohibits an untroubled self-identity'.[30] Already assaulted by these changes in metaphysical and psychological understanding, any conceptualisation of home that requires definite origins or immutable selfhoods also faces the challenges posed by the histories of colonialism, fascism and post-war nationalism; and the mass displacements, diasporas and cultural encounters that followed.

So what are our options, at least in terms of the *attitude* to home we might take? Are we necessarily as homeless as Moravia's "modern man", Riccardo? Are we left with a choice only between some pragmatic form of mourning or melancholia: living with our loss, but experiencing the world (in mourning) or ourselves (in melancholia) as impoverished? What attitude to the (im)possibility of home might my reading of *Le Mépris* suggest?

*Le Mépris* is not directly concerned with the "divided subject", nor with nationalism. Instead, it is in part a response to the apparent collapse of cinema production, the ambitions of film as mass art, and, with them, many of the hopes of the Nouvelle Vague. And yet, we can also understand the film as a response to wider psycho-historical conditions in which we are all, to varying degrees, exiles. *Le Mépris* enacts a particular attitude to a modernity in which there is no stable home to which to return. This film, as we have seen, exemplifies a kind of freedom that Kristeva has described:

> since he belongs to nothing the foreigner can feel as appertaining to everything, to the entire tradition, and that weightlessness in the infinity of cultures and legacies gives him the extravagant ease to innovate.[31]

There is no Ithaca to look upon at the end of *Le Mépris*. But – with the bitter-sweet freedom of exile – Godard and his collaborators had by then already translated a range of materials and made a new location: creating a film which revels in the history of cinema, creates something strikingly distinctive with that history, whilst mourning its loss.

Home may no longer be conceivable as a 'fixed residence', and yet human desires for home recur. Perhaps we can reconceptualise the spaces 'where one finds refuge, rest, or satisfaction' without subscribing to the forms of delusion and violence that so easily accompany attempts to re-establish homes in conditions of psychic and social exile. This would be to understand homes not as sites of origin or permanent refuge, but as cultural spaces: homes produced through shared practice; provisional but habitable spaces of history and value. Whilst we cannot exactly live inside a film beyond the two hours of its duration, nor exactly can we be at home in the world. And perhaps films, like other spaces we create together, provide both examples and resources with which to create the provisional structures of mourning, memory, pleasure and opportunity in which to live.

## Notes

1 *The Oxford English Dictionary*, Second Edition (Oxford: Clarendon Press, reprinted 1991).
2 Ibid.
3 Ibid.
4 Ibid.
5 Homer, *The Odyssey*, trans. E.V. Rieu (London: Penguin, 2003), 90.
6 Ibid., 21.
7 See, for example, ibid., 33 and 311–13.
8 Ibid., 151.
9 Ibid., 225.
10 Ibid., 306.
11 Ibid., 254.
12 Ibid., 111.
13 Nancy Sultan, *Exile and the Poetics of Loss in Greek Tradition* (Lanham, Boulder; New York, Oxford: Rowman & Littlefield, 1999), 25.
14 Ibid., 25.
15 Alberto Moravia, *A Ghost At Noon*, trans. Angus Davidson (Middlesex: Penguin, reprinted 1976), 15.

16 Ibid., 15.
17 Ibid., 176.
18 Ibid., 13.
19 Ibid., 195.
20 Ibid., 181.
21 Ibid., 5.
22 Ibid., 142.
23 Ibid., 170.
24 *The Oxford English Dictionary.*
25 Moravia, *A Ghost At Noon*, 91.
26 *The Oxford English Dictionary.*
27 Ibid.
28 Ibid.
29 Sigmund Freud, *The Uncanny*, trans. David McLintock (London: Penguin, 2003).
30 Elizabeth Bronfen, *Home in Hollywood: The Imaginary Geography of Cinema* (New York: Columbia University Press, 2004), 244.
31 Julia Kristeva, *Strangers to Ourselves*, trans. Leon S. Roudiez (New York: Columbia University Press, 1991), 32.

WALTER STABB

# Producing Prokosch: Godard, Levine, Palance, Minnelli and a lament to lost Hollywood

At every stage of Jean Luc Godard's career, from his days as a critic on *Cahiers du cinéma* through the Nouvelle Vague and the Dziga Vertov Group to the later self sufficient modes of production, he has been concerned with the relation between art industry and commerce in film. One might therefore expect that his portrait of a film producer will be complex and nuanced. However, it has been widely accepted in both popular and academic writing on *Le Mépris* that Godard 'sent up Levine as the ignorant Hollywood mogul'[1] and that the character Jerome Prokosch represents 'a stab in the back of *Contempt*'s legendary vulgarian producer Joseph E. Levine.'[2] This approach to the film has left many to dismiss Prokosch as a completely negative caricature – a personal character assassination and gross stereotype constructed from on-set conflicts. This reading denies Godard's wider analysis of the crisis in cinema during the 1950s and early 1960s in *Le Mépris* and his reconfiguration of Vincente Minnelli's work in melodrama that sought to explore the collapsing Hollywood studio system in *The Bad and The Beautiful* and *Two Weeks in Another Town*. It also undermines the virility and agency that Jack Palance brings to the role, which contrasts sharply with the central protagonist Paul's 'weakness, his irresoluteness, his lack of self.'[3]

By 1963 Levine was a prominent American show business figure featuring occasionally in national publications like *Esquire, Fortune* and *Life* and satirised in *Mad* magazine as 'Joe LeVenal – Hollywood's latest producing genius.'[4] Famous as the distributor of a series of *Hercules* peplum imports and as a bombastic marketeer Levine was also the subject of the Maysles brothers' documentary *Showman* released in 1963. François Truffaut asserts Godard 'always displayed a distain for total fiction.'[5] Godard himself states '*reportage* is only interesting when it's inserted in fiction, but fiction is interesting only when it is verified by reality.'[6] *Le Mépris*' central protagonists operate on the boundaries of fiction; Fritz Lang plays the great director Fritz Lang and Bardot is always as much Bardot as she is Camille. In the same way there are links between Levine and Prokosch. Early in the film we are told that "Joe Levine is calling at one from New York" and given Levine's high profile

Godard may well have decided prior to production that he would insert some of his own producer's identity into Prokosch. However to over emphasise the link, as I believe film historians have done, is to deny other elements in Godard's creation of Prokosch.

Levine as a distributor turned producer was acutely aware of the economics of film markets. In 1961 he went on record in *Variety* stating 'I'm going heavy on the art-type stuff. The market is saturated with spears and sandals and I've had it.'[7] He followed through on this statement, purchasing and selling *Two Women*, a film which would serve as a production package template for *Le Mépris* as it featured a celebrated European director Vittorio de Sica, voluptuous beauty Sophia Loren and was based on a novel by Alberto Moravia. Levine's attempt to replicate this formula in production to reap box office return seems less intelligent in the light of Godard's criticism:

> he's doing a picture with me and Moravia, but he hasn't even read the script; he spent a million dollars to buy a novel he never read, to make it directed by me. I've made five pictures since *Breathless*; he never asked to see them, and doesn't know which direction I'm going now.[8]

The conditions on set were primed for disaster. In his 1961 foray into the production of *Sodom and Gomorrah* Levine had lost heavily and felt Robert Aldrich had gone out of control, he was therefore anxious to keep the film on budget and schedule. This was extremely difficult for Godard who was a director acutely aware that 'the important thing in film is to control the money'.[9] For Godard it was crucial to be able 'to spend money according to your own rhythm and pleasure' as with control of a film budget 'real power isn't in the amount but in the time in which it is spent.'[10] This principle of production and desire for freedom would bring the director and producer into conflict.

Prior to *Le Mépris* Godard had eschewed conventional industrial cinema pre-production practice, preferring to create dialogue and scenes on a day-by-day basis and raise money on the basis of scenarios, journalistic articles and ideas rather than formed scripts thereby encouraging spontaneity and improvisation. According to Coutard:

> [Godard] had difficulty making this film. That was because it adhered closely to cinematographic traditions. Since the Americans were involved, we had to follow a set work schedule. We had to send a daily telex to Levine to assure him that things were going to plan. That really upset Godard, since he couldn't do exactly as he wanted. Sometimes he didn't feel like doing anything at all. We were working with an Italian crew, and the Italians were eager for us to work within the American system.[11]

When considering to what degree Levine's production methods frustrated Godard's creativity and how this encouraged the notion of Prokosch as purely a negative stereotype of the Hollywood film type it is crucial to acknowledge that 'crisis was Godard's method of invention'.[12] Godard used his difficulties with Levine and his opposing views of cinema to inform his own exploration of the industry's crisis and charge it with emotion. Godard draws heavily on Minnelli's *Two Weeks in Another Town* in *Le Mépris*. Godard rated the film, which was widely received as a critical failure, in his top ten of 1963[13] and would have been aware that during its production 'Minelli and his collaborators found themselves caught up in the same kinds of dilemmas *Two Weeks* was documenting'[14]... 'it is a film in which creative impotence and exhaustion are at the very core of the project' ... 'they are also its subject.'[15] It is easy to believe that Godard used his frustrations with Levine's enforcement of conventional film production methods and the difficulties this caused between himself and his Italian crew to mould Prokosch as a force of incessant demands. Prokosch attempts to command Paul and Camille, repeatedly insisting on responses to his forceful questions – 'Yes or No?' However, while this belligerent behaviour may link back to Levine its primary function in the film is to expose the emotional stasis Paul and Camille appear trapped in from their mechanical opening scene.

It was not just the battles with Levine that Godard channelled into the character of Prokosch. With the large budget and transnational production also came notable stars Brigitte Bardot and Jack Palance. It has been claimed that the genius of Godard's direction in *Le Mépris* is his ability to channel Bardot's contempt for the film's production process into her role as Camille. A similar analysis can apply to Godard's antagonistic relationship with Palance. Godard draws both a seething frustration and a bristling restraint out of Palance. Brought to life in Prokosch are the confidence and presence of Palance the star, tempered by an underlying discomfort, best exemplified by the flow of languages on both set and screen that leave Palance alienated.

Palance was unhappy with Bardot's lack of punctuality on the first day of filming and with the fact that she was treated with more deference than him.[16] He also 'took great exception'[17] to Godard's minimal and logistical direction. Eventually 'Palance would speak to neither Godard nor Bitsch, who were both fluent in English, but insisted on addressing all his remarks to the Italian grip, who knew no English at all.'[18] It is Godard's managing of Palance's star quality on screen and star attitude on set that makes the role so complex and intriguing. Godard thrives on the challenge of Palance, responding with direction that advances his art. Palance's machismo, anger and threat are on display as he stalks across the frame, apparent in his thrusting, griping physical performance. The unwanted physical attention that both Paul and Camille receive from Prokosch in the opening act of the film demands a response and it is this demand which brings the contempt in their relationship to the surface.

In contrast to the painfully indecisive Paul, Prokosch is a man of action. Lang's withering comment, 'Finally Jerry you get a taste of Greek culture' as Prokosch throws the film canister across the projection room, is mocking. The action nonetheless provides a moment of vitality. The adopted pose of the discus thrower provides an allusion to the statue of Neptune who reappears in the aftermath of Prokosch's aggressive departure from Cinecitta with Camille at his side and again as he roars off to the villa with Camille in a speedboat. The statues remind us repeatedly of the various layers of adaptation in the film, and one of these links back to Palance's performance in *The Big Knife*. As Charlie Castle he acts out a similar spinning motion in celebration of his wife's promise to return to the marital home. Godard is playing up to Palance's screen persona as a man of agency. These repetitions of movement draw on his physicality. In *The Big Knife* the amoral Hollywood studio boss gropes Palance and blackmails him, demanding his signature on a movie contract stating, 'I need your physical presence on the lot. I need your body.' Levine was a producer very much aware that sex sells. As an importer of peplum movies in which 'one of the dominant themes is virile strength'[19] and distributor of the Hercules movies in which muscle men and ex-boxers feature, he was fully aware of the box office pull of the muscular male body. In these films, 'directors patently linger on their actors' physique, often highlighting it by drawing a parallel with statues.'[20] Palance, a former boxer, functions as an object of sexual desire. His figure, like Bardot's, is framed by the shapes of the classical statues that appear in the film and remind the viewer of his oiled massages and revealing boxing attire in *The Big Knife*.

Goddard's restrained and choreographed direction of Palance in the role of Prokosch also invites a reading of the character as a classical protagonist. Minnelli had encouraged Kirk Douglas to play down the physical aspect of his performance as producer Jonathon Shields in *The Bad and the Beautiful* so that it could operate as restrained force 'he played against his strength.'... 'You knew the strength was there.'[21] Like Prokosch, Shields is 'an active and goal-orientated protagonist in the classical sense.'[22] Minnelli, clearly an influence on Godard, employs 'a "queer" modernist aesthetic'[23] from within the opulence of the Hollywood studio system. 'Minnelli's cinema is not primarily one of the face or of the object seen in isolation, but a cinema of the body in motion'...'The body itself, however, does not give the appearance of enjoying unrestricted freedom but frequently seems to be moving in a choreographed fashion, the action carefully staged in accordance with the precise framing and movements of the camera.'[24] Godard redeploys the techniques of Minnelli's classical Hollywood cinema in his presentation of Prokosch to provide a commentary on its demise that cannot be simplistically dismissed as completely negative.

The notion of the heroic Prokosch, the peplum Hercules, is apparent in Godard's framing. Prokosch is introduced on the stage of Cinecitta. Filmed from a low angle below the 'Teatro 6' sign he exudes a dramatic authority and is framed in a style much closer to the spectacular hero than the other weak protagonists. A recurrent visual motif in *Le Mepris* is the decentred figure pacing the borders of the wide cinemascope frame. Palance's imposing body appears less marginal even when the shot is fairly wide. On Capri as Prokosch asks 'Why don't you come up to the villa with me and leave them here to talk' he is again filmed from a low angle. In this medium close-up the epic landscape is subordinate to him in the frame, his arms point, grip and swing across the cliffs. In the following scene by contrast the camera tilts up the cliff as it holds Paul as a tiny figure in the top left of the frame, dwarfed by the epic Mediterranean location. The voice-over has Lang's comment, 'A producer can be a friend to a director. But Prokosch isn't a real producer. He's a dictator.'

In these two scenes we can see both the importance of Godard's framing and of Lang's commentary in the construction of Prokosch for the viewer. Fritz Lang devised much of his own dialogue in the film[25] and is the character that provides the most commentary on Prokosch. Lang's statements construct the link between fascism and the producers' economic dominance in the film. Godard links Paul to Ulysses through Ulysses's equally pathetic relationship to the environment in the film within a film. The classic Hollywood or peplum film would typically present its hero at key moments in a series of low angled close-ups, resplendent at the centre of the frame. In contrast Ulysses's arrival at Ithaca is filmed as a long shot. Over a relatively extended duration we see the small figure struggling to climb out of the sea and up the rocks, 'the film within the film fails to bring the Homeric ethos to life.'[26] Prokosch manages to manipulate Paul into his reading of Ulysses and Penelope as a failed marriage. Godard's framing collapses Paul and Ulysses into what Lang resists, a 'modern day neurotic' neither in harmony with his environment or like Prokosch able to dominate it with theatrical poses and loud pronouncements.

*The Bad and the Beautiful* opens with a camera run through, the director mounted on the crane ends the shot with his lens pointing at the viewer. This scene is self-consciously echoed in the opening title sequence of *Le Mépris*. Godard's reworking of Minelli is consciously less celebratory: Hollywood's golden age is over and the huge lot at MGM has been substituted for an almost deserted Cinecitta, but both scenes clearly convey that these are movies about 'picture people' and cinema. *The Bad and the Beautiful*'s Jonathon Shields, a star making and insatiably success driven producer played by Kirk Douglas is 'a composite of people – David Selznick and so on, an awful lot of people, the legends of Hollywood.'[27] In three acts Shields deceitfully shapes the careers of a director, a star and a writer within the Hollywood studio system for his own ends. Like Prokosch, who malevolently predicts Paul will sign a contract to write for him because he has 'a very beautiful wife' and manipulates the couple to gain time alone with Camille, Shields influences and dominates his collaborators. Interestingly Shields's machiavellian actions benefit the director, star and writer and the film closes with them all agreeing to make another picture. The conclusion in this self-penned MGM love letter is that the nefarious and commercially minded producer brings success to the artists around him and that he is necessary in film production. The same conclusion is not drawn in *Le Mépris*. The camaraderie of the studio system is lost to 'the ephemeral, artificial and polyglot style of transnational cinema, here represented primarily by Prokosch.'[28] However Prokosch's machinations cannot be taken as purely an obstacle to creativity and Godard's reconfiguring of Minnelli's mildly critical attempts to grapple with the end of a golden age of production mean that the role of producer still maintains some sense of positive dynamism. Lang, the films voice of reason, accepts compromise and the working conditions of Prokosch and Hollyood. Despite repeating Brecht's reservations and criticisms of its practice of lies he is aware of the producer's necessary role.

In *Le Mépris* 'The story is of the cinema, of the battle between a producer who represents the claims of commerce and a director who is struggling for his art'.[29] In a fascinating collapse of art and reality Prokosch demands more nudity and spectacle in the film within the film whilst Levine was 'furious' and demanded re-shoots on *Le Mépris* because he 'wanted to see Bardot's bottom.'[30] But the simplicity of relying on the paradigm; art/commerce, good/bad, director/producer denies both the collaborative complexity of cinema production and Godard's intelligence as a director who uses the character Prokosch not just to ridicule the role of the producer but to contrast and examine the failings of the 'artists' on set. 'The re-shoots demonstrate clearly the difficulty of any aesthetic which would simply oppose creativity and money'[31] because upon their completion Godard commented 'I find it very good now, and I wouldn't remove it. There was some talk once about removing it for the censors, and I wouldn't have it.'[32] For Godard the commercially minded problems posed by Prokosch became an opportunity not a constraint, a typical response in Godard's filmmaking practice. This is informative when considering his presentation of Prokosch, however problematic the character's ignorance and commercial desires appear, his dynamism operates as catalyst in forcing the resolution to Camille and Paul's unhappy relationship and in pushing onwards the production of the Odyssey.

It is clear that Prokosch represents the commercial and the industrial in contrast to the artistic in *Le Mépris*. Introduced on the huge film lot of Cinecitta, an Italian remaking of the dream factory, Prokosch drives the revving sports car that separates Camille from her husband and traverses the sea in a roaring speedboat where Ulysses flounders. It is also apparent that he is ridiculous, his manner is pompous and hyper-masculine, his assertions incorrect and inappropriate. The barren studio lot presents the crisis of cinema and Prokosch meets his death on the highway. *Le Mépris* was Godard's first venture into the realm of big budget film making and through a solely negative reading of Prokosch many have drawn the conclusion that in terms of his own filmmaking Godard rejects completely the industrial model of film production and the big budget, Hollywood, transnational project. Retrospective writing often takes this angle, Godard is described as a director 'who loved American films as much as he hated the industry that produced them'[33] and Michel Marie argues that a:

> strong aversion to big budgets remained a constant concern of the New Wave. When . . . Godard agreed to compromise by hiring the most expensive star for an international co-production with producers Joe Levine and Carlo Ponti he repeatedly stated that, discounting the salary paid to the main actress, his was a low budget film.[34]

This analysis seems to ignore the huge benefits and possibilities that Godard saw major financial backing could bring to his cinema in the form of star power and technical freedom. Godard claims he embraced the star factor of Bardot as a means of gaining a bigger budget. 'I could not have made the picture without her; it was an expensive one, and I wanted to do it in an expensive way.'. . . 'I thought I was going to have a lot of trouble with her. I considered her the *real* producer. But on the contrary it was very nice with her, and I have trouble with the producer.'[35] This could be dismissed as hype for the film. According to Coutard Bardot's 'courtiers'[36] in hair, make-up and wardrobe did cause problems on set, but at least in terms of pre-production and her use as a tool for generating investment Godard appears excited by the prospect of Bardot the star.

Godard is quite clear when he asserts 'I always say, the dream of the New Wave when you've been a critic and then you start making films, my personal dream, then and now, has been to make a film with a five-million-dollar budget on the larger MGM set in Hollywood.'[37] 'People have always believed that the Nouvelle Vague means cheap films as opposed to expensive ones. It is, simply, good film as opposed to bad film'.[38] To ignore the cinematic possibility that a big production offered and to read into Prokosch nothing more than an outright rejection of industrial film practice is to ignore Godard's love of Hollywood cinema. Discussing the character Paul's reverence for the cinema of Griffith and Chaplin 'in the United Artist days' Godard states 'Today we are in the habit of separating the industrial side of the cinema from the aesthetic side. In that period the two were not separated. I think that they ought not to be.'[39] Coutard's extremely technical camera work, *Le Mépris*' opulent locations, the star players and the cinemascope print all represent a tension between economic opportunity and artistic restriction that the character Prokosch embodies.

Reading Prokosch as a negative character because he is an American producer in opposition to the European artists Lang and Paul is to fail to acknowledge the nuances of Godard's characterisation. Godard's real biting critique of new modes of production are not related to nationality, transnational production, industrial studio production or independent producers per se, they relate to an increasing ignorance of the real knowledge of cinema amongst producers and an increasing emphasis on commerce and marketing rather than creative producing. Godard states:

> An editor knows the kind of paper his book is printed on. A producer doesn't know the kind of film his films are made on . . . He is not interested in what he is doing, He is only interested in giving money, selling it, and getting money again.[40] . . . when Zukor and Goldwyn were beginning they knew *everything*. When you speak to old producers, they knew they were *fighting*.[41]

Levine was a working producer on *Le Mépris* but he was more widely recognised as a distributor, what Sam Fuller would call a 'movie mujik'. . .'men who serve camouflaged arsenic-on-the-rocks to neophyte writers and directors.'[42] Godard differentiates between the two:

> I shouldn't speak too negatively about producers, because the exploiters and distributors are much worse. The producers, basically, are like us . . . They're on the same side we are . . . The distributors and exploiters are not in love with what they're doing. I have never seen a producer who didn't love his metier. Compared to an exploiter, the worst producer is a poet. Mad, imbecilic, innocent, or stupid – they are sympathetic[43]

Godard detests the functionaries that show no passion for cinema and are not even engaged enough to understand the projects they are packaging, 'They are financiers, capitalists, interested in manufacturing their product. But I don't blame them for being merchandisers, I blame them for not knowing what their merchandise is'.[44]

In *Le Mépris* Godard is lamenting the drop in Hollywood production standards that have arisen with the collapse of the studio system. Minnelli's *The Bad and the Beautiful* and *Two Weeks* provide rich inspiration for Godard because they operate as 'both a work of mourning for the creative producer of the past while pointing toward the creative director of the present and future'[45]. In *Le Mépris* Lang turns down Levine's offer of a drink by saying, 'include me out, as Goldwyn a "real" Hollywood producer once said.' 'Godard characterises Prokosch through the pomposity of his manner and diction'[46] most clearly in his pronouncements of faux Confucian wisdom redolent of Californian self-help nonsense. 'To know that one does not know is the gift of a superior spirit. Not to know and to think that one does know is a mistake.' This statement links to Godard's comment on the changing landscape of cinema production 'At one time, they [producers] didn't know that they knew nothing. Today they know it.'. . .'80 percent of the producers are completely lost. They can't succeed with either big films or little intellectual films. Everything is mixed up.'[47] For Godard what has been lost in the new confused landscape of cinema is the craft in the industry, the popular art in the commercial. 'The producers say: Godard – he talks about Joyce, metaphysics, or painting, but he will always have with him a commercial side. I don't say this at all – I don't see two things, I only see one.'[48] Godard and Levine hold oppositional ideas about cinema:

> When I was discussing Le Mepris with Joseph Levine, I learned little by little that the words did not mean the same things to him that they did to me. – He is not a bad man; but I am not either. When we say "picture" it doesn't mean the same thing at all.[49]

However to conclude from this that Prokosch is a completely negative caricature of Levine ignores Godard's collaboration with Palance and Lang, the influence of Minnelli and the complex themes in *Le Mépris*. It also does a disservice to Godard's invention and subtlety of characterisation and is refuted by the director when he states, 'I try now to be a little closer to my characters, not to judge them, not to propose them as models (good or bad), not making up types or prototypes which correspond to specific ideas.'[50]

## Notes

1 'Godard Only Knows' *Observer* Review Section, 26th November 2000, 11.
2 James Verniere, 'Film Shows Comic Contempt For The Industry', *The Boston Herald*, 22nd August, 1997, 4.
3 Toby Mussman, 'Notes on *Contempt*', in *Jean-Luc Godard: A Critical Anthology*, ed. Toby Mussman (New York: Dutton, 1968), 156.
4 A.T. McKenna, 'Joseph E. Levine: Showmanship, Reputation and Industrial Practice 1945–1977' (Nottingham University Ph.D Dissertation, 2008), 120.
5 François Truffaut, 'Interview with François Truffaut (Second Extract)', first published in *Cahiers du cinéma 138* (1962), in *The New Wave*, ed. Peter Graham (London: Secker & Warburg/BFI Education, 1968), 104.
6 Jean Luc Godard, 'An Interview With Jean-Luc Godard by *Cahiers du cinéma*', first published in *Cahiers du cinéma* (December 1962), trans. Rose Kaplin, in *Jean-Luc Godard: A Critical Anthology*, ed. Toby Mussman (New York: Dutton, 1968), 119.
7 'Levine Going Arty; To Drop Spear and Sandals Films,' *Variety* (November 1961) quoted in McKenna, 'Joseph E. Levine', 182.
8 Herbet Feinstein, 'An Interview with Jean-Luc Godard', in *Film Quarterly*, vol.17, no.3 (Spring, 1964) University of California Press. http://www.jstor.org/pss/1210901 (Accessed 19/12/2009), 9.
9 Jean Luc Godard, *Introduction à une veritable histoire du cinéma* (Paris: Éditions Albatros, 1980), 174. quoted in Colin MacCabe, *Godard: A Portrait of the Artist at 70* (London: Bloomsbury, 2004), 34.
10 Godard, *Introduction à une veritable histoire du cinéma*, quoted in MacCabe, *Godard*, 34.

11 Raoul Coutard, Interview on *Contempt* DVD, Criterion Collection, 2002.
12 Colin MacCabe, *Godard: A Portrait of the Artist at 70* (London: Bloomsbury, 2004), 150.
13 'Godard's Top Ten – *Cahiers du cinéma*'. http://www.theauteurs.com/topics/1200 (Accessed 20/12/2009).
14 Joe McElhaney, *The Death of Classical Cinema: Hitchcock, Lang, Minnelli* (New York: State University of New York, 2006), 142.
15 McElhaney, *The Death of Classical Cinema*, 143.
16 Coutard, Interview on *Contempt* DVD.
17 MacCabe, *Godard*, 152.
18 MacCabe, *Godard*, 152.
19 Michèle Lagney, 'Popular Taste: The Peplum', in *Popular European Cinema*. ed. Richard Dyer & Ginette Vincendeau (London & New York: Routledge, 1992), 171.
20 Lagney, 'Popular Taste: The Peplum', 171.
21 Richard Schnickel, *The Men Who Made The Movies* (Chicago: Ivan R. Dee, 1975), 261.
22 McElhaney, *The Death of Classical Cinema*, 169.
23 McElhaney, *The Death of Classical Cinema*, 162.
24 McElhaney, *The Death of Classical Cinema*, 162.
25 Gretchen Berg, 'The Viennese Night: A Fritz Lang Confession Part Two', first published in *Cahiers du cinéma* (June 1966), in *Fritz Lang Interviews*, ed. Barry Keith Grant (University Press of Mississippi, 2003), 66.
26 Robert Stam, Audio Commentary on *Contempt* DVD, Criterion Collection, 2002.
27 Schnickel, *The Men Who Made The Movies*, 261.
28 Robert Stam, Audio Commentary on *Contempt* DVD.
29 MacCabe, *Godard*, 156.
30 Coutard, Interview on *Contempt* DVD.
31 MacCabe, *Godard*, 154.
32 Jean Luc Godard & François Chalais, 'Le Coup De Mepris' *Cinepanorama* (1964) on *Contempt* DVD, Criterion Collection, 2002.
33 'Godard Only Knows' *Observer* Review Section, 26th November 2000, 11.
34 Michel Marie, *The French New Wave: An Artistic School*, trans. Richard Neupert. (Oxford: Blackwell, 2003), 57.
35 Feinstein, 'An Interview with Jean-Luc Godard', 9.
36 Coutard, Interview on *Contempt* DVD.
37 Godard & Chalais, 'Le Coup De Mepris' on *Contempt* DVD.
38 Godard, 'An Interview', in *Jean-Luc Godard: A Critical Anthology*, 119.
39 Jean Collet, 'Interview With Jean-Luc Godard', first published in *Cinema d'Aujourdhui* (September 1963), trans. Toby Mussman, in *Jean-Luc Godard: A Critical Anthology*, ed. Toby Mussman (New York: Dutton, 1968), 139.
40 Feinstein, 'An Interview with Jean-Luc Godard', 9.
41 Feinstein, 'An Interview with Jean-Luc Godard', 9.
42 Richard Koszarski, *Hollywood Directors: 1941–1976*. (New York: Oxford University Press, 1977), 347.
43 Godard, 'An Interview', in *Jean-Luc Godard: A Critical Anthology*, 112.
44 Feinstein, 'An Interview with Jean-Luc Godard', 10.
45 McElhaney, *The Death of Classical Cinema*, 170.

46 Robert Stam, Audio Commentary on *Contempt* DVD.
47 Godard, 'An Interview', in *Jean-Luc Godard: A Critical Anthology,* 112.
48 Godard, 'An Interview', in *Jean-Luc Godard: A Critical Anthology,* 109.
49 Feinstein, 'An Interview with Jean-Luc Godard', 9.
50 Collet, 'Interview With Jean-Luc Godard', 147.

RAPHAËLLE J. BURNS

# Experimenting with Cinema in Godard's *Le Mépris*: The Past and the Present Between Possibility and Impossibility

## Introduction

In many respects *Le Mépris* by Jean-Luc Godard stands out from the rest of his œuvre. *Le Mépris* is an uncharacteristically big budget film for Godard and the closest he ever came to the Hollywood mode of production, it is also undoubtedly his most faithful and explicit adaptation of a pre-existing novel. Although the film comprises a genuine and thorough questioning of spectacular narrative cinema as well as of the forms of adaptation, translation and citation such a cinema implies, *Le Mépris* remains nonetheless the most coherently narrated film Godard has ever filmed. In the following pages I suggest that the unique quality of this film lies not only in the richness of its themes, critiques and self-reflection but above all in the very modes in which these themes are interwoven. What does Godard's daring experimentation with cinematic techniques and new materials expose and to what effect, through and at the cost of the illusion of narrative and logical continuity? Taken at face value the film seems to narrate the breakdown of a relationship, one man's search for the reasons and truth behind his wife's contempt for him. But Godard manages to suggest – less with words or theory than with images in themselves – how this entrapment in causal continuity can be radically challenged through cinematic techniques and montage. The broken link between humans and truth, humans and the gods, which the main character Paul desperately seeks to mend is for Godard, it would seem, to be re-appropriated not by a ceaseless search for truth and knowledge but through the acknowledgment of this break, through the recognition of appearance as such, of the world simply as it is and of the past unfinished. As such the past does not contribute to a sense of coherent causality and tragic inevitability but exists as a time always contemporaneous with the present, exposed in its pure availability.

At the heart of *Le Mépris* lies a very peculiar and provocative engagement with time, the past, and more specifically the past of cinema. Godard achieves this by directly engaging the themes of adaptation and origin and by circling around the image of a fleeting instant in which love can turn into contempt and possibility into impossibility. While he takes the event of this impossibility seriously he remains faithful throughout to the notion of possibility, most importantly of cinematic possibility. All the characters in the film appear to be steeped in contempt: Camille feels contempt for Paul, Prokosch for Lang and his cinema, Lang for Prokosch and modern cinema, and Paul for himself through the gaze of Camille. But as Godard films these impossibilities he manages to make visible through cinema, how cinema can safeguard and reveal the forgotten potentiality at the heart of all experience and perception.[1] This article investigates the intrinsic link between Godard's cinematic reflection on cinema and his exploration of forms of temporality and potentiality. From the very first scene, Godard poses what is at stake in the film for both him and for the spectator. While this reflection is in a sense already lost to the 'shipwrecked'[2] individuals whose story is about to be narrated, he challenges the viewer to a different experience of the images and actions within the film.[3]

The particular relation to the past that Godard experiments with in the film prefigures in some respects the more developed, theoretical approach of his later *Histoire(s) du Cinéma*. He makes use of novel cinematic techniques (filming in CinemaScope, travelling shots, colour filters, montage, repetition) and experiments with old ones (sound, music, flashbacks, actors). He also experiments with citation (imagistic and literary), translation and adaptation. In doing so he attempts to expose these means as such, to reveal their role in cinema and the role they can give to cinema. Through the exhibition of the medial character of these processes he is able to challenge the seemingly inevitable relegation of the past to tradition and the present to convention.

Godard uses a wide range of artistic devices in *Le Mépris*. Notably, he explores the potential for linguistic multiplicity in cinema and exploits an increasingly blurred distinction between fiction and narrative, documentary and reality, actors and characters, author and creation. What does Godard thereby achieve? What is effected through the 'real' presences on screen of Brigitte Bardot, Fritz Lang, Jack Palance and of course Godard himself (through the figures of Paul and Lang's assistant)? The appearance of these spectres of reality within the fiction of the film seem to contribute to Godard's attempt to move away from an epistemological relation to truth and knowledge towards an ontological and cinematic one, participating in Godard's nascent exploration of the poetic possibilities of cinema to 'make the invisible visible',[4] to reveal the immanence of thought *in* the image and not beyond it. Born within spectacular cinematic modes of production, *Le Mépris* becomes the opportunity for Godard to stage his own defiant opposition to the narrowing effects of the media industry of his time. He is clearly attacking the requirements to reduce the media to the presentation of fact, what has been without its possibility, and critiquing the resultant veiling of the power of images for the sake of pure profit and spectacle.[5] In a sense *Le Mépris* presents us with Godard's own Odyssean journey, cinema's voyage home to its own proper dwelling, its *ethos* and condition of possibility: potentiality and the exhibition of appearance as such. Godard presents us with a cinema able to make the real once again possible and to make the possible real not by representing that cinema to us (indeed the cinemas of Lang and Prokosch present no such sense of possibility) but by bringing it into being experimentally through his own work.

## Cinematic Means Made Visible

In the opening scene of *Le Mépris,* a voice is heard listing (selectively) the film credits. The somewhat inelegant expressions "c'est d'après", "il y a", "il y a aussi" seek no effect other than to announce the film for what it 'is' that is to say to exhibit it as the product of a process of construction and creation. But Godard's suggestion in the next scene, through the use of colour filters and incomplete shots – that Bardot's enumeration of her body parts cannot exhaust nor totalise her presence on the screen, that reality cannot be exhausted in a single shot – except perhaps at the cost of sealing its fate tragically hints at the possibility that the previously listed credits cannot successfully grasp the film as a totality either. The opening credits are immediately followed by a (pseudo)-quote by Bazin "Le cinéma substitue à notre regard un monde qui s'accorde à nos désirs. *Le Mépris* est l'histoire de ce monde".[6] Somewhat perversely however, this quote is spoken just as the fictional camera turns to look into the real camera. Thus, just as the viewer is told that cinema can present her with a world in accordance with her desires, she is made to feel her own act of looking more keenly than ever.

As the film unfolds, Godard's reflection on cinema is conducted on the one hand through a self-reflexive use of cinematic technique itself and on the other through the narration of the decline of classical cinema (as represented by Lang) and the rise of modern, psychological and spectacular cinema (as represented by Prokosch). Paul Javal sits unhappily and neurotically between these two antagonistic figures, oscillating between the two, hoping that by understanding the past he might be able to find his own identity in the present.

Aumont writes "[Godard] was constantly tempted by classicism, but also to an equal degree, by another, very different desire for mastery – a kind of mastery which precisely can be engendered only by a reflection *on* classicism".[7] The analogies that can be made between the character of Paul and Godard himself bring to light the experimental side of Godard's endeavour. But these resemblances are only partial, for if Paul is tempted by classicism he cannot reflect *on* classicism and cannot thereby overcome the tragic and fatal separation of the modern and the classic which modernity seems to have imposed. Godard on the other hand, relentlessly explores the inexhaustible nature of the classic and its power to continue poetically into the modern.

## The Cinema: Epistemology Versus Ontology

One of the key aspects of Godard's films, in this respect, is the suspension of the illusion of knowledge, the illusion that the past can be fixed and understood once and for all. He does not side with any of the characters in *Le Mépris*, not even Lang. For Godard neither Homer's *Odyssey* nor classical cinema can be relegated to a past that is altogether past, it is rather their ability to *return* in the form of citation, always with a difference, a possibility to be and show otherwise which for him marks their past-ness. This critique of the epistemological paradigm of knowledge and truth is further elaborated in *Le Mépris*. First in the refusal to provide any comfortable 'oversight' to the viewer, in the misalignment of the perspectives of camera, spectator and characters and in the refusal *within the image* of some of the key technical tropes that make a total comprehension possible (for example the complementary use of shot and reverse-shot, or shots narrating a clear subjective continuity). Secondly, in the film's use of dialogue as it alludes to the problematic nature of epistemological truth (for example Camille's retort to Paul in the apartment scene: "And of what use would the truth be to you?"). Thirdly, in his clear lack of interest in revealing through Lang's film what a "true" classical interpretation of the *Odyssey* might look like. Fourthly, through the distortion and manipulation of traditional techniques such as the flashback, in which conventional chronological narrative time is confounded, in which absolutely nothing is explained or clarified, and in which images can return differently revealing their indeterminate being as such. And finally, with Paul's inability to see "en deça" (on this side of images) in his desperate urge to understand what is "au delà" (beyond appearances).[8]

Godard sees in cinema the potentiality to restore what has become hidden from view when too much weight is given to conventional modes of seeing, narrative continuity and a quest for certainty. In this film the potentiality of cinema is neither theorised nor put into words, it is explored through cinematic technique itself and passes through the necessary stages of experiment and of cinema reflecting on cinema. What can be made to appear in cinema is therefore not epistemological truth but cinematic ontological truth.

## Actor and Persona, Fiction and Reality: The Exploration of a Relationship

While Godard's critique of the epistemological paradigm of truth and history seems to posit him firmly on the 'side' of Bardot/Camille in the film, many elements hint at his partial identification with the character of Paul (his Godardian hat, Camille's wig which is none other than Anna Karina's in *Vivre sa vie*, the dialogues Anna Karina claims were often inspired by their own).[9] Furthermore, his portrayal and exploitation of Bardot as Camille is ambivalent to say the least, containing elements of both appreciation and critique. By withdrawing from established ways of being and seeing, by challenging and manipulating Bardot's fame and charisma as well as the dominant structures of subjectivity and desire of spectacular cinema, Godard makes the plurality and potentiality of the image as such become conceivable and visible. The film elevates Bardot to a role far more complex than any other she was made to play, yet succeeds in its own experimentation largely at her own expense.

There are also many allusions to theatre in *Le Mépris*. Prokosch's caricatural and theatrical style and demeanour, particularly in his first entrance and on the several occasions when he loses his temper, as well as Paul's dreams of writing for theatre are but two of the most obvious. As Aumont has noted, in *Le Mépris* "Godard relies much less on improvisation than in any of his other films, and exploits stereotypes as well as psychological and dramatic conventions to an unaccustomed degree".[10] Godard himself noted that he always tried to consider his actors as real people, always taking into account the actors existence as actor in the elaboration of his films. He relies partly on the history, real lives and fame of his actors to construct his film. For him therefore Camille *is* BB, Prokosch *is* Palance, Lang *is* Lang and Francesca *is* Giorgia Moll, just as the film credits at the beginning of the film lead us to believe, each of them holding in their name multiple references to other cinematic forms and histories. Similarly to his treatment, both faithful and unfaithful, of adaptation, translation and citation, his usage of the 'reality' of his actors whilst sometimes respectful can sometimes border on total manipulation. But once more this is a form of experimentation, reminiscent of the way in which the characters in the Commedia dell'Arte have to experience the mutual dissolution of actor and persona in order to escape from grip of traditional ethical and narrative classifications.[11] This contagion between theatre, film and reality is one Godard seems very keen to explore and does so here through the exploitation and critique of stardom as the spectacular side of this contagion. He explores the relation cinema has and could have with reality, exploring the constant to and fro between the styling of a character and the styling of a star, the metamorphosis of a film and the metamorphosis of its participants.

## What Contempt Does

If, as I noted earlier, Camille removes herself from an epistemological regime of experience, the aura of mystery with which she surrounds herself in her refusal of traditional structures of subjectivity, desire and narrative prevents her from fully taking the measure of this removal. She exploits her capacity to inspire in Paul the neurotic experience of desire as lack. The enigmatic and indecipherable character of Camille, her status as guardian of a secret, captivates Paul's vision to the point of saturation making it impossible for her herself to overcome the tragic impossibility of contempt. But Godard, through the use of long shots, close-ups, cuts and juxtapositions invites the spectator to eschew this saturation. The camera makes its presence felt by an insistent framing, changes in tempo, interruptions and juxtapositions both auditory and visual.[12] In doing so it insists on its inability to capture the totality of a scene by letting the characters dance in and out view. Viewers are incited less to register an absolute failure to communicate between the characters, as they are to experience their own inability to settle on and register once and for all what they are seeing. Indeed, MacCabe writes of Godard's refusal to "master space", whether visually or psychologically: "It is the ability of the camera to explore fully the visual space of a conversation that convinces the spectator that they have also understood the psychology of the characters. The spectator of a Godard film, on the other hand, is always aware of a shot as a shot, as a particular angle on reality, and of the characters as characters, that is to say as patterns of behaviour which cannot be unified under some notion of a subjective psychology".[13]

This refusal to master space goes hand in hand with a refusal to master movement but instead to exhibit it as such. The intricate and incessant ballet-like movements of the characters amongst themselves in the film are not simply a technique used by Godard to show the disintegration of communication. More importantly they act as the unsaid, the in-between of all the attempts at communication of which the film is made. As Agamben puts it "if dance is gesture, it is so, rather, because it is nothing more than the endurance and the exhibition of the media character of corporal movements. *The gesture is the exhibition of a mediality: it is the process of making a means visible as such*".[14] Nothing is exhibited in these movements except the fact of exhibition itself. It is the unsaid which acts as the origin, the condition of possibility of saying, the unseen which acts as the origin, the condition of possibility of all seeing and it is this indeterminacy immanent to image, voice and body which, beyond the concrete reality of the story, Godard – through cinema – seeks to render visible.

None of the characters seeing with contempt in the film are able to overcome the impossibility this contempt creates. Only Lang perhaps holds a more serene position, but he too has resigned himself to the impossibility of continuing beyond his last resistance, to the idea that the classical past might be grasped authentically. Perhaps only Francesca, in spite of her dejection in the face of all the brutality and contempt around her, remains at times aware of the possibility through linguistic translation (another form of adaptation) of seeing anew, in-authentically, always differently, openly. If the mundane everyday translations seem to bore her to desperation and carelessness, Hölderlin she translates for Lang with care, enthusiasm and attention. Perhaps it is because in poetry a glimpse of something altogether different to everyday communication can be caught, an abandonment of the constraints of conventional forms of narrative and communication. Languages can bring with them different modes of seeing, in the same way as images can, but this can perhaps only be grasped in between two languages (in translation) and in between two images (in montage or adaptation) and where they cease to communicate anything else than their own communicability. Once again we see that Godard is more interested in exploring what contempt does (restricting our ways of seeing and our modes of being) than in why and how it first came into being (a putative explanation that would seal a tragic fate).

## Of Origins and Being in *Le Mépris*

Lang quotes Dante in *Le Mépris* "Apprenez quelle est votre origine, vous qui n'avez pas été faits pour être mais pour connaître et contempler la vertu".[15] This can be considered an appeal to cinema to seek out and return to its origin. Paul, incapable of coming to terms with the idea of a return brimming with possibility and creativity, seeing it instead only as a desperate attempt to understand and fix the past once and for all, can see only closure as he recites the closing lines of Dante's verse "Déja la nuit contemplait les étoiles, et notre première joie se metamorphose en pleurs".[16]

Godard takes Lang's position even further however, for as I have noted even Lang seems to hold a rather too secure point of view on the past. If Prokosch embodies a new cinema based on the notion of desire as lack – the producer always wants "more" but he knows not of what – Lang represents a classical view which would have it that in the past desire was complete, wholly in accordance with nature. But Godard takes neither of these two views, both of which establish a relationship of fixity and certainty with the past. Instead Godard's camera reveals these views as partaking in the same tragic impossibility, or fatality (in the literal sense: the film ends with death), and implies that a world which would be in harmony with our desires, for Godard the world of cinema, of montage and of poetic experiment, is neither a "take it or leave it" world nor a world always lacking, but one in which the real would be once again made possible and the possible made real.

This position echoes his effort to reveal a modality of experience neither akin to Paul's extreme neurosis, his desire to understand, his inability to choose between different interpretations, his constant over-psychologisation, nor to Camille's extreme, complete, instinctual and therefore irreversible experience of contempt (Godard once said of Bardot that you have to take her in one block) both of which constitute the two sides of the tragedy which is *Le Mépris*, the marking of their impossibility to live experience as experiment.

On the use of adaptation in *Le Mépris*, Joanna Paul[17] writes that by concealing, withholding and postponing what the *Odyssey* might actually look like if filmed by the faithful classical film director, Godard implicitly critiques the view whereby there could be a genuinely faithful adaptation. But if Godard is an adept of mistranslation and misquotation, of putting tradition to new uses, he does so in the name of experimentation and wholeheartedly against the temptation to use it for facility or for profit – characteristics of the newly developing cinematic and mediated world in which he lived. If cinema in modernity betrayed itself by concealing the power of images in the name of narration-spectacle, this does not mean that the latter form cannot reveal the former. Michel Marie claims that *Le Mépris* is Godard's most conventionally linear and narrative film,[18] but this may well be to his credit, as he boldly takes on the difficult task of eroding conventional forms and productions from within.

When asked about the place of Godard in the history of cinema Jacques Rancière once commented: "With the films others made, Godard makes the films they did not make".[19] Although this comment was made in a discussion of Godard's later *Histoire(s) du Cinéma*, already in *Le Mépris* Godard questions the notion of citation as homage, in reverence to the great founders of film. In his work citation is decidedly irreverent, an experiment with the potential of each image, each technique, each creation, to return again and again, always differently showing new things and showing itself as such. Bergala cites Godard on the fact that he would often claim to never have invented anything but always only cited others, for this he saw as the essence of cinema: revealing and concealing what is always already there, in potentiality, in the image[20]. Indeed, already in 1963 cinema for Godard was not about invention but about experimentation.

## Conclusion

By the end of the film we sense that by using cinema to open up new ways of seeing, Godard saves himself from melancholy neurosis, mere nostalgia and mourning in the face of the decline of classical cinema. That the last scene is just the filming of a wide expanse, the supposed vision of a homeland, might be seen to suggest that although this is a film recounting the collapse of both a relationship and of classic cinema, nothing – not even death – can resolve the past into being either fully understood, fully known or even fully complete. That in his very last shot of the blue sea, Odysseus' homeland is nowhere to be seen might be taken to suggest that the proper homeland to which all things must return, the origin, is not distinct from the present but immanent to it, unfolding within it, always open. And thus, the proper dwelling of cinema need not be mourned as an irretrievable past but always already returned to as its own immanent condition of possibility: the power of the image *as* image. In this, Godard firmly situates himself between the old and the new, between images, not pathetically, fearfully or neurotically like Paul but experimentally in the use and possibilities of techniques and creations, old and new.

It may seem a little hasty to read such optimism into *Le Mépris*, a film that differs little from Godard's other films with regard to its portrayal of characters consistently failing to produce or create anything, capable only of destruction, consumption, failure and collapse. Nonetheless, although by the end of the film we have witnessed the collapse of both the couple and the film, the last shot is a shot of the act of filming, which can continue freely as experiment even if it is doomed to remain unfinished. To always leave something unfinished, unsaid is perhaps precisely that which all artists must aspire to if they hope to continue to experience the potentiality of the human imagination.

Youssef Ishaghpour in a published interview with Godard on *Histoire(s) du Cinéma* suggests that "The raw material is limited partly perhaps because you didn't have access to a lot of things, but in another way it seems like a necessity, because no form can be created without what is the elementary basis of form: recurrence, going back, repetition, all differentiated, and it's the work on the image, but also on sound, the words, the musics, it's the whole montage that makes that impression possible through the metamorphosis of a limited whole."[21] This could also be said of *Le Mépris*, to the extent that through experimentation with some of the most basic elements of film (image, sound, language) and the use of montage, stoppage and repetition, Godard relentlessly brings to the fore the unsaid, the presupposed being-image of the image. Finally, as I have shown, that Godard's shots are always haunted by borrowed gestures, images and words, circling around a point where cinema touches the zone of indistinction between reality and fiction, is each time a reminder of and an invitation to experience the secret communication between, the indivisibility of, art and life as part of the same *experimentum vitae*.[22]

## Notes

1 See Chapter 1, L. Bersani and U. Dutoit, *Forms of Being: Cinema, Aesthetics, Subjectivity* (London: British Film Institute, 2004) for more on potentiality in *Le Mépris*.
2 'Interview with Godard', in *Cahiers du Cinéma*, 146 (1963).
3 One can see here the influence of Brecht on Godard's work. For more on this see C. MacCabe, *Godard: A Portrait of the Artist at 70* (London: Bloomsbury, 2004).
4 Bersani and Dutoit, *Forms of Being*, 1.
5 G. Agamben, *Image et Mémoire: Ecrits sur l'image, la danse et le cinema* (Paris: Editions Desclée de Brouwer, 2004), 92.
6 "Cinema substitutes for our look a world in accord with out desires. *Le Mépris* is the story (or history) of that world." (my translation).
7 J. Aumont, 'The Fall of the Gods: Jean-Luc Godard's *Le Mépris* (1963)' in S. Hayward and G. Vincendeau (eds), *French Film: Texts and Contexts*, (London: Routledge, 2000), 225.

8 In the long apartment scene in the middle of the film, Paul asks Camille "Why are you looking pensive?" and she replies "Because I'm thinking, imagine that". During the flashback in this scene, we also hear Paul's voice saying "The truth as to her behaviour was still to be elucidated taking no account of appearances." (my translation). See Bersani and Dutoit, *Forms of Being*, 6–7 for a detailed study of the contrast between the "en deça" and "au delà" of images.
9 MacCabe, *Godard*. See Chapter 3 for an account of Godard's shifting modes of presence within his films.
10 Aumont, 'The Fall of the Gods', 220.
11 Agamben, *Image et Mémoire*, 124.
12 M. Marie, *Comprendre Godard: Travelling avant sur À bout de souffle et Le Mépris* (Paris: Editions Armand Colin, 2006). The author notes the loud superimposition of music or the way in which the apartment scene evolves not linearly but in intensities, to name but two examples.
13 MacCabe, *Godard*, 155.
14 G. Agamben, *Means Without End: Notes on Politics*, trans. V. Binetti and C. Casarino (Minneapolis: Minneapolis University Press, 2000), 58.
15 "Consider your origin you were not made to be but to pursue virtue and knowledge." (my translation).
16 "Already the night contemplated the stars, and our first joy turned to tears." (my translation).
17 J. Paul, 'Homer and Cinema: Translation and Adaptation in Le Mépris' in A. Lianeri and V. Zajko (eds), *Translation and the Classic: Identity as Change in the History of Culture* (Oxford: Oxford University Press, 2008) 149–165.
18 Marie, *Comprendre Godard*.
19 J. Rancière, 'Jean-Luc Godard, La religion de l'art. Entretien avec Jacques Rancière' in *CinémAction* 'Où en est le God-Art?', 109 (2003), 106–112.
20 A. Bergala, *Nul Mieux que Godard* (Paris: Editions des Cahiers du Cinéma, 1999)
21 Y. Ishaghpour and J-L. Godard, *Archéologie du cinema et mémoire du siècle: Dialogue*, trans. J. Howe, (Oxford: Berg, 2005), 11.
22 See Agamben, *Image et Mémoire* generally for a discussion of the concept of *experimentum vitae* in relation to cinema and L. Lagier, *Godard, l'amour, la poésie* (DVD, Documentaire Point du Jour, 2007) for an account of Godard's own evolution through his films.

BURHANUDDIN BAKI

# Cinema at the Intervals of Cinema

The critical, theoretical and philosophical reflections that follow belong to a meditation on how the relation of difference proper to the cinematic image constructs itself in Jean-Luc Godard's work. I limit myself by only pursuing this question in terms of the following problematic: what is at stake for the ontology of the cinematic image when a film, such as Godard's, presents itself as just a network of citations and, moreover, explicitly foregrounds its entirety to be as if it was none other than a network of citations? My intention here, in other words, is to think through the connection between the textual ontology of the quotation and the differential relationality of the cinematic image. My main filmic reference will be *Le Mépris* [*Contempt*] and my main theoretical reference will be several relevant statements made by Godard in various interviews.

That Godard's films are littered with lines, images, gestures and techniques lifted from other films and media – be it from some poem, novel, essay, song, lyric, painting, photograph, sculpture, and so on – is well-known and something the director freely acknowledges, and acknowledges as something positive. 'It's very good to steal things,' he says. 'Bertolt Brecht said art is made from plagiarism'.[1] Sometimes, all the lines in Godard's dialogues are wilfully lifted from other texts. This is true, in a sense, for any film and text. Godard's work, moreover, draws attention to its own quoting instead of obfuscating it, to the repeated employment of this stylistic trope, oftentimes overtly illustrating, sometimes parodying, the passion for citation in his film (for example, in *Le Mépris* with Jeremy Prokosch's repeated referencing of his little red book). It would be a useful exercise to catalogue meticulously and classify many of the intertextual allusions that appear in *Le Mépris* and in Godard's entire œuvre, and search for patterns, structures, commonalities and fault-lines – and then comment on them, with the hope of saying something 'enlightening', 'deep' or at least 'interesting' about his work in general. This would be a noteworthy contribution to Godardian and cinematic scholarship, and the form of the hypertext or the online wiki would, at this moment, seem to be the one most suited for organising and presenting such a material. Nevertheless, at some point during the execution of such a project, we can be sure, even with the various archival, cross-referencing, pattern-recognition and search engine technologies readily at hand, that the task will eventually appear to us as infinite or almost infinite. One will always have the impression of being able to read forever. We can easily argue that this is the case not only for Godard's films, but for any 'great work of art', and *Le Mépris* is well-regarded by critics today to be one of the director's principal masterpieces, so much so that Colin MacCabe famously proclaimed it to be 'the greatest work of art produced in post-war Europe'.[2]

Reading and listening to what Godard has revealed about his own logic of citation, we cannot help but consider the practice behind it to be surprisingly crude and innocent, even 'unsophisticated'. Sometimes he cites without realising he is citing, without realising he is repeating something he has read, seen or heard. This not-knowing is itself extraordinarily 'innocent', sometimes wilfully so. '[T]o me quotes and myself are almost the same. I don't know who they are from; sometimes I'm using it without knowing [...] It has something to do with me, but I don't know what exactly'.[3] Sometimes he misremembers and misattributes his sources, as in the case of the quote that opens *Le Mépris*, 'The cinema substitutes for our gaze a world more in harmony with our desire', a line that, despite sounding like something André Bazin would write, was never written by the great film critic, but by Michel Mourlet in a *Cahiers du Cinéma* essay.[4] Sometimes, Godard even purposely changes the words, phrasings and formulations of his quotations in order to fit his contexts, to make it his own, or to add something to it. A statement in literary theory (by Maurice Blanchot, for example) might become one in film theory after replacing the word 'literature' with 'cinema'. Colin MacCabe has made the case that Godard does not even read many of the texts from which he lifts his quotations, and that he reads only the 'strategic' portions of a book – the table of contents, the introduction, the epilogue – searching only for some gist in the form of a 'sound bite' that he will be able to use or transmute.[5]

'I skim over books and novels, and sometimes a sentence strikes my imagination,' Godard claims. 'I put it in my notebook, then I check to see whether this phrase might fit in'.[6] This would imply that, for him, the value of a possible intertext is measured less on the institutional prestige it would afford, less on the fact that it originated from works by authors or artists of great cultural, aesthetic or intellectual worth, and more on what might be called its 'technological power', its possibility for provoking some thought that might be useful for a future work. In fact, Godard did not even consider Alberto Moravia's *Il disprezzo*, the novel on which *Le Mépris* is based, to be a great work of literature. Still, as he famously told the director Paul Schrader, 'What's important isn't what you take – it [is] where you take it to'.[7]

Let us pursue this point further by trying to understand its implication to our current images of the filmmaker and film viewer. The image we have of the artist then becomes that of an 'engineer', a 'technician' for converting memories into works of art. The knowledge and memories the artist has acquired – from the film watched; the books read; the paintings, photographs or sculptures seen; the music listened; the sensations experienced; and the people with whom he fell in love – all serve as resources to be churned and woven together into the fabric of the created text. This is even more apparent in the editing phrase in film production: a certain amount of footage has been supplied by the cameraman, actors, stage director, production designer, film archivist, etc., and the task of the director as editor is to 'quote' from them by constructing a suitable permutational arrangement. Since this passion for quoting is explicitly foregrounded in Godard's work, we become more aware of the use of the archive as a resource: this technological possibility of memory and history, and this technicity of remembering. The image of the cinematic technician brings to mind the image of the scientist, and Godard has often compared his activity in 'cinematic alchemy' to that of the experimental scientist, who is, in the Lévi-Straussian sense, a bricoleur. 'I mix images and sounds like a scientist,' Godard claims. 'The mystery of the scientific is the same as the mystery of the artistic'.[8] Colin MacCabe compares Godard to the Leibnizian arithmetician who multiplies together different 'prime numbers of social reality' in his attempt at creating cinema.[9]

An interlocking hyper-textual assemblage of symbolic nodes and lines of allusions, constantly shifting and re-negotiating themselves, manifests itself before us in the film, demanding to be decoded, appropriated and interpreted. The demand is for the film viewer to 'hunt the reference', to become a decoder and a genealogist. Watching a film or making one becomes, among others, an act of retrospection, an ethical act of redemption that demands us to think another relation between the past and the future, and a different relation with respect to the impossible other. This mirrors Paul's reaction in Moravia's novel to the enigma of his wife's contempt for him, which is indicated by his almost obsessive analysis of his situation, an examination that we can sense is without end. Confronted with this genealogical jungle of forking and criss-crossing codes, the work of the reader then becomes the work of the cartographer, the map-maker. When this work is coupled with the task of writing some critical essay, the reader will then have to find some logic to the diagram, some path that traverses through all or almost all the nodes of the network (a 'Hamiltonian path', to use the mathematical term), to flatten and iron out the crumpled topology and uncurl it into some linear narrative form: a quest that unlike the Odyssean story that inspired *Le Mépris*, is without origin or end – an unsolvable 'cross'-word puzzle.

But then Godard says this: '*Le Mépris* proves in 149 shots that in cinema, as in life, there is nothing secret, nothing to elucidate; one has only to live – and make films'.[10] His carefree and almost cunning use of quotations in his films does not make a mockery out of this interpretive strategy of hunting and elucidating references. By orienting our attention to its own structure as a network of citations, *Le Mépris* engages with the possibility and impossibility of its own reading, with the possibility of a cinematic encounter or event. The nocturnal obscurity at the heart of the image, the opacity at the heart of what makes cinematic signification possible, what permits any interpretation, any reading, even of the most leisurely kind, to take place: this is what Godard's cinema brings into play. Films, thenceforth, only seem to be made in order to allow the labour of cinema, as some sovereignty without essence, to accomplish itself by the articulation of its own question. Art is not just a mirror, a 'reflection of reality', but 'the reality of reflection,' says Godard.[11]

The beginning of *Le Mépris* already indicates this with its title sequence, a long take of a long take being filmed at the Cinecittà back lot. Showing itself, this shot also shows itself showing. The spatial distance between the seeing subject (the viewer's eyes) and the object seen (Raoul Cotard and his Franscope camera) at the screen's left-hand side becomes narrower and narrower until at some point, a self-reflexive 'flip' occurs and it is the object that is staring at the voyeuristic subject, causing the latter to tremble in shame. What ends up being shown, if I might be permitted to employ Heideggerian vocabulary, is the *lethe* at the heart of *aletheia*, the abyss that locates itself in the very reality and texture of the image itself. In this shot, it is the anonymous, obscure and ever-shifting 'origin' of cinema itself that is being 'shown'.

This is the image as the movement of the image, as the image in movement. This is *cinema at the intervals of cinema*, a cinema that is barely cinema, that hovers just pass the bordering threshold where it becomes itself. Cinema here becomes the meditation of its own event.[12] Its announcement is suspended just infinitesimally past that border between the unseen and the seen, between the invisible and the visible, between the night and the day.

Godard has often stressed the necessity of equating cinema with its own movement. 'To me, movies *are* movement,' he says. 'It's going from the unseen to the seen, and from the hidden part of the iceberg to the seen part. It's crossing. The screen is a border between me and the audience'.[13] For him, this movement is precisely what allows for the scene of the human, which remains forever nomadic and without identity. 'To me, being a human being is being between two places. It's the movement that's important, not the remaining in one place'.[14] In an interview with Jonathan Rosenbaum, Godard even went so far as to say that only in this neutral and dispersive in-between zones of movement do things really exist. They constitute the precondition for a real and 'authentic' existence. 'I like to think of myself as an airplane, not an airport [. . .] A lot of tourists, when they go from New York to Honolulu, don't think that between New York and Honolulu they still exist, even if it's a 10-hour flight. To me, what exists is *mainly* between'.[15] Moreover, the radical medium of cinema is for him the one best suited to create and bring about the creation of such movements and scenes. Unlike sculpture and painting, film is a revolutionary art because 'it is the sensation of movement, and such a sensation doesn't exist with a Grecian urn'.[16] As Colin MacCabe writes, 'What cinema, or the camera, does is to allow the possibility of representing reality, of seizing it in a language which is continuously variable'.[17]

Hence: the extraordinary lightness of Godard's images, which seem to be dancing *À bout de souffle*. Hence, also: the extraordinary radicality and innovation of his cinematic technique. 'He foils our calculations and disappoints those who worship him too readily,' writes Serge Daney. 'Godard has always kept moving, in every sense of the word, within a film-world that is still big enough to allow you to move about and show your restless energy'.[18]

Yet, despite this emphasis on the radical relation of difference in his work, despite the rebelliousness of his cinematic style, Godard remains in many respects a traditionalist. Novelty, for him, comes hand in hand with the old. When asked why he placed such emphasis on newness and innovation in his films, Godard answers by repeating T.S. Eliot's proposition that 'everything which is really new is by that fact very traditional'.[19]

In fact, nowhere is this need to acknowledge the past more clearly illustrated than in Godard's passion for quotation, for alluding and for paying homage to films and texts that came before him. *Le Mépris*, which is as cinematically adventurous as any other film by him, mentions the works of, among others, Alfred Hitchcock, Howard Hawks, Orson Welles, Fritz Lang, Homer and Friedrich Hölderlin (and one can go on listing endlessly). We are, thus, understandably confused in regards to Godard's position as both a radical filmmaker and as a traditionalist. He appears to be neither simply an avant-garde artist nor a classicist but hovers at that neutral and more radical null-space in between. Reminding us of the temporal dynamics of Walter Benjamin's Angel of History, Serge Daney has called this ambiguity 'the Godard paradox':

> [L]ike many formal inventors, he [Godard] advances back-to-front, apprehensively, facing what he is leaving behind. He is not so much the man who opens doors as the one in whose gaze a previously familiar and natural landscape changes with hindsight: he is worn down by an alarming feeling of alienation and overcome by the mystery that occurs when one feels that one no longer knows how to do things.
>
> This sums up the Godard paradox. He is caught between a recent past and a near future (unlike prophets who can easily combine archaism and the future), he is crucified between what he can no longer do and what he cannot yet do, in other words, he is doomed to the present.[20]

We can thus further approach the image of the artist as a kind of machine, computer or electronic circuit that produces cinema as its output while taking history or, more precisely, the history of cinema, as its input. What happens in the feedback loop between the output and input holds the obscure secret of artistic production itself – which is, perhaps, the most mysterious of questions, beyond all computation or mechanics. This is a history of cinema that is constantly engaged and fascinated with itself, that perpetuates by repeating itself through the silent force of an essential difference. Rather than being created only with the intention of communicating some external idea or imparting some personal expression, the Godardian image, which appears to be generated by its own sonorous qualities and self-resonances, perpetuates by feeding off itself. Its movement, which is neither simply that of continuity nor discontinuity, constitutes neither a total rupture nor a simple repetition of what precedes it. It achieves its rupture precisely by engaging with what comes before it.[21]

Let me end by suggesting that more can be said about this dispersive and ambiguous ontology of cinema if we reflect back on the strange disaffected ontology of the quoted text, which is comparable to that of the footnote or the parenthetical remark. The intertext is neither there nor not there in the film – or is both there and not there. Belonging neither to the film nor to its original source, the intertext is a supplement that playfully intrudes and yet also continues the thematically and structurally complete text into which it intervenes.[22] Hence: the impression of lightness and breathlessness that sometimes appears when a quotation is introduced. We are more aware of this lightness when an intertext appears in a film – particularly when we are watching in a movie theatre, as we are not given the luxury to pause and to think before the next image appears.

Critical theory for the past few years has supplied a useful thematic through which to think this presence-absence, this undecidable ontology, materiality and temporality: the ghost. According to the well-known analysis, the ghost assumes a mode of existence that is neutral with respect to the life-death and presence-absence dichotomies. We are perpetually hovering between two mutually exclusive choices: taking the ghost as dead, as belonging to the past to which it testifies, or taking the ghost as alive, as present in the time in which is appears to us. We cannot accept the former because the ghost is obviously not identical to the absent person that shares its name. But we cannot accede to the latter either since one cannot be both a ghost and yet remain wholly alive and present at the same time. As the living dead, the ghost enters into and disrupts what is present and what is real. It is neither there nor not there.

This does not simply mean that all films are, directly or indirectly, horror films or ghost stories (even though one can easily approach the projection of the cinematic image on the screen as a kind of spectre). Remember that Godard changed the ending of his film by removing the 'ghost at noon' scene at the end of the Moravia novel. In the original text, Molteni describes encountering the living ghost of his now dead wife on a boat by the sea.[23] We can speculate that maybe Godard re-inserted a modified version of this scene into the middle of his film as those interruptive and parenthetical shots of Camille running through the woods or lying naked on white and blue carpets: scenes that bring into question our everyday state of affairs with temporality and ontology by being neither a flashback of Paul's previous memory of her nor the expression of some hopeful futurity. Like quotations, these shots are part and not part of the film. Camille has become spectral in another way.

We can thus generalise that the Godardian image can only show itself in all its invisibility and hollowed-out lightness by placing itself in quotation marks or parenthesis: as 'cinema', a cinema suspended and distanced from itself by receding within the lightness of these scare quotes as if in irony, as if ashamed of asserting itself. Placing anything within scare quotes allows one to use it without owning it, without positing or negating it: to say without saying and to show without showing. It does not situate itself forward as some advancing site of plenitude but like an empty quotation, or nested collection of empty brackets,[24] haunting the trace of its own mark by absenting its own name. From this, and from watching many of Godard's works, we cannot help but infer that his cinematic Odyssey was to provide a new meaning to give to the word 'filmmaking'. There is no image to show; 'there is nothing secret, nothing to elucidate; one has only to live – and make films'. Godard would like to make movies where it would only be a matter of 'showing', where 'showing' is not limited to its function as a transitive verb, and that its proper labour is accomplished in the suspended middle voice where its transitivity is forced to flow back into itself. One shows an image, but the object remains in quotation marks, so that its visibility will obscure while maintaining the sovereignty of its invisibility.

## Notes

1 Gene Youngblood, Interview with Godard in 1968, collected in *Jean-Luc Godard: Interviews*, ed. D. Sterritt (Jackson: University of Mississippi Press, 1998), 23.
2 Colin MacCabe, *Godard: A Portrait of the Artist at 70* (London: Bloomsbury, 1996), 56.
3 Alison Smith, Interview with Godard in 1966, collected in Sterritt, *Interviews*, 184.
4 This was noted by Jonathan Rosenbaum in 'Trailer for Godard's *Histoire(s) du Cinéma*', *Vertigo* 7 (1997), 19. The essay in question is Mourlet's *'Sur un art ignoré'*, *Cahiers du cinéma* 98 (1959), 34.
5 MacCabe, *Godard*, 399.
6 Gerald Peary, 'In Praise of Jean-Luc Godard', *Boston Phoenix*, Oct. 31-Nov. 7 (2002).
7 Jonathan Rosenbaum, Interview with Godard in 1980, collected in Sterritt, *Interviews*, 100.
8 Penelope Gilliatt, Interview with Godard in 1976, collected in Sterritt, *Interviews*, 72.
9 MacCabe, *Godard*, 63.
10 Tom Milne, '*Le Mépris* (Review)', *Sight and Sound*, 39:3 (1970), 164.
11 Youngblood, Interview with Godard in 1968, 29.
12 To avoid confusion, when Godard affirms the sovereignty of cinema, he is not making the gesture of the typical aesthete by asserting the credo of *l'art pour*

*l'art*. At least, this is not his later stance once he moved on from his so-called 'film buff' period. The cinematic labour does not intend to satisfy some ornamental function or provide some sensuous pleasure. When cinema becomes its own question, this does not mean it becomes equated with its own organic becoming or autonomous teleological development.

13 Annette Insdorf, Interview with Godard in 1980, collected in Sterritt, *Interviews*, 90.
14 J. Cott, Interview with Godard in 1980, collected in Sterritt, *Interviews*, 91.
15 Rosenbaum, Interview with Godard in 1980, 104.
16 Gilliatt, Interview with Godard in 1976, 83.
17 MacCabe, *Godard*, 79.
18 Serge Daney, 'The Godard Paradox', in *For Ever Godard*, eds M. Temple, J.S. Williams & M. Witt (London: Black Dog, 2004), 70.
19 Youngblood, Interview with Godard in 1968, 24. Here, Godard is probably referring to Eliot's essay 'Tradition and the Individual Talent' (1919).
20 Daney, 'The Godard Paradox', 71.
21 John Drabinski has explicated further this tension between continuity and discontinuity in *Godard Between Identity and Difference* (London: Continuum, 2008).
22 For more on the ambiguous textuality of the quotation in Godard, please refer to L. Hill, 'A Form that Thinks: Godard, Blanchot, Citation', in Temple, *For Ever Godard*, 396–415.
23 Earlier English translations of Moravia's book titled it *A Ghost at Noon* instead.
24 That is to say: quotations that quote nothing but other quotations, which themselves quote other quotations all the way down to the void. The symbolic equivalent would be pairs of inverted commas or brackets that contain nothing but either the void itself or other brackets, all the way down to the void – a sets of sets, or a 'multiplicity of multiplicities', to use Alain Badiou's well-known formulation.

ANNA MANUBENS

# Godard's Lingering Camera From *Le Mépris* to *Passion* and Back

*To Alexander Düttman*

In the opening scenes of *Le Mépris*, after meeting Jeremy Prokosh, the American producer that hired him, Paul Javal is invited to see extracts from the film which he is meant to give a twist to. In a small projection room at *Cinecittà*, he is confronted with a first series of shots where the characters are statues. It is exclusively as a result of the camera movements around the statues that motion and time enter these sequences. In fact, the stillness of the statues allows for the foregrounding of the role of the camera's point of view. This very brief projection is testament to the connotative potential of the camera moves and exemplifies the statement made by Fritz Lang, the director of the film, as a prologue to the images: 'Each image should have a definite point of view'. Indeed, as the different characters – statues – appear on the screen, the camera's positioning propitiates different reactions in the spectator: Minerva's protection is inferred by a lateral move that gives the impression that the statue is panning the horizon and Neptune's threat is dramatised by a low-angle shot which contrasts with the identification with Ulysses enabled by a frontal close-up (see Figure 1).

Commenting on Rossellini's treatment of the museum statues in *Journey to Italy* (1954), Laura Mulvey makes an observation that could suit Lang's statues-starred sequences in *Le Mépris*: 'Movement emerges out of stasis, it is as though Rossellini imagined that his camera would be the magic means of bringing life to those blocks of stone.'[1] It is not coincidental that the Italian director is among Godard's pantheon of cinema masters and, more significantly, that *Journey to Italy* is one of the clearest influences of *Le Mépris*. In addition to the similar shooting of statues in both films (the manner in which the camera movements give the impression of them being living stones), *Journey to Italy* and *Le Mépris* also share the identification between the flesh and blood characters and their petrified *alter egos*. In the former, the crisis in the relationship between Ingrid Bergman and George Sanders is echoed by the petrified bodies unearthed in Pompeii's archaeological site. In the latter, the triangle formed by Ulysses, Minerva and Neptune is superimposed on the one formed by Javal, Prokosh and Camille.

**Figure 1** Stills from *Le Mépris*, dir. Jean-Luc Godard, 1963

It is worth looking into Alain Resnais and Alain Robbe-Grillet's *Last Year in Marienbad* (1961) to further examine the effect caused by the singular interplay between sculptures, characters and the camera surrounding motion. The first encounter between Robbe-Grillet's lovers, A and X, is witnessed by a sculptural couple. "Remember – will later recall X – very close to us there was a sculptural group, a man and a woman, dressed like classical statues, whose unfinished gestures seemed to represent a precise scene. You asked me who those figures were; I answered that I did not know. You made a few suppositions, and I said that it could also be you and me."[2]

X's comparison between the statues and the living couple is not a mere flirtation strategy; it is a remark which is in synchrony with Robbe-Grillet's choice of the atmosphere of the film: inside this enclosed, suffocating world, both men and things are under the same sort of spell.[3] His intended analogy between individuals and things finds its epitome in the opening scene where one could say that human figures are *sculpturised*. Throughout a long *plan-séquence*, a voice-off accompanies the camera's entrance into a hotel salon where the action has been frozen. Within this still scenario the camera travels fluidly and at ease among the bodies, the sculptures and the architectonic volumes that compose the interrupted scene, homogenising them all. This ambience matches the aesthetic of the Nouveau Roman as a mode of narrative where 'things are simply "there" and such meanings as people discover beneath their *surface* are inventions which ascribe coherence and significance to a neutral and non-signifying universe.'[4] The allusion to a surface will become increasingly relevant to the present examination. However, at this stage, it should suffice to observe that Resnais' cinematic strategies seem to correspond to a will to restore a surface to the characters. A restoration that could either be causing or resulting from the characters' aspect of statues.

To a certain extent, Godard's acknowledged avoidance of psychologism also takes recourse to an analogy between statues and characters whose most distinct manifestation is accomplished in the character of Camille. The

**Figure 2** French theatrical release posted for *Et Dieu… créa la femme*, dir. Roger Vadim, 1956

voluptuous Lolita that Bardot embodies in Roger Vadim's *Et Dieu… créa la femme* (1956) is transformed by Godard into a reserved and cryptic Camille (see Figure 2).

In contrast with Bardot's usual register of attitudes, her role in *Le Mépris* demanded an entirely different set of manners. Her new repertoire of postures connotes concealment which, as well as strongly evoking the female statues that appear in the film. Thereby the statues' impenetrableness redoubles Camille's isolation. Probably the highest degree of identification between the statues and her is reached in the apartment scene where a sculpture that stands in the young couple's living-room functions as Camille's visual alter-ego and recalls the kind of postures that

**Figure 3** Stills from *Le Mépris*, dir. Jean-Luc Godard, 1963

she adopts throughout the film. Moreover, during the scene, the copper figure becomes her double whenever Bardot is out of the frame (see Figures 3 and 4).

However, in relation to *Last Year In Marienbad* Camille's equivalence with the statue does not attain the form of a *sculpturisation* of the character as it is the case there. The difference lies in the fact that in *Le Mépris*, as in *Journey to Italy*, the isolation of the camera movements is only executed over stone or copper figures while in *Last Year In Marienbad* the camera pans indistinctively around sculptures or stilled characters. This camera movement gives the impression that the character is turned into a sculpture but most importantly achieves a specific alteration of duration and progression. The camera journeys through stilled actions are neither a cinematic frozen image – since temporality is carried on by the camera moves – nor a pretended photographic stillness where the camera would remain as still as the action. The combination of stilling the action and initiating an isolated camera motion splits temporality into two: that of the action and that of the camera. It is this specific rupture that this essay aims to examine in order to identify the solo choreography of the camera as having an effect on temporal progression and as a means to restitute a kind of surface.

Although missing in *Le Mépris*, the use of this singular combination of stillness and movement is recurrent in Godard's later film *Passion* (1982). In *Passion*, Jerzy is directing an eponymous film that stages famous paintings of Western tradition including Ingres, Rembrandt or Goya. Very often, during the process of reconstruction, the camera seems to take advantage of the stilled motion of the figurants to circulate around them in a way that echoes Resnais' opening scene (see Figure 5).

**Figure 4** Stills from *Le Mépris*, dir. Jean-Luc Godard, 1963

In 'The Work of Art in the Age of Mechanical Reproduction', Walter Benjamin poses a question that seems especially relevant to the theme of *Passion*: 'How does the cameraman compare with the painter?'.[5] According to Benjamin, their difference lies in the relationship, or more accurately, in the *distance* that they maintain – or not – with regards to reality. Benjamin associates the painter with a magician and the cameraman with a surgeon. The *distance* that the curing magician preserves with regards to its patient is suppressed by the surgeon's penetration into his/her body. The former preserves the apprehension of reality as a total picture while the latter moves among its organs.

Benjamin's approach of the cameraman as a surgeon – which is not by chance a profession connected to science – is linked to a quite epistemological understanding to film. He conceives film as a medium that allows a "deepening of apperception", where things can be "analysed much more precisely", and as being able to extend our field of perception.

> By close-ups of the things around us, by focusing on hidden details or familiar objects, by exploring commonplace milieus under ingenious guidance of the camera, the film, on the one hand, extends our comprehension of the necessities which rule our lives; on the other hand, it manages to assure us of an immense unexpected field of action.[6]

**Figure 5** Still from *Passion*, dir. Jean-Luc Godard, 1982

Through Benjamin's scope, *Passion* could be regarded as a penetration of painting, an exploration of its details and connections made possible by the cinematic power of incision. However, Godard's conception of close-ups departs from a strictly epistemological understanding:

> A beautiful face, as La Bruyère wrote, is the most beautiful of sights. There is a famous legend which has it that Griffith, *moved by the beauty* of his leading lady, invented the close-up in order to capture it in greater detail.[7]

For Godard, the close-up is not as much concerned with inspection or clarification, as prompted by emotion and beauty. As if the camera movement of getting closer embodied Griffith's attraction to the actress' beauty. It is worth drawing the reader's attention into a constellation of notions that is slowly forming since the thesis of this analysis will stem from their progressive articulation. Benjamin's depiction of close-ups as devices that abolish distance – as chirurgical penetrations – implies that a surface is being transgressed. It will be argued that Godard's legendary reading of close-ups and especially the connection of the camera moves to *beauty* and *desire* allow the inversion of Benjamin's statement: certain camera moves can create and preserve the surface.

## Beauty and Lingering

Extending Godard's idea that Griffith was 'moved by beauty' and recalling Godard's statement when presenting *Passion* in Cannes – 'Cinema is the last representative of beauty'[8]- Kant's account of the aesthetic pleasure associated to beauty constitutes a second point of departure to approach the camera's choreography within stillness.

> This pleasure is also not practical in any way, neither like the one arising from the pathological basis of the agreeableness, nor like the one arising from the intellectual basis, the conceived good. Yet it does have a causality in it, namely to *keep* [us in] the state of [having] the presentation itself, and [to keep] the cognitive powers engaged [in their occupation] without any further aim. We *linger* in our contemplation of the beautiful, because this contemplation reinforces and reproduces itself.[9]

For Kant, beauty is not a quality on the side of the object but a feeling of pleasure that is absolutely deprived of any instrumental or practical value, while remaining bound to a certain effect: our will to remain within it: to *linger* within it. This permanence in the contemplation is not a mere visual fixity but is characterised by a dynamic reengagement of the viewer's faculties and the reproduction of the beautiful presentation. It is this contemplative dynamism that the camera seems able to transmit, when panning around the "tableaux vivants" of *Passion*.

Kant also refers to a form of pleasure that arises out of '[keeping] the cognitive powers engaged in *their* occupation'. Through this scope, the camera circulations within a stilled scene can be understood as the suspension of the action flux in favour of the lingering will prompted by beauty. The camera movements materialise the engagement of the spectators' cognitive powers in front of a beautiful instant extracted from time flux. Jerzy's camera allows a cinematographic restoration of a sense of duration in perception.

In addition, the camera moves around Rembrandt's *Nightwatch* to provide a point of view that is constantly changing and thus a multiplication, or re-enactment, of our contemplative encounters with the painting. Thereby, *Passion*'s sequences are also faithful to Kant's depiction of the desire to remain in – or within – beauty as a desire to '*keep* [us in] the state of [having] the presentation itself'. *Passion* manages to accomplish the spectator's will to linger in contemplation by both retaining the instant and activating a dilated temporality for apprehension through the camera motion.

Furthermore, Kant exposes pleasure as being disconnected from any kind of directionality or goal beyond itself: one wishes to linger in the contemplation of the beautiful without "any further aim". In order to get deeper into the examination of the relationship between perceptive lingering and the absence of an aim beyond it, it is worth recalling Freud's use of the term "linger" in his description of perversion[10]. The manner in which he introduces the idea of "deviation" from the "aim" is a very valuable scope when looking at Godard's interests and usage of cinema.

## Perversion and Lingering

Freud describes the "normal sexual aim" as being the 'union of the genitals in the act of copulation'[11]. From that viewpoint, a perversion – which etymologically contains the idea of "turn about" – is a sexual activity that deviates from normative sexual aims by altering the normal succession of behaviours that should establish a progression from encounter to copulation. Freud distinguishes two modes of perversion:

> Perversions are sexual activities which either (a) *extend*, in an anatomical sense, beyond the regions of the body that are designed for sexual union, or (b) *linger* over the intermediate relations to the sexual object which would normally be traversed rapidly.[12]

The perversion produced by lingering (b), is related to the impediment of gradual progression culminated in copulation: a tendency to 'linger over the preparatory activities and to turn them into new sexual aims that can take the place of the normal ones.'[13] In fact, a certain amount of lingering is not necessarily perverse 'provided that in the long run the sexual act is carried further.'[14] Perversion occurs when there is a substitution of the "normal aim" by transitory stages.

In order to examine to what extent the camera movement around stilled action could be compared to a perversion – a "turn about", a deviation – from the usual aim, it is necessary to identify what would a "normative" cinematographic progression be.

In 'The Death Drive: Narrative Movement Still' Laura Mulvey draws a comparison between the forward-moving direction of cinematographic progression and that of narrative:

> Cinema's forward movement, the successive order of film, merges easily into the order of narrative. Linearity, causality and the linking figure of metonymy, all crucial elements of story-telling, find correspondence in the unfolding, forward-moving direction of film.[15]

Taking this analogy as a starting ground, she will then apply Peter Brooks' identification of a Freudian death drive in cinema. Exactly as narration 'needs a motor force to start up out of an inertia, to which it returns in the end'[16], Mulvey's cinematic take on the death drive locates stillness and stasis at the beginning and at the end of the film, where she identifies different motives of stillness that range from more conceptual ones (marriage, death or revelation) to more visual ones (frozen image or passing clouds).

However, in considering the Freudian notion of "perversion" in relation to the "forward-moving direction" of film there is an alternative location and function that can be attributed to stillness. A generation and use of the latter that is not necessarily located at the opposite extremes of the film, but rather within it so that stillness becomes a mode of subversion of film's forward pulse. In other words, a lingering in stillness that stands against the normative and thus narrative progression of film.

The understanding of cinema as being a forward-moving narrative, haunts and harasses Jerzy throughout *Passion*. Formulated by different characters in the film, he is recurrently confronted to the same question: 'What is the story?'. Although Jerzy never answers the question, the most useful response is to be found in Patrick Bonnel's answer:

> [...] this composition is full of holes, of wrongly occupied spaces. Do not examine the construction nor the shots severely. Do as Rembrandt: look at living beings, carefully, for a long time, at the lips ... and in the eyes.[17]

Due to the fact that Jerzy's film has no story beyond the capture of the process of composition of each staged painting, the lack of narrative becomes a theme in *Passion*. In fact, it is Godard's *Passion's* meta-theme too since the overall film could also illustrate Bonnel's answer which is ambiguously constructed so that the spectator does not really know whether he is referring to the composition of the "tableau vivant", or to that of Godard's film as a whole. Godard's narrative composition can be said to be 'full of holes, of wrongly occupied spaces'. As Colin McCabe formulates it: 'The film has both too many stories and too few. (...) But each one of these is told in abbreviated, almost farcical scenes.'[18] The scenes at the recording studio are abruptly juxtaposed to those from the nearby hotel where the film crew is staying, and to those from the factory where some female figurants work.

This fragmentary juxtaposition of sequences could be read under the light of what Jacques Rancière calls Godard's 'aesthetic of suspension'[19]. According to him, the French director emancipates images from their traditional representative function. In Rancière's terms, images fulfil this function when they "are subordinated to the causal relationality of the plot; when they 'present its visible effects inviting us to understand their causes and set in motion specific effects, thereby enhancing the perception of the cause-effect connection.'[20]

In opposition to the representative function, Rancière identifies in Godard a *suspension* of the shot, its withdrawal from its illustrative function in relation to the plot in favour of an alternative relationship between visibility and signification. A mode of signification based on 'not determining it, of rendering infinite the relationship between visibility and signification and thus paralysing the logic of action. Such is the aesthetic form of suspension, the suspension of action by pathos.'[21]

Rancière's article focuses on Godard's episode "Introduction à la méthode d'Hitchcock" included in *Histoire(s) du cinéma* (1998), where Godard extracts some of Hitchcock's most famous shots from their original plot, and recomposes them in a different sequence of images. Hence he effects a literal suspension – deracination – of the image from it original plot. Even though suspension is neither so drastic nor so obvious in *Passion,* it can be argued that the camera's lingering motion assists in the effectuation of that "aesthetic of suspension".

In the first studio scene, the progressive zoom-in into the central feminine character of Rembrandt's *Nightwatch,* isolates her from the rest of the composition but also cuts the continuity between her and the action that is taking place around her. As a result, the spectator can hear the action that remains outside the frame while he/she struggles to connect it to what is shown inside the frame. Similarly, at Isabelle's house, while a worker's meeting is being held, the camera remains uninterested by the vehement discussion that is taking place. Instead, it conducts a fragmented journey over the various still poses that the women adopt, sending the spectator back to the atmosphere of the "tableaux vivants" (see Figure 6).

By moving around stillness, Godard forces a visual deviation from the progression of the plot. This lingering – this permanence in situations that, as Freud would say, 'should be traversed rapidly' – produces what Rancière identifies as 'paralysing the logic of the action.' Through detention and dilation a perverse substitution of the fragment over the visual and narrative continuum is achieved.

This substitution is caused by a similar kind of power as the one that Barthes attributes to the *punctum* of a photograph: a detail that 'overwhelms the entire of my reading; an intense mutation of my interest.'[22] The *punctum* is a mode of looking at a photograph that Barthes opposes to the *studium.* The latter is a kind of "human interest" a disposition in the viewer to engage as a 'docile cultural object, in what the photograph has to say, for it

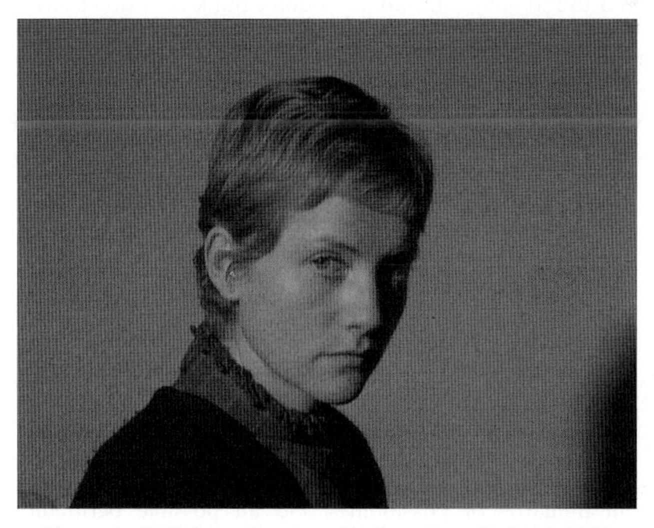

**Figure 6** Still from *Passion,* dir. Jean-Luc Godard, 1982

speaks.'[23] On the contrary the *punctum* is a 'detail that attracts me'[24], like a supplement that is at once 'inevitable and delightful.'[25] Godard's camera lingering over random elements are proposing to the spectator a *punctum*-driven gaze by capturing the "delightful" detail instead of providing the visual codification required for the construction of a narrative, a *studium*. This desire-driven choice recalls the opening quotation of *Le Mépris*: "cinema substitutes to our gaze, a world that is in accordance with our desires".

In fact, whereas the *studium* is meant to mobilise a kind of "unconcerned desire", the *punctum* is described as a 'wound, a prick, this mark made by a pointed instrument (. . .) that accident which pricks me (but also bruises me, is poignant to me).'[26] To the warmth of the former, the second appeals to a higher intensity of desire in its more overwhelming form.

Finally, Barthes' definition of the *punctum* provides the means to understand Rancière's idea of the 'suspension of action by *pathos*'. On one hand, it evokes the idea of pain or affectation (wound, prick, mark) implicit in the term 'pathos'. On the other, it alludes to the empathic stimulation of the viewer. This rapture of the viewer's attention 'withdraws the usual blah-blah, to shut [his] eyes, to allow the detail to rise its own accord into *affective* consciousness.'[27] Suspended from its responsibilities with regard to narrative progression, the image awakens the viewer's associative power for an extension of the visual's possible significations.

This mobilisation of affective associations is what leads Barthes to conclude that the *punctum* requires the involvement of the viewer. However, according to Barthes this potential of participative addition is restricted to the field of photography:

> Do I add to the image in movies? I don't think so; I don't have the time: in front of the screen, I am not free to shut my eyes; otherwise, opening them again, I would not discover the same image; I am constrained to a continuous voracity; a host of other qualities but not *pensiveness*.[28]

On the contrary, the Godardian lingering camera over stilled scenes seems to counter 'the continuous voracity' of the spectator in favour of what Raymond Bellour has called – in connivance with Barthes – the 'pensive spectator'.[29] Therefore, it appears reasonable to look at Godard's contouring camera motions as a strategy that allows a reflexive – and even digressive or perverted – spectator. As Jerzy tells to Hanna in *Passion*: 'Take advantage of the fact that the sentence is not over to start talking, to start living.'[30] At this stage it seems very adequate to transcribe Godard's observation on the effects caused by the stilling of a shot.

> We realise that depending on the way we stop a shot that we have filmed, different milliards of possibilities and all possible permutations become apparent (. . .) We realise that there are loads of different worlds inside the

> movement of a women (. . .) galaxies which are different each time and that we have jumped from one to another by a series of explosions.[31]

*Passion* gives the impression that Godard took up the challenge to restore to the instant all its possible permutations. By a use of the camera that selects still-motion scenes to linger around them, it is as though he was opening up a time for wandering – for 'keeping our cognitive powers engaged'– within the potential significations of the image. *Passion* proposes a mode of visual composition that conducts images to exceed their contingency and subjection to the continuum of narrative. Thereby it encourages a less functional and practical mode of relating to images.

In *La pensée et le mouvant*, Henri Bergson signalled that practicality narrows perception because the necessity of action over the word constrains our field of vision.

> Perception is cut out from a wider whole by practical life needs. (. . .) In the immensely wide field of our virtual knowledge, we have picked everything that interests our action on things, to turn it into our present knowledge [connaissance actuelle], we have neglected the rest.[32]

However, for Bergson, the artistic disengagement with pragmatism offers a possibility to experience an alternative mode of apprehension of the world.

> But, every now and then, by a fortunate accident, some men whose senses or conscience are less adherent to live, appear. Nature has forgotten to bound their faculty to perceive to their faculty to act. When they look at something, they see it for itself and not for themselves. They no longer perceive in view of action: they perceive [only] to perceive – for *nothing*, just for *pleasure*. (. . .) It would be a matter of *diverting* this attention for the practically interesting side of the universe and return it to that which is almost [pratiquement] useless.[33]

Bergson's description of artistic perception coincides with the qualities that can be allocated to Godard's motion around stillness: the aesthetic pleasure of lingering associated with beauty, the emancipation of the image from its representative practicality and the perverse deviation – diversion – from the action's logic of plotting. All these strategies address to the viewer an invitation to engage in an mode of perception that is not conditioned by the need of action. It is quite significant that the advertising slogan for *Passion* was 'It is just a matter of looking [Il n'y a qu'à regarder]'. [34]

To that goal, the use of paintings in *Passion* is especially relevant. Since painting is intuitively more closely associated with contemplation than cinema, Godard's spectators more readily accept the lingering of the camera within the paintings and the subsequent suspension of the action.

However, Godard progressively conducts the viewer to maintain the contemplative capacity beyond the paintings, towards the prosaic reality of the hotel and the factory. 'Passion is not interested in the meaning of the paintings. It is interested in their organisation of space and in the light which can render everyday reality of the sun over the Lake Geneva, or the movements of Isabelle Huppert as she works in the factory, just as luminous.'[35]

Indeed, despite the fragmentation of the film, there is a strong visual continuity between the studio scenes and that of the factory or the hotel. For instance, during the domestic meeting between factory workers, one of them asks Isabelle to bring the light closer. The way in which she positions the lamp and places herself under the light blatantly reproduces the obsessive preoccupation with light witnessed in the previous studio scenes.

Complementing the film's slogan "il n'y a qu'à regarder", "voir [seeing]" is a recurrent leitmotiv in *Passion*. Isabelle insists on the fact that "il faut *voir* ce qu'on va dire [we need to *see* what we are going to say]"; an observation that perfectly fits Godard's parallel project *Scénario du film passion* (1982). Trying to move away from the usual problem of translation from textuality to imaginery that affects scriptwriting, *Scénario du film Passion* intends to be a visual script. In it, Godard performs the constitution of *Passion* as a movement from one image to the other according to visual criterias instead of narrative ones. It is this same movement from one image to the other that is made apparent in *Passion* and that explains the visual continuity across fragmented scenes.

Therefore, what Godard offers to the spectator is not as much content as a different mode of composition that allows for an alternative perceptive disposition. Such perceptive disposition makes possible the spectator's tolerance to unspecified meaning. As Rancière puts it: 'releasing images from stories increases their power of infinite interconnection within a space whose aesthetic name is *mystery*.'[36]

Observed from this viewpoint, Godard's lingering camera releases cinema from the epistemological function that Benjamin prescribed to it. In opposition to the surgeon's hermeneutical penetration of reality, Godard preserves its mystery. It is as though the camera choreographies around stilled action would be generating a surface that holds mystery within images. Although the first impression conveyed by the lingering shots is that we get closer to the internal fabric of images their effect is the exact opposite.

In "The Hole and the Zero: Godard's vision of Femininity" Laura Mulvey identifies in Godard an attitude towards cinema that often recalls that of the relation of masculinity towards the feminine body. It is worth underlining a distinction that she makes between unveiling and penetration. While the former alludes to a dichotomy between surface and secret, the latter, she argues, considers the surface, not as 'a mode of production or something that it overlays, but into a celebration of the fetishisation of surface as such.'[37]

When Godard lingers around a *punctum*, the surface – the image's resistance to straightforwardness – is not as much pierced as made apparent and celebrated. In *Passion*, the visual wandering around stilled sequences cuts them from a narrative 'raison d'être' and in doing so creates a kind of impenetrable confinement surface. The patina is not there to be removed but rather to allow the viewer to enjoy the possibilities opened by facing the unknown. Godard's sophisticated camera movements could thereby be considered as a form of caress of that surface.

In *Le temps et l'Autre*, Lévinas identifies the relationship with the absolute unknown – the Other – as a relationship with mystery. What is more, the only mode of relation with mystery is the caress. Although his use of the term exceeds the scope of this exploration, it is a very suggestive formulation in relation to Godard's relationship with images.

> The seeking of the caress constitutes its essence by the fact that the caress does not know what it seeks. This 'not knowing', this fundamental disorder is essential to it. It is like a game with something slipping away, a game absolutely without project or plan, not with what can become ours or us, but with something other, always other, always inaccessible and always still to come. (...) It is made up of this increase of hunger, of ever richer promises, opening new perspectives onto the ungraspable.[38]

The possibility of understanding Godard's lingering camera as a cinematic caress over the surface that this very caress is constituting, takes up Mulvey's suggestion that there is in Godard an attitude towards cinema that reproduces the masculine fetishisation of the feminine as the mysterious and unknown Other. From that framework, in *Le Mépris*, Camille has all the attributes to sustain and maintain the masculine pleasure of lingering in mystery. The most literal reference to the masculine celebration of the surface is Javal's gentle hitting of the copper statue's breast. The empty echo makes palpable how cryptic Camille remains to him and materialises the surface that seals her mystery (see Figures 7 and 8).

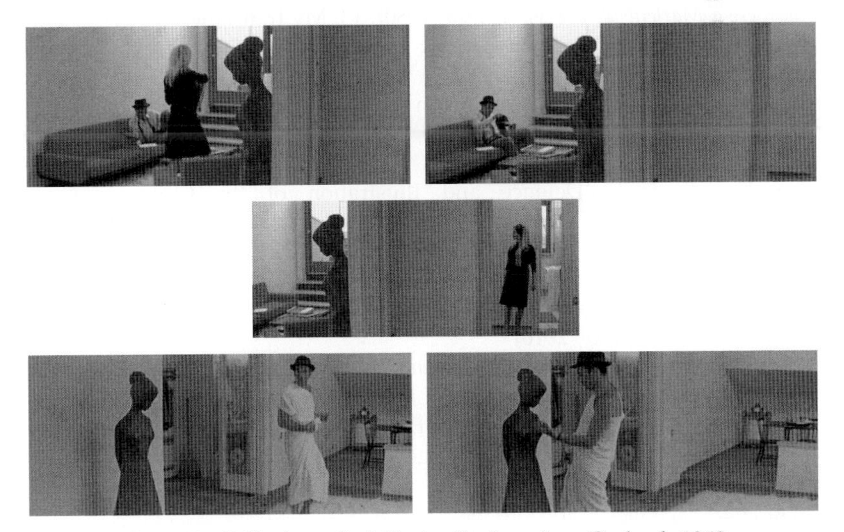

**Figure 7** Stills from *Le Mépris*, dir. Jean-Luc Godard, 1963

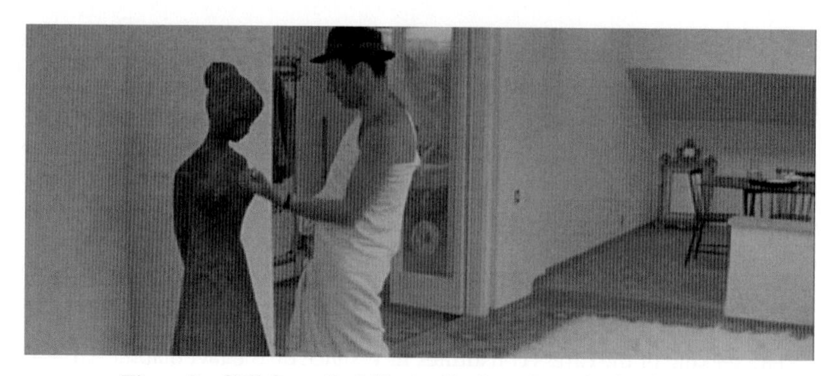

**Figure 8** Still from *Le Mépris*, dir. Jean-Luc Godard, 1963

Javal's lingering over – caress of – the feminine mystery mirrors the relationship that Godard's lingering camera has with reality.

## Notes

1. Laura Mulvey, 'Roberto Rossellini's Journey to Italy', *Death 24x a Second* (London: Reaktion, 2006), 116.
2. « Rappelez-vous, il y avait tout près de nous, un groupe de pierre, un homme et une femme vêtus à l'antique, dont les gestes inachevés semblaient représenter quelque scène précise. Vous m'avez demandé qui étaient ces personnages, j'ai répondu que je ne savais pas. Vous avez fait plusieurs suppositions, et j'ai dit que c'était vous et moi aussi bien ». Alain Robbe-Grillet, *L'année dernière à Marienbad*, (Paris: Minuit, 1980), 58. My translation.
3. « À l'intérieur de ce monde clos, étouffant, hommes et choses semblent également victimes de quelque enchantement ». Alain Robbe-Grillet, *L'année dernière à Marienbad*, (Paris: Minuit, 1980), 13. My translation.
4. Alain Robbe-Grillet, *For a New Novel: Essays on fiction* (New York: Grove Press, 1965), 15–24, 25–47 My emphasis.
5. Walter Benjamin, 'The Work of Art in the Age of Mechanical Reproduction', in *Illuminations* (London: Pimlico, 1999), 226.
6. Ibid., 229.
7. Jean-Luc Godard, 'Defence and Illustration of the Cinema's Classical Construction', *Godard on Godard*, ed. Tom Milne (London: British Film Institute and Secker & Warburg, 1972), 28. My emphasis.
8. *Duplex Cannes Godard et extraits de Passion* http://www.ina.fr/art-et-culture/cinema/video/I00004857/duplex-cannes-godard-et-extraits-de-passion.fr.html [Accessed: 03 January, 2010]
9. Immanuel Kant, *Critique of Judgement*, trans. Werner S. Pluhar (Cambridge: Hackett, 1987), 68. Brackets included in Pluhar's translation.
10. Sigmund Freud, *On Sexuality: Three Essays on the Theory of Sexuality and Other Works*, trans. James Strachey, ed. Angela Richards (London: Penguin, 1977).
11. Ibid., 61.
12. Ibid., 62.
13. Ibid., 68.

14 Ibid., 69.
15 Laura Mulvey, 'The Death Drive: Narrative Movement Stilled', *Death 24x a Second* (London: Reaktion, 2006), 69.
16 Ibid., 70.
17 « C'est parce que cette composition est pleine de trous, d'espaces mal occupés. N'examinez sévèremnet ni la construction ni les plans. Faites comme Rembrandt: regardez les êtres vivants attentivement, *longuement*, aux lèvres... et dans les yeux. » *Passion*, dir. Jean-Luc Godard, 1982. My translation.
18 Colin MacCabe, *Godard: A Portrait of the Artist at 70* (London: Bloomsbury, 2004), 277.
19 Jacques Rancière, 'Godard, Hitchcock and the Cinematographic Image', in *Forever Godard*, ed. Michael Temple, James S Williams and Michael Witt (London: Black Dog, 2004), 214–241.
20 Ibid., 216.
21 Ibid., 220.
22 Roland Barthes, *Camera Lucida: Reflections on Photography,* trans. Richard Howard (London: Vintage, 2000), 45–49.
23 Ibid., 43.
24 Ibid., 42.
25 Ibid., 47.
26 Ibid., 27.
27 Ibid., 55.
28 Roland Barthes, *Camera Lucida: Reflections on Photography,* trans. Richard Howard (London: Vintage, 2000), 55.
29 Raymond Bellour, 'The Pensive Spectator', in *The Cinematic*, ed. David Campany (London: Whitechapel, 2007).
30 « Profite que la phrase n'est pas faite pour commencer à parler, pour commencer à vivre. » *Passion*, dir. Jean-Luc Godard, 1982. My translation.
31 « On s'apperçoit qu'un plan qu'on a filmé, suivant comment on l'arrête tout à coup il y a des miliards de possibilités, toutes les permutations possibles (...) on s'apperçoit qu'il y a des tas de mondes différents à l'intérieur du mouvement de la femme (...) des galaxies à chaque fois différentes et qu'on passé de l'une à l'autre avec une série d'explosions. » Jean-Luc Godard, 'Défence et illustration du decoupage classique', in *Godard par Godard*, ed. Alain Bergala (Paris: Éditions de l'étoile & Cahiers du Cinéma, 1985), 462. My translation.
32 « La perception est découpée par les besoins de la vie pratique dans un ensemble plus vaste. (...) Dans le champ immensément vaste de notre connaissance virtuelle nous avons cueilli, pour en faire une connaissance actuelle, tout ce qui intéresse a notre action sur les choses; nous avons négligé le reste. » Henry Bergson, *La pensée et le mouvant*, (Paris: PUF, 1990), 151–152. My translation.
33 « Mais, de loin en loin, par un accident heureux, des hommes surgissent dont les sens ou la conscience sont moins adhérents à la vie. La nature a oublié d'attacher leur faculté de percevoir à leur faculté d'agir. Quand ils regardent une chose, ils la voient pour elle, et non plus pour eux. Il ne perçoivent plus simplement en vue d'agir: ils perçoivent pour percevoir – pour *rien*, pour le *plaisir*. (...) Il s'agirait de *détourner* cette attention du côté pratiquement intéressant de l'univers et de la retourner vers ce qui pratiquement ne sert à rien. » Henry Bergson, *La pensée et le mouvant*, (Paris: Publications Universitaires de France, 1990), 153. My translation.

34 Jean-Luc Godard, 'L'amour du cinéma et rien d'autre', in *Passion* (Paris: L'Avant-Scène, 1989), 84. My translation.
35 Colin MacCabe, *Godard: A Portrait of the Artist at 70* (London: Bloomsbury, 2004), 279.
36 Jacques Rancière, 'Godard, Hitchcock and the Cinematographic Image', in *Forever Godard*, ed. Michael Temple, James S Williams, Michael Witt (London: Black Dog, 2004).
37 Laura Mulvey, 'The Hole and the Zero: Godard's Visions of Femininity', in *Fetischism and Curiosity* (Bloomington: Indiana University Press; London: British Film Institute, 1996), 83.
38 « La recherche de la caresse en constitue l'essence par le fait que la caresse ne sait pas ce qu'elle cherche. Ce « *ne pas savoir* » ce désordonné fondamental en est l'essentiel. Elle est comme un jeu avec quelque chose qui se dérobe et un jeu absolument sans projet ni plan non pas avec ce qui peut devenir nôtre et nous, mais avec quelque chose d'autre de toujours autre, toujours inaccessible, toujours à venir. (. . .) Elle est faite de cet accroissement de faim, de promesses toujours plus riches, ouvrant des perspectives nouvelles sur l'insaisissable. » Émmanuel Lévinas, *Le temps et l'autre* (Paris: Publications Universitaires de France, 1983), 72. My translation.

LAURA MULVEY

# *Le Mépris* (Jean-Luc Godard 1963) and its story of cinema: a 'fabric of quotations'

In *Le Mépris* the cinema has a central presence on various different levels. The making of a film has brought the central characters together and the dramatic processes of film-making are often shown on screen, as a backdrop to the human drama. But woven into this overt presence is another story about the cinema: its histories and its contemporary crises. Only occasionally explicitly reaching the surface of the film, this story is concealed in signs, images and allusions. The unifying thread that ties these oblique references together is the world of *cinéphilia,* Godard's formative years as a critic for the *Cahiers du cinéma* and the films and directors he had written about and loved during the 1950s. That world had, by 1963, moved into a past tense: the Hollywood studio system that had produced the *politique des auteurs* had aged and had been overtaken by industrial changes; Godard was no longer a *cinéphile* critic but a successful New Wave director. But through allusions and quotations the world of *cinéphilia* seeps into *Le Mépris,* mediating between past and present. As quotation necessarily refers backwards in time, Godard evokes a now-ended era with an aesthetic device that always comes out of the past. Thus, in *Le Mépris,* form (quotation) is appropriate to its content (history).

But, on the other hand, quotation is a key modernist formal device, fragmenting a text's cohesion, disrupting traditional forms of reading by introducing other layers to a linear structure. As Peter Wollen puts it in his discussion of quotation in Godard's *Vent d'est*:

> One of the main characteristics of modernism . . . was the play of allusion within and between texts . . . The effect is to break up the heterogeneity of the work, to open up spaces between different texts and types of discourses . . . The space between the texts is not only semantic but historical too, the different textual strata being residues of different epochs and different cultures.[1]

These kinds of insertions also necessarily address the reader/spectator and generate two possible directions of engagement: one remains with the text's overt meaning while the other takes a detour into a latent and more uncertain terrain. To reflect on the passing references, especially if they are not underlined or emphasised by the film's action, involves a step aside from the main line of the film's narrative. The temptation is to pause, to attribute a reference to its source, or attempt to trace it until the trail is lost, as opposed to following the forward flow of a text. So, for instance, when I analyse, later in this essay, further associations triggered for me by the posters in Cinecittà, I will be giving priority to certain background images over the crucial narrative moment when Camille and Jerry meet, when Paul betrays Camille and the theme of 'contempt' begins. Mikhail Iampolski describes the relationship between quotation and the spectator's detour in the following terms:

> The anomalies that emerge in a text, blocking its development, impel us towards an intertextual reading. This is because every 'normative' narrative text possesses an internal logic. This logic motivates the presence of the various fragments of which the text is made. If a fragment cannot find a weighty enough motivation for its existence from the logic of the text, it becomes an anomaly, forcing the reader to seek its motivation in some other logic or explanation outside the text. The search is then constructed in the realm of intertexuality.[2]

I would like to reflect on those moments when references to the cinema within *Le Mépris* intrude and direct the spectator away from the internal logic of the text, its manifest narrative, and towards 'other explanations'. To my mind, when followed up, the 'anomalies' begin to form a network, relating back to a latent, other story of the changes that had overtaken and were overtaking the cinema. The anomalies do, of course, take on multiple shapes or forms, deviating from a strict concept of 'quotation'. Iampolski sums up this multiplicity when he points out that an 'anomaly' takes the form of a fragment which means: 'what is traditionally considered a quote may end up not being one, while what is not traditionally seen as a quote might end up being one'.[3]

Godard's 'taste for quotation' has often been commented on and he himself uses the phrase in a long interview in the special *Nouvelle Vague* issue of *Cahiers du cinéma* (168, December 1962). He says, in relation to *À bout de souffle*:

> Our earliest films were simply films made by *cinéphiles*. We could make use of whatever we had already seen in the cinema to deliberately create references. This was particularly the case for me. [. . .] I constructed certain shots along the lines of ones that I already knew, Preminger's, Cukor's etc. Furthermore, Jean Seberg's character follows on from *Bonjour Tristesse*. I could have taken the last shot of that film and added an inter-title Three Years Later . . . It comes from my taste for quotation that has always stayed with me. In life, people quote things that appeal to them . . . So I show people quoting: except I arrange their quotations in a way that will also appeal to me.[4]

Quotation, Godard seems to be saying, offered a point of cinematic transition in his trajectory from *cinéphile*/critic to *cinéphile*/director, from the days of the *Cahiers* to those of the *Nouvelle Vague*, from loving a particular shot to using it in his own films. About thirty years later, this lifelong partiality for quotation culminated in *Histoire(s) du cinéma*. *Le Mépris*, released in 1963 as a comparatively large budget fiction film with corresponding production values, adapted from a quite conventional novel, benefits from the retrospective shadow cast by *Histoire(s)*. Not only are both made up of a tissue of film quotation and reference, both were also made during transitional periods in film history. Looking back at *Le Mépris* from this perspective, its juxtaposition between cinema history and quotation gains in significance, the fiction dominates less, the characters give way to their emblematic casting and the network-like structure, central to the *Histoire(s)* aesthetic, becomes more visible. Furthermore, *Histoire(s)* draws attention to the place *Le Mépris* itself occupies in film history, how close it lies, in 1963, to 1950s Hollywood, both as a time of industrial decline but also the decade in which the last great studio system films were still being made. It was these films that Godard loved in particular and that provided his formation as a director (as he points out in the 1962 interview). But the presence of history draws attention to an aesthetic shift. Quotation in *Le Mépris* is no longer simply 'a taste'. It enables an elegiac commentary on the decline of one kind of cinema while celebrating another, the style that Godard had himself developed within the context of the French New Wave. Summing up this situation, Michel Marie says:

> The aesthetic project of *Le Mépris* is entirely determined by the context of the end of classical cinema and the emergence of new "revolutionary" forms of narrative.[5]

It was Alberto Moravia's novel *Il Dizprezzo* (1954) from which *Le Mépris* is adapted that gave Godard, in the first instance, the necessary film-within-a-film framework from which to develop his own themes and reflections. The novel was based on Moravia's own real-life encounter with the Italian film industry when, as a journalist, he visited the location of Mario Camerini's 1954 spectacular *Ulisse* (a Lux Film production with Kirk Douglas as Ulysses, also starring Silvana Mangano and Anthony Quinn). *Il Dizprezzo* uses a film production of *The Odyssey* as the setting for a tight group of characters (producer, director, screen-writer and screen-writer's wife). The setting brings together the story of a film in production, a marriage in decay and intellectual debate about Homer's epic poem. The novel shows no interest in either the mechanics of film-making or the history of cinema. Godard, however, makes the most of the way that, unlike a novel, a film about a film in production is necessarily self-referential and thus modernist. But above all, Godard inserts into the adaptation of the human story, his story of the cinema.

To reiterate, the latent story in *Le Mépris* makes visible a break in film history: on the one hand, there is the new flourishing cinema of the New

Wave and Godard's own modernist, innovative style and, on the other, Hollywood cinema of the 1950s, and the flourishing *cinéphilia* it had fostered in Paris, both of which had declined by the beginning of the 1960s. Thomas Schatz sums up the radically changed conditions in the Hollywood industry that lay behind the disappearance of the films valued by the *politique des auteurs* critics:

> Gone was the cartel of movie factories that turned out a feature every week for a hundred million movie-goers. Gone were the studio bosses who answered to the New York office and oversaw hundreds, even thousands of contract personnel working on the lot. Gone was the industrial infrastructure, the "integrated" system whose major studio powers not only produced and distributed movies but also ran their own theatre chains.[6]

In the first instance, these changes were set in motion by the Paramount Decree of 1948. The Federal Government wanted to break the restrictive practices inherent in Hollywood's vertically integrated system of production, distribution and exhibition. After the Decree, the studios had to sell their cinemas. The old financial mode of self-investment, through which production was supported by box-office returns, was gradually replaced by individual package deals put together by independent producers, stars and increasingly powerful agents and agencies, with the increasing participation of banks and other outside investors. Furthermore, during the 1950s box office receipts declined due to the rise of television (from $80 million c. 1950 to below $20 million c. 1960) and the industry struggled for survival. It was in this context that Hollywood began to invest in spectacular historical blockbusters. In *Le Mépris*, the conflict between Fritz Lang, representing old Hollywood, and Jerry Prokosh, who represents the new breed of producer associated with 'package deals', gestures to this history. And the film of *The Odyssey* does, of course, represent the new focus on the big movie that would, with luck, pull off a major box office hit; this was very different from the returns made from 'a feature a week' that had sustained the Hollywood genre system and its auteur directors.

Several of the directors whose films Godard had reviewed on their release during the 1950s, and who had special significance for him, were caught up in the blockbuster trend. The impact can be seen, for instance, in the case of Anthony Mann. In one of his last *Cahiers* reviews of a Hollywood film (92, February 1959) Godard argued that just as Griffith had invented the cinema in each frame of *Birth of a Nation*, so Mann had reinvented it in each frame of *The Man of the West*. Ultimately, he claims, Mann had created a work of modern cinema. I dwell on this moment as exemplary of Godard's aesthetic and critical investment in his key directors. But as conditions in Hollywood changed (as evoked above), Mann would go on to direct the spectacular *El Cid* in 1961 and manage to continue to make films with overblown casts, budgets and limited cinematic possibility for at least most of the 60s. He was more fortunate than others. Some favourites of the *politique des auteurs* who had regularly produced movies year after year during the post-war period, such as Sam Fuller, could no longer find work in the Hollywood film industry, only occasionally managing to make a few independent productions over the coming decades. Nicholas Ray made no more movies after *King of Kings* in 1961 and *55 Days at Peking* in 1963. Joseph Mankiewicz, for whom Godard had a particular admiration and whom he had described, as early as 1950, as 'one of the most brilliant of the American directors', was in 1963, directing *Cleopatra* (ironically for a director with a particular talent for spare, witty dialogue and sophisticated direction of actors).[7] This long decline is vividly reflected in the *Cahiers du cinéma*'s annual list of the 'Ten Best Films of the Year'. Dominated throughout the 1950s by their favourite Hollywood directors, by 1958 only three Hollywood films appear, Mankiewicz's *The Quiet American* stands at number one, Preminger's *Bonjour Tristesse* at number three and *The Man of the West* at number five. The following year, no Hollywood films are included in the Ten Best list.

## The Cinecittà triptych: the studio lot, the screening room, the posters

The story of cinema in *Le Mépris* is vividly laid out through a kind of 'pre-story' at the beginning of the film and is clearly marked by use of quotation. Leaving aside its subsequently inserted 'prologue', *Le Mépris* opens with three sequences set in Cinecittà, the film studios outside Rome, which were as evocative of the Italian film industry as Hollywood for the US or Pinewood for the UK. Together, the three sequences form a triptych in which the 'old' that Godard loved, especially Hollywood, is enunciated through the 'new' he believed in. In his book on Fritz Lang, Tom Gunning uses the screening room sequence in *Le Mépris* to discuss the complex question of film authorship. He says: 'The film-maker functions less as a scriptor than as a fashioner of palimpsests, texts written over other texts creating new meanings from the superimposition of old ones'.[8] For all three of the triptych sequences, the concept of palimpsest has special relevance, evoking the way that quotation and reference create layers of time, bringing something from past into the present, which then inscribes the present onto the past. In a similar but different manner, ghostly rather than textual, the actors too have meaning layered into their present fictional roles. As Jacques Aumont puts it:

> Jack Palance, Georgia Moll and Fritz Lang are vehicles, in the flesh, of part of the past, of history. They are living quotations and, already survivors of a vanished world . . .: through them, Godard quite consciously evokes not only his own immediate past as *cinéphile* – *The Barefoot Contessa*, *The Quiet American* – but a more distant, already heroised and mythic past . . .[9]

In the first sequence of the triptych, the studio lot stands idle and deserted. Francesca (the producer's assistant) explains to Paul (the screen writer):

'Jerry has sent everyone home. Things are hard in the Italian film industry at the moment.' Jerry, the American producer, then appears on the edge of the sound stage and proclaims, in long shot and as though addressing a vast audience, that he has sold the studios for real estate development. And Francesca's final remark: 'C'est la fin du cinéma' carries the sense of crisis beyond Cinecittà to the general decline of industrial cinema by the late 1950s and even to the question of cinema itself. The studio lot is itself, to adapt Aumont's terms, 'a vehicle, a part of the past, a history' and, as such, might be understood as mise-en-scène as quotation. Poignantly, the scene is set in the lot belonging to Titanus (the studio that had produced Roberto Rossellini's *Viaggo in Italia* in 1953) and which was, in actual fact, just about to be demolished. The fate of Cinecittà corresponds to that of the Hollywood studios at the time, more valuable as real estate than for film production.

The second sequence of the Cinecittà triptych brings together the central group of *Le Mépris*'s characters who all, fictionally, belong to the cinema through their various roles in the production of *The Odyssey*. It is here that Godard introduces most intensely the aesthetic of quotation. Set in the studio screening room, the confined space is criss-crossed by quotation and reference of all kinds: spoken, enacted, written, personified, discussed. Francesca and Paul join Prokosh, the producer, and Fritz Lang, the director, to watch rushes from their production of *The Odyssey*, (part Italian peplum, part Hollywood spectacular). The conversation between the characters enables Godard to juxtapose references to the contemporary state of cinema and classical European culture; and these two themes are reiterated, on the one hand, by literal quotations from European literature, on the other, by the presence of figures with an emblematic association with Hollywood. And Louis Lumière's grim prediction, written in large letters under the screen, 'Le cinéma est une invention sans avenir' creates a link to the elegiac spirit of the first and third sequences.

Central to the screening room sequence are the rushes, shots of the statues of the gods or snippets of the story composed more in tableaux than in continuity. As bits of cinema, they are short and finite, as indeed are rushes, but they take on the aesthetic characteristics of quotation: fragmentation and repeatability. Several commentators have pointed out that the style with which the statues are filmed, accompanied by Georges Delerue's music, strikingly quotes the filming of the statues, accompanied by Renzo Rossellini's music, in Roberto Rossellini's *Viaggo in Italia*.

While the literary quotations are, by and large, overt and attributed, the conjuring up of Hollywood is more complex, here taking place through the signifying properties of the actors as living quotation. Fritz Lang, as the fictional director, obviously brings his own cinematic history with him, but so do Jack Palance (as Jerry Prokosh) and Giorgia Moll (as Francesca) who also represent, metonymically, particular Hollywood films that had significance for Godard. Michel Piccoli (as Paul Javal) brings to this collective of signifiers a particular resonance of Paris: as an actor, he evokes the French New Wave; as a character, he evokes Parisian *cinéphilia*.

As well as having appeared in Italian peplum productions, Giorgia Moll had played the French-speaking Vietnamese heroine in Joseph Mankiewicz's *The Quiet American*, thus creating a direct link to one of Godard's favourite directors. He had reviewed the film on its release with his usual admiration but was also disappointed that Mankiewicz's intelligent, elegant script was imperfectly realised as film (*Arts* 679, July 1958). In *Le Mépris*, Giorgia Moll plays Francesca Vanini, a character invented by Godard (she is not in the Moravia novel) whose name refers directly to Roberto Rossellini's latest film *Vanina Vanini*, (which will represent him on the line of posters in the third sequence). As Prokosh's interpreter, she comes to stand for living quotation in a different sense, repeating the words of others, translating, often very freely, between the mono-linguistic Paul and Camille on the one hand, and Prokosh on the other. As well as her own native language, Italian, with Lang she can speak English, French or German and gains his approval for her recognition and translation into French of his quotation from the German poet Hölderlin's 'The Poet's Vocation'.

Jack Palance brings Hollywood into *Le Mépris* in several ways. As a star in his own right, he represents the Hollywood star system as such. But he also represents a link, both as a star and through his fictional character, Jeremiah Prokosh, to a cluster of Hollywood films-about-film that had been made in the 1950s, all of which include an unscrupulous and exploitative producer or studio boss. In the first instance, Palance would, for Godard, have linked back to Robert Aldrich's 1955 film *The Big Knife*, an adaptation of a Clifford Odets play about the conflict between a star (Palance) struggling to maintain his ethical principles in the face of the power and persistent bullying of the studio boss, played by Rod Steiger. Palance thus brings with him a double quotation: he is the star who had played the role of a star, while in *Le Mépris*, in the persona of Jeremiah Prokosh, he references the character personified by Steiger. Furthermore, as Michel Marie points out, Prokosh is a direct descendant of Kirk Edwards, the megalomaniac, casually brutal and sexually predatory Hollywood producer in Joseph Mankiewicz's 1954 *The Barefoot Contessa*, a film that had been highly prized by *Cahiers du Cinéma*. Palance's chiselled, mask-like features (due to plastic surgery after being wounded in World War II) and his slow, almost Frankenstein-like movements recall Warren Stephen's stony, almost motionless performance as Kirk Edwards. To these two 'Hollywood on Hollywood' films should be added Vincente Minnelli's 1952 *The Bad and the Beautiful* in which Kirk Douglas plays the prototypically unscrupulous, if more engaging, producer Jonathan Shields.

Although Prokosh has been said to evoke Godard's real-life producers Carlo Ponti and Joe Levine, the iconographical legacy of these Hollywood movies is very strong. But, as well as inscribing these traits and characteristics, Godard uses Prokosh specifically to signal the decline in Hollywood production values in the face of cynicism, philistinism and a taste for kitsch. A throwaway remark of Fritz Lang's indicates that Prokosh is not, for him, within the true tradition of Hollywood independent production. Refusing his invitation to have a drink, Lang quotes a famous Goldwynism (Sam Goldwyn tended to mix up language): '"Include me out", as Sam Goldwyn a real producer of Hollywood once said'. And Prokosh's first appearance in Cinecittà underlines the new commercialism. While Godard's citation of the Hollywood-on-Hollywood films puts *Le Mépris* within this 'sub-genre', evoking a tradition of films of self-reference (that does, of course, pre-date the 1950s), he is also clearly gesturing towards the industry's uncertain future, underlined by the Lumière quotation. The decline, he seems to imply, was already there in the beginning.

Fritz Lang is first introduced to the film by the most well-known anecdote of his career. Paul tells Francesca that Goebbels offered Lang a privileged position in Universum Film AG (UFA), to which he had replied by leaving the following day for Paris and then the United States.[10] Godard follows this up with an enacted confrontation between Lang and Prokosh in the screening room. In a moment that seems anomalous and strange, Prokosh violently interrupts the screening, claiming that the images on the screen were not in the script. Lang brings the argument to an end, saying calmly: 'Naturally, because in the script it's written and on the screen it's pictures, motion pictures it's called.' According to Tom Gunning, this is a re-enactment of a confrontation between Lang and Eddie Mannix, his first US producer.[11] Both these anecdotes show Lang confronting authority; but one is given its place in Lang's biography, while the other floats, functioning dramatically as a fragment but without explanation. Together, these two anecdotes represent two very different kinds of quotation, the attributed and the 'to-be-deciphered', both with very different aesthetic implications.

If Prokosh, in his *Le Mépris* role, is emblematic of changing Hollywood, Lang stands, in stark contrast, for a long history of the cinema, some of its most outstanding films and its more generally changing fortunes. Born in 1890, shortly, that is, before the cinema and making his first film in 1919, Lang and cinema matured, as it were, side by side. Due to the *Mabuse* films, *Metropolis*, and his prolific output during the Weimar period, as a 'living quotation' he brings to *Le Mépris* the memory of aesthetic achievements of German silent cinema, then, with *M* in 1931, early experiment with synch sound. (It might be worth remembering, in the context of the late 1950s blockbuster, that Lang had almost bankrupted UFA in 1927 with his spectacularly expensive spectacular *Metropolis*.) In 1933, he joined the stream of exiles from Nazism who then contributed so much to Hollywood during the years of the studio system. From *Fury* in 1936 to *Beyond Reasonable Doubt* in 1956, he made a film, sometimes two, every year (except one). Although he was, by and large, successful (unlike some of his compatriots), he too found it increasingly hard to direct by the mid-1950s. In Germany, in the late 1950s, he directed his own versions of 'spectaculars':

*The Tiger of Eshnapur* and *The Indian Tomb* as well as an attempt to return to the *Mabuse* cycle. By the time he appeared in *Le Mépris*, he had made no films for three years; on the other hand, as an early pantheon director of the *politique des auteurs*, his critical status had risen in France and Luc Moullet's book *Fritz Lang*, that Camille reads and quotes from in the apartment sequence, had been published in 1963. Godard treats Lang reverentially, himself acting the role of the fictional director's assistant. He frames and films Lang so that his literal presence takes on the mythical quality due to an old man, no longer employable but, more than any other director still living at the time, stretched across and emblematic of this complex cinematic history. Still wearing, as a badge of belonging and distinction, the monocle that signifies the old days of Weimar, Lang is quotation as embodiment, summoning up the past and inserting it into a present to which he no longer belonged.

In the third sequence of the triptych, these themes are realised and confirmed. Outside the screening room, the characters act out their scene in front of a wall of posters: Howard Hawks's 1962 *Hatari!*, Godard's own 1962 *Vivre sa vie*, Rossellini's 1961 *Vanina Vanini* and Hitchcock's 1960 *Psycho*. Apart from Godard, the three were great directors celebrated and defended during Godard's time as a *Cahiers du cinéma* critic, but all were, by this point in time, nearing the end of their careers. Appropriately, Godard inserts the figure of Fritz Lang into this series of '*hommages*'. Framed alone, in front of the posters, Lang walks quite slowly towards the camera as he lights a cigarette and, emphasising the mythic nature of this portrait shot, music briefly appears on the sound track. In the next couple of shots, Paul, as a *cinéphile*, brings cinema directly into his conversation with Lang. Lang brushes aside Paul and Camille's admiration for *Rancho Notorious* (1952), 'the western with Marlene Dietrich', with 'I prefer *M*'. But Paul persists and mentions the scene in which Mel Ferrer (as Frenchie Fairmont) allows Marlene Dietrich (as Altar Keane) to win at chuck-a-luck. This was a favourite moment of Godard's, to which he refers specifically in his general discussion of the Western in his *Man of the West* review. The citation of *Rancho Notorious* has its own relevance to the posters that frame the conversation between Paul and Lang; the film is itself about ageing but mythic figures of the West (Frenchie Fairmont and Altar Keane) who have become part of its legend, just as these directors have become part of the legend of Hollywood as told by the *Cahiers du Cinéma*.

But this sequence is also the one in which Brigitte Bardot, as Paul's wife, Camille, first appears. As she stands against the backdrop of posters, she personifies new cinema, a new kind stardom, as well as a new kind of glamour, European as opposed to Hollywood. In the last resort, she stands for the personification of cinema. If Godard tends to fuse cinematic beauty with that of his female star, this is particularly so in *Le Mépris*. But the presence of the *Vivre sa vie* poster creates its own distinctive chain of female beauty reaching back across the history of cinema. Later in the film, Camille wears a black wig, bobbed in the style worn by Anna Karina in *Vivre sa vie*, which in turn cites Louise Brooks. Much admired by the director of the Cinémathèque Française, Henri Langlois, for an insouciant seductiveness in films such as Hawks's 1928 *A Girl in Every Port* to Pabst's 1929 *Pandora's Box*, Louise Brooks might be seen as a pre-figuration of Godard's fascination with feminine beauty that fused wih the beauty of the cinema.

The bracketing of Hawks and Hitchcock conjures up André Bazin's ironic term 'Hitchcocko-Hawksianism' to describe the dedicated supporters of the *politique des auteurs* at the *Cahiers*. Both directors had started their supremely successful careers in the 1920s and had flourished under the studio system but with comparative independence (Hitchcock, of course, arriving from Britain in the late 30s). But both were old by the time of *Le Mépris* and would only make films occasionally until the 1970s. Although he was to make two more films (*Anima nera* in the same year and *Italia anno uno* in 1974), Rossellini's career in cinema was also just about over. From 1961 to the end of his life in 1977, apart from a few documentaries, he would work exclusively for television. *Vanina Vanini* was adapted from a novella by Stendhal. Set in Rome during the Risorgimento (Rossellini had celebrated its centenary the previous year with *Viva l'Italia*), the story bears witness to Stendhal's love of Italy and his fascination with its struggle for liberation. As if to emphasise its significance, Godard had 'Francesca Vanini' summoned by name over an intercom a few seconds before the film's poster appears on the screen.

In this concluding section, I would like to exemplify ways in which quotation can set in train further lines of thought that might be particular to the spectator. A quotation or reference might trigger associations for the spectator that go beyond the specific textual context and produce an 'extra-textual reverie'. Thus for me personally (and, very likely, others), thinking about *Le Mépris* in the light of *Hatari!* and *Psycho* unexpectedly draws attention to coincidences of narrative and theme. Like *Psycho*, *Le Mépris* is separated into two distinct parts; the first takes place over the course of one day during which the ordinariness of everyday life is overtaken by catastrophe: Marion's crime and death in one case, the loss of Camille's love in the other. Although the second part of *Psycho* is not, as in *Le Mépris*, streamlined into a single day, both films are overshadowed by fate: what might seem a minor ethical failing (on the part of Paul and Marion) is punished beyond reason by 'the gods' of narrativity. The relevance of *Hatari!* is more thematic and has less to do with narrative structure. The film repeats one of Hawks's preferred story settings: a small group of people are arbitrarily thrown together in some isolated situation, in which death and love intermingle with the group's internal dynamics. The Hawksian group has a certain resonance for *Le Mépris*: here again a small group of people are thrown together by the chance contact of their profession creating a drama of professional and personal conflicts and loyalties.

I would like to end by reflecting on the particular importance of *Viaggio in Italia* for *Le Mépris*, due not only to the filming of the statues of the gods, but also more generally to the story of a marriage in crisis. Here the latent references to cinema history link specifically to the modernism of quotation as a formal device. Godard confirms the relevance of Rossellini's film very precisely: at the end of the 'audition' scene, the group leave the cinema and pause to talk outside, allowing a poster for *Viaggio in Italia* to be clearly seen in the background. *Viaggio* introduces another kind of palimpsest in its relation to *Le Mépris*. In the first instance, the story of Paul and Camille's marriage re-inscribes that of Emilia and Riccardo from the novel *Il Dizprezzo*, creating another temporal layer, just as any adaptation must necessarily hover behind its retelling. In *Viaggio in Italia* Alex and Katherine Joyce are an English couple staying in Naples whose marriage, quite suddenly, falls apart. During one of their embittered exchanges, Katherine turns to Alex with the words: 'I despise you'. But just as Godard uses the quarrelling couple in *Le Mépris* to quote *Viaggio*, so Rossellini inserts into his film, without acknowledging the source, the troubled marriage in James Joyce's 'The Dead'. Katherine retells Joyce's story as though transposed to her own memory. She reminds Alex that she had once been loved by a young man who had then died; his sensibility and his poetry continue to haunt her and irritate Alex, contributing to their deteriorating relationship. Although Rossellini uses the story for his own fiction, making no hint of its status as citation, it shares something of Iampolski's anomaly, inserting, due to a feeling of excess or oddity, a kind of blockage into a text. Katherine's monologue is quite long and furnished with a few details that belong to the original. Ultimately, Rossellini does provide a clue to its source through the couple's name: Joyce. The layering of references to a marriage in crisis across the Moravia's novel, Rossellini's film and Joyce's story creates an intertextual network that ends most appropriately with Godard's *Le Mépris*.

From this perspective, the presence of *Viaggio in Italia* in *Le Mépris* does considerably more than cite a director of the greatest importance to Godard. In *Viaggio*, the memory of the dead young man acts as a figure for a more general metaphor of haunting, but it also acts as a figure for the ghostly nature of quotation itself. The relationship of *Le Mépris* to *Viaggo in Italia*, and its specific reference to Joyce, generate a fragile link to his *Ulysses*, his retelling of *The Odyssey* into the great epic of modernist literature, itself a palimpsest of quotation and reference. These links bear witness to the significance of quotation as a modernist strategy and the way that a citation from the past works as an aesthetic device precisely for the destruction of tradition and the generation of the modern.

The blurb that accompanied the London Consortium's seminar on *Le Mépris* specifically mentioned the film as 'a fabric of quotations'. The phrase, coming from Roland Barthes's 1967 essay 'The Death of the Author', is a reminder that Godard's prolific and stylistic use of quotation and reference pre-dates its theorisation. The origin of the phrase, however, is also a reminder that the search to trace the fragment and the anomaly to its source can never stabilise the uncertainty of meaning or pin down the intention that lies at the heart of quotation. Important and minor instances will always remain overlooked, hidden and locked. But, all the same, Godard's use of allusion and reference, palimpsest and living quotation creates a layered form of film reading. The experience of watching the film, for me, a *cinéphile* formed by the *Cahiers politique des auteurs*, involves the triggering of memories and the recognition of the special significance of films and directors cited. For instance, the sudden, unmotivated and anomalous reference to Nicholas Ray's *Johnny Guitar* leads me back to the particular emotional resonance the film had for *Cahiers*-influenced *cinéphiles*. And the reference links back to Godard's earlier film *Le Petit Soldat* in which he quotes dialogue between Joan Crawford and Sterling Hayden ('tell me lies') and forward to its nearly invisible but key place in *Pierrot le Fou*. It is because Ferdinand had allowed the maid to go to *Johnny Guitar* that Marianne comes to baby-sit and they meet again 'after five years'.

If the latent story of cinema exists, as in a palimpsest, in another layer of time and of meaning outside that of the fiction, enabling a detour into the quite different discourse, it also doubles back on an allegorical level into the film's manifest content. Just as the spectator struggles to decipher the film's quotations, so Paul struggles to decipher Camille. Alongside, or overshadowed by, the enigma of Camille and her desirability are signs and clues suggesting that the cinema has a similar status for Godard as enigma and elusive object of desire. And on this allegorical level, Paul and Camille's lost love and their mutual inability to understand their emotional history relates to Godard's sense of loss at the disappearance of the cinema that had formed him so completely. Just as Paul promises at the end of the film to become the writer he had always wanted to be, out of the ruins of his lost love, so Godard turned into a New Wave director, out of the ruins of his love of 1950s Hollywood cinema. As always for Godard, the beauty and inscrutability of his female star and of cinema are fused in his aesthetic and erotic sensibility. Ultimately, the use of quotation in *Le Mépris* shifts the uncertainty of emotion to the spectator. The uncertainties of attribution, the abrupt anomalies that erupt into the text, leave the spectator with a sense of yearning for understanding, always conscious of just missing a point, contented with some moments of satisfied recognition. In addition to its modernist significance, its layering of the text (as formal device and latent story), quotation puts the spectator into the situation of longing and loss that characterise the 'feeling' of the film as a whole.

## Notes

1 Peter Wollen, 'The Two Avant-gardes', in *Readings and Writings: semiotic counter–strategies* (London: Verso 1982), 102.

2 Mikhail Iampolski, *The Memory of Tiresias. Intertextuality and Film* (San Francisco and Los Angeles: University of California Press, 1998), 30.
3 Ibid., 31.
4 *Jean-Luc Godard par Jean-Luc Godard* (Paris: Editions Pierre Belfond, 1968), 28.
5 Michel Marie, *Le Mépris* (Paris: Editions Nathan, 1990), 14.
6 Thomas Schatz, *The Genius of the System. Hollywood Film-making in the Studio Era* (London: Faber and Faber, 1998), 4.
7 Rather strangely, given his later dismissive comments about *Il Disprezzo*, Godard says of Mankiewicz 'I would not hesitate to accord him as important a place as that occupied by Alberto Moravia in European literature'.
8 Tom Gunning, *Fritz Lang* (London: The British Film Institute, 2000), 6.
9 Jacques Aumont, 'Godard's *Le Mépris*', in Susan Hayward and Ginette Vincendeau (eds), *French Film: Texts and Contexts* (London: Routledge, 2000), 176.
10 Tom Gunning analyses this anecdote and demonstrates that Lang elaborated it considerably over the years (*Fritz Lang*, p. 8–9).
11 Ibid., 6.

# Index